THE INSIDE TRUTH OF R

True life experiences from a former British Police Detective Constable.

This edition published 2018
by Copyright @ Howell Jackson LUNN

Cover design by Chris Williams
williamsgraphics.co.uk"

I write this book for my dear wife, three sons and in loving memory of my late mother and father and parents in law. I also wish to thank all the kind relatives and friends who have participated in helping formulate this book with their kind help and advice.

PREFACE OF BOOK

This is the second book I have written also entitled - The Inside Truth of Real Policing. This time it again reflects and portrays all the hard work and interesting issues of everyday police duties in the role of a sub-divisional Detective Constable. This was a role where I was fully operational at all times when working within the CID right up to the time of my retirement. I had left school as stated having no academic qualifications, coming from a basic background like most ordinary people of hard working parents. What an achievement I had reached well beyond my ultimate goal, in not only having been a fully experienced uniform police officer and coroner's officer but had all the success of being a plain clothes detective for a period of some 18 years.

I did not want promotion through the ranks just to be professional in all I did and in the role I enjoyed. To work for some senior officers who had integrity and experience was a first class privilege, rather than against the background of the opposite kind of supervisory staff. Where the over promoted individual had nothing to be proud of other than being a continual embarrassment to the police force and his or herself. I just thank God there were not too many of them.

Being in CID and working extremely irregular hours tested every avenue of our marriage and as stated previously I cannot praise my wife enough for all the love, patience and tolerance provided through her strong support. In addition to our sons who were aware of the dedication I had continued to give the job in all areas of criminal work. Who suffered the indignity of some of their class mates, in the latter part of their education and with other members of society all because of the job I was doing or were just jealous or anti-police. Even some officers in CID did not have the same dedication as me and fellow colleagues and sadly this included some senior officers.

As I worked within this role I was in a better position than ever to still identify wasters and shirkers compared to the self-motivated officers who were always the same hard working kind covering up for those with poor standards and lazy attitudes. In those days I think it was a matter of who you knew instead of what you knew, as familiarity breeds contempt which enabled some senior officers to close their eyes to the poor work, if any work at all was done, by some of their so called favourite officers. Sadly this situation still applies today I believe, in a whole range of public sector employment where possibly some of these staff would never get a job in private industry, allowing the more experienced always having to cover for these individuals.

Eventually through changes in many practices a large amount of these poor quality and underperforming staff have since been removed or have retired from their roles as performance targets were introduced. I think its speaks for itself, why did they have to introduce these methods when after all if proper supervision had been there in the first place all would have been totally unnecessary. I can take pride in always supporting the keen hard working uniform officers and never taking any glory away from them which they richly deserved. In most cases submitting full reports of their action in order true merit could be awarded accordingly.

As in my first book no locations of where I worked have been given, other than serving within the police service of the British Isles. Names appear in pseudonym of all colleagues mentioned including myself. This is to respect privacy for everyone. Any other person referred to, including victims witnesses or offenders have not been identified in complying with The Official Secrets Act and The Human Rights Act. Again in many chapters I have made comments on several issues which I have based on my own judgment and experience, all being in my view only and not wishing to cause any individual any offence. I understand other people may have other views or theories which is accepted and appreciated in a free democratic society. In writing true stories it is only fair and a matter of principal that I include some instances of poor and unprofessional work and behaviour that took place during my service, which I have portrayed honestly and accurately. To me it would be grossly wrong not to include such details but never once do I undermine the truly magnificent work experiences I encountered with the utterly professional people that I worked with. Without such stories this would not be an accurate reflection of all events that took place during my police service.

Back then in 1980 many changes were to take place in the form of interviewing procedures either contemporaneous notes or interviewing suspects under audio and video recording facilities. With the role of the Crown Prosecution Service forever having increased responsibilities and the introduction of disclosure of evidence before interview to the defence. When at a time there was no robbery squad, burglary squad, fraud team, murder or child indecency teams, detective officers were experienced in all these different areas of crime. One thing was for certain as the years went on throughout my service the deterrent to commit crime has become less and less, where in many cases there does not seem to be any punishment and prison is every bit as much a holiday camp for serious villains which comes with a five star rating. It is expected that some people quite rightly argue that there is a selection of wrong people locked up, with many of the ones who deserve prison given freedom, so I wonder where we go from here and will we get the balance correct for the future.

In preparing the contents of this book I have re-lived all my true life experiences, some sad, some funny and unforgettable moments that will stay with me forever. Some people may consider my phrasing of sentences is not all within the full tradition of the perfect English language. I write how I speak after all we are individuals in life. The grammar in this edition has been corrected and I thank people for their comments and although I am not perfect, never has this ever stopped me in being successful. I suppose over the years there were far too many senior officers who would have made better English teachers as their main qualities in the police force appeared to be enforcing rigidly the scrutiny of reports. Just a pity some were not as highly qualified in detecting all crimes and bringing offenders to justice. No different to being gifted in solving serious problems within the community based on common sense, or being able to speak on the same level with all the people from so many walks of life you deal with every day in operational policing. Sadly far too many were far too pompous in their approach and manner being incapable of achieving this level of experience thus could not detect a smell yet alone a crime.

In these books I have told stories that actually happened in my career, no different to very similar stories that have appeared in the news in all forms of the media. In addition to stories of very similar police work in feature films and television dramas. In addition many instances of criminal behaviour is highlighted in numerous programmes showing the work of crime profilers in the United Kingdom and also the U.S.A, which are all part of highly informative television documentaries. Whist mindful of divulging any possible secrets of policing affecting any present day duties, no information is given that has not appeared in media previously, or aired before in these type of books or films. Many incidents or crimes detailed could not now however be committed in present day due to a change in police procedure or new legislation in various areas where the law has changed, in some cases definitely for the better.

In addition there a few examples in this book where bad language is typed, it is hoped this does not cause offence as it reflects the truth of what was said in all of the relevant circumstances. I have hoped to have shown the variety of work which was undertaken by detective officers in a sub divisional CID office, in some cases offering at all times support for our uniform colleagues with whom we would not in many cases have been able to have done our job so effectively.

Howell Jackson LUNN - Served 1970 – 1998

LIST OF CHAPTERS

CHAPTER 01

APPOINTED TO THE RANK OF DETECTIVE CONSTABLE

I had now achieved 10 years' service and had completed a successful 6 months attachment to C.I.D. This was backed up with a further temporary attached period of 4 months, each time working under different supervision at two other stations within the same division.

During this short but busy attachment I received information that the man wanted for the offence of living off immoral earnings of prostitution was in custody. He had been committed to prison for a number of offences and other criminal charges and was on remand to Crown court. Together with another officer I arranged to interview him in prison where I was informed he wanted to cooperate.

This was the offender in the previous chapter who eluded the uniform beat officer I had given information to about the nurse stealing purses at the hospital. This officer stated he knew the offender but the man in custody stated he recognised the uniform officer even though he was in plain clothes and ran straight past him. Pity this officer did not have the same talents. He came clean about all the activities, running the four prostitutes and hiring cars. He admitted along with the others receiving good money from their activities of being on the game and being paid for sex.

He was a likeable villain and I had dealt with him previously and recalled the time when I was keeping observations on him. If you recall he actually confronted me stating I was watching him, as detailed in a former chapter. This man stated I really pulled the wool over his eyes in that I really convinced him that he was messing up another case I was dealing with. I falsely told him I was watching a stolen vehicle and to get out the way. He laughed and stated I even said sorry to you and all the time you were watching me and all the others. That was crafty and we both had a good laugh together about it. He made a full written statement on his involvement and was later charged at his next appearance at court. He later pleaded guilty and was sentenced to imprisonment for this offence and all the other matters. The galling issue was this un-observant uniform officer who failed to identify him and make an arrest caused an incredibly complicated file to be split, creating massive time preparing paperwork for committal to crown court.

I eventually was in line, for the next vacancy which took place a couple of months later where I was appointed Detective Constable. Again I had to serve a 12 month probation period, but I had made it. My dream had come true mainly thanks to Monty who gave me the strength and drive, telling me to go first for it. Within 12 months he was appointed Detective as well, but working from another station. Needless to say we remained good friends throughout our service and up to present day.

The downside to all this, which again I also saw as a challenge, was the C.I.D. Office I moved to had recently been taken over with a new senior officer, Detective Inspector Brian MOUNT, a fair honest and likeable man, who had the very necessary role of getting rid of the dead wood. This was an exception to the general rule, as he was a former uniform officer who rose through the ranks with his first posting at his current rank to CID. Not everyone would fit into these criteria as you will see in various examples later illustrated. One thing to this officer's credit was that he recognised real experience and those who were hardnosed good working investigators, who left no stone unturned in their quest for the truth.

When I arrived it did not take long to see the reason why, half the office were carrying the remainder of the staff. Most were mainly dead wood who had over stayed their welcome and had become bitter and twisted. They had hung their boots up, a phrase I often used to illustrate they had all passed their sell by date. It was if I was playing a role in the television program Life on Mars which was exactly the role that I portrayed. I had the task of working in the same office as Dc GLOVER, who had stuck the knife in many times previously when he tried to obliterate my information given on the Social Club robbery, but to me that was history. I was constantly aware of his jealousy and continual back biting and tried to maintain a low profile, but do my job to the best of my ability.

One issue that was quite disturbing was the fact that at every opportunity Dc GLOVER in my first few years in this department, targeted new recruits and other officers transferring to this subdivision where he warned them discreetly to give me a wide birth, in other words brain washed them as if I had some contagious disease. He would portray me in an extremely bad light that I lacked experience and was untrustworthy and any other defamation that came into his mind. When challenging some of the recruits and new staff, it was virtually impossible to obtain any vindictive evidence against him but I could sense from those indoctrinated I had to tread carefully. Compared to all this injustice, fighting crime and locking up offenders was the easy part for me. I just did not know what I had done to upset him. I just had to move on and give myself and everyone else a clean sheet and prove to them I was more than ready for succeeding in my new post.

After all I had earned my promotion as it was then called as today it is merely just a transfer to another department. I walked through the front doors of the station an established and successful thief taker. No it had nothing to do with meeting the Chief Inspector or Superintendent on the golf course, or joining the Masons, just good old fashioned dedicated police work got me the role. I did not slide in through the side door either, like they did on the Regional Crime Squad or Stolen vehicle squad as a step to getting into C.I.D. Not that some officers from those areas were not good, but I had gone down the correct track. I had passed my Interview Boards had a good knowledge of the criminal law and could hold my head high, but even with all this, I still had plenty to learn.

I always remember my first case, a testing point to see how good you were, all I could do was go with the evidence using all my practical and investigative skills. We had a report of theft of

£1000 in cash over a period of time at a local Sub- Post office in a busy little village in a suburb of our area. This business was run by two delightful sisters both spinsters and in their mid-sixties who thrived on good customer service but were at their wits end with this serious dilemma which needed resolving as they were emigrating to mid-west America. The pressures of not only moving to the other side of the globe, but having to settle down in a strange and alien environment where they were opening up a similar business. What a daunting challenge you just had to take your hat off to this incredible pair of ladies who were full of confidence and so richly deserved to succeed in their new exciting venture. This discrepancy hung over them like heavy cloud, without a proper result their future was in jeopardy. It all pointed to a middle aged woman who always worked one of the tills who had been out of character with them for some reason. She was one of two other staff who we also had not ruled out.

As with any enquiry it is important to keep an open mind and go with your instincts as far as you can. With a woman detective on attachment we both went to the premises the one morning shortly before opening. The lady arrived and we identified ourselves and informed her she was under arrest on suspicion of theft of money. She would have been the last person you would have thought responsible, a neat, tidy and efficient person in her mid- forties. During interview I stated we would examine all the books leaving no stone unturned, and from experience sometimes we always found more discrepancies than initially first thought. She immediately admitted that she had taken just over a £1000 and pinpointed the amount to £1045 exactly. She explained how she did it and was adamant that was all she had taken. She made the excuse her husband had lost his job. We were shown evidence by her of keeping false records. If not for her honesty about what she had done wrong, we may never have got to the truth as she could have easily blamed everyone else. The proprietors were both realistically aware of this and so grateful we had solved the problem. They left for America their nightmare over. Their dreams had finally come true. The lady received probation and of course lost her job.

Another interesting and clever crime back then involved a team of four men who were connected with theft and unlawful encashment of giro cheques. This crime would be absolutely impossible to commit these days, but back then in the early 1980's it was a thieves paradise as with all kinds of fraud involving so many banking issues. Over the years the banking profession has tightened up completely with customer identification and today these types of offences would be virtually impossible to commit.

These individuals had a good knowledge of the occupants of several multi-storey flats. They worked out who were in receipt of unemployment benefit by looking out at local social security offices. On the day giro's were normally sent out they would go to all the addresses they had targeted and place newspaper under the doors. Most of the main entrance doors to individual flats were draughty with gaps at the base, due to constant changes in tenancy and a newspaper was slid under the doors to catch and retrieve any mail posted through the letterbox. The big advantage to a really ingenious plan was the fact the postman started his round extremely early, shortly after 6.00am. Most people who were not working would have no need to get up at this time of the day. In turn the offenders would then follow the postman discreetly on his round and retrieve the mail which had been pushed through the letter boxes and steal all the giro cheques all in the name of male persons.

The next move was to produce identification in the name of the person entitled to cash the giro and the way this was done was to open a small saving account a building society in the nominal sum of a £1.00. They would give the name and address obtained from the giro and for security the passbook was posted back to the address given. No other form of security checks were made back in those days, so it was easy, they just retrieved the pass book the same way they had stolen the giros. Then when they went to the main Post office in town they had identity in the form of the building society savings book and were paid out the full amount of the giro in cash. This they did with numerous people over several weeks without any detection and the gang netted several thousands of pounds. If only they could have put their talents to more honest purpose.

Naturally these were extremely difficult times for the victims being the poorest people in society some having children. It was if it was a personal robbery without any violence against each and every one of them, who were desperate and virtually had no money. This was a sickening crime, for the thieves were robbing the people most in need who had no one else to turn to. The authorities were very rigid in enforcing the policy that the giro had been issued and cashed in their name and they could not prove to any satisfaction that they had not received payment, so no allowance or refund was awarded. They certainly were unaware a savings account had been opened in their names. The full scale of the fraud did not come to light immediately as several isolated thefts were not reported until we started building a pattern. It was only then that the authorities realised there was a major problem and with Christmas fast approaching it was only our determination that encouraged duplicate payments to be made, directly in person to those poor victims in urgent need of help. To catch a criminal you had to think like a criminal and the pressure was on to catch those responsible. I made a personal visit to see the people in question where I made brief enquiries into their thefts, but more importantly noting their descriptions so I would be aware of this when checking the identity of those cashing the stolen giro cheques. This was also just in case there was any collusion with the actual thieves, but there was no evidence to support this and of course this also helped to eliminate them from any involvement.

At about the appropriate time I was in the post office and out of public view, when one of the offenders presented the stolen giro producing the identification that had been obtained by deception. He was paid the cash and I noted his dress and full description. I had seen him previously in and around the town centre. I decided not to strike at that time but see if anyone else came into the same premises. Not before long another man purporting to be the person entitled to cash a giro using false documents was paid the amount of the giro in cash. I also noted his dress and full description. In those days not all premises had security cameras installed. As he left the post office I followed and kept him in distance. Interestingly enough he went and met up with the other man who had cashed the giro earlier, who was outside a shop a few blocks away. I was able to get to the plain unmarked police vehicle and followed them both as they walked about a mile to a local housing estate, where I saw them enter a house on the corner. At this point I called for assistance and two other detectives arrived together with a uniform fast response vehicle with other officers. We covered all exits and were allowed entry into the address. Inside I saw both men who had been in the post office and arrested them for theft and deception offences.

They were in the main lounge and two other men were present who were also arrested. A thorough search was made and several building society passbooks in names and addresses of other people were found. It transpired we had the whole team and although some were uncooperative initially, we eventually obtained the truth and all admitted responsibility. The total amount of money obtained exceeded £8,000 and although the true owners of all of the giro's had their monies finally refunded, it did not compensate for the unnecessary stigma they endured, or some being completely without money over the previous Christmas period. This reflected in the sentences later given at Crown Court where they all received varying custodial periods in prison, between 12 months and 4 years which they utterly deserved.

CHAPTER 02

WORKING WITH DEAD WOOD

I had experienced many criminal cases during my early years in C.I.D and some of the dead wood officers side moved, and had been replaced but still I had to put up with Dc GLOVER and his tantrums of jealousy. As my desk began to get full with a heavy workload I needed to be organised and plan, incorporating each case into individual folders. To be efficient you had to be on top of your game, as you could easily get into a mess if you failed to take responsibility, a downfall waiting to happen for many a disorganised detective.

After all no matter what the circumstances of the crime involved, whether very serious or not, every victim deserved completely the best of your efforts and skills in trying to detect the matter. However priority was always given to detecting firstly the most serious of crimes and then followed by action in looking at the less aggravating matters. Not that the lesser crimes would be unimportant as either way I would leave no area of investigation unchecked as I would thrive on building where possible the road to detection.

As for Dc GLOVER he was still in the office, it was just sad a person of his service could not adapt to change and became so bitter. At every opportunity he attempted to belittle me in front of all the staff by putting all his rubbish work into folders on his desk, which I had always done as part of my work pattern. This form of copycat mickey taking was just another example of how childish and immature this man was. It was important to locate and find paperwork quickly, which not only helps everyone and saves important time searching for certain documents in your absence. This was a task virtually impossible for such disorganised and lazy people like Dc GLOVER who really had the capability to do better. He just could not adapt to the changes of the modern policing world, and sadly had given up, showing resentment and bitterness often reminiscing the past instead of moving on and being positive with the future. I just bided my time as it was soon approaching the situation where I was more than ready for pay back. One such example where his lack of judgment was obvious involved a complaint from a Director of a Company where monies totalling £50,000 had been stolen over a 12 month period, in present time this amount would be equivalent to several hundred thousand pounds. He attended with another associate Company Director and between them were six large cardboard boxes of evidence to examine.

I had a methodical system when I was shown the ingredients of any fraud there would always be offences be it theft or false accounting. When I was showed any method used I would get the person who was to give evidence, draw up a schedule of the discrepancies. These transactions had taken place over various dates and cross referencing would be made, throughout all the several copies of bookwork and to me this greatly simplified things for easy understanding of the fraud.

Like with all office fraud it normally starts when a member is entrusted with petty cash. They borrow and fail to put it back, before knowing they are out of their depth and without realising allow it to escalate from just hundreds to thousands of pounds over a period of time. This one clerk for the company used to ask the Directors to jointly sign cheques which she had written out for £100. This was used towards petty cash purchases and as stated she started using this money as her own. It got to the point where before cashing the cheque, where she had written in words one hundred pounds, where the word [one] was written, it was made to look like a one but more like [our] with a bit of a squiggle in the handwriting. After the cheques had been signed by both of the directors she then altered the details. She then inserted the letter [f] making the word four, and with the figure [1 [as shown in 100 changed it to [4] making the total cheque for £400 instead of £100. She did this for a complete cheque book.

Not realising the full extent of her activities the Directors then both jointly signed blank cheques, as they felt she could be trusted. This was the ultimate prize the perfect recipe for theft. She had worked for them for a period of some three years and had completely gained their trust and could just help herself continually taking money at every opportunity, which was precisely what she did. Without any annual audit she remained free until eventually discrepancies were found which meant complete disaster for the company. Unfortunately I had to ask Dc GLOVER to assist and to my dismay when the woman was arrested, he allowed the husband to sit in on the interview. Despite voicing my objection to him privately, he just pulled rank which at that time I had no control over. I thought to myself how naïve this was, just completely unprofessional. I was still in my first year of probation within C.I.D. and could not cross the line. In those days any interview with an accused notes would either be taken at the time or as soon after the interview had ceased. There was no way to conduct any lengthy interview without making notes, especially when I had to show the suspect all the cheques she may have written and note any replies.

I started to make notes and it was obvious I was irritating Dc GLOVER and before long he just got up and walked out of the Interview room, leaving me alone to continue. Again this was another example of his unprofessionalism and as infuriating as it was, I had to maintain control, in any case it showed his consistency in being narrow minded and immature. I thought what if the husband is involved in disposing of the proceeds, so why the hell is he even in the room. This however was an avenue that I could not change or justify, due to Dc GLOVER allowing him there in the first place. I would have preferred a solicitor to have been present instead. Nevertheless I persevered until I had gone completely through all the documents. She admitted writing almost all of the cheques with the exception of a few which she could not recall or identify her writing. She was charged with specimen offences whilst full committal proceedings to Crown Court were prepared. In the meantime she was freed on bail.

Within 3 months, I received a further complaint involving a separate company where I established the same woman had commenced employment again where there were discrepancies involving monies. Apparently she had lied to this new firm about her last job and they were unaware of her impending predicament.

She was again arrested and admitted her involvement in another separate theft of £1000 and was charged. Again in present time this amount would be equivalent to well over ten thousand pounds. This time she did not have her husband present on any interview and both cases were linked together.

Whilst waiting for the matter to reach Crown Court, there was an unusual twist in the case. The wife of one of the Directors who trained this clerk, who was a Company Secretary with another firm, was herself sent to prison for embezzlement of monies. She had also admitted writing some of the cheques which the Clerk had denied responsibility, so it was of the utmost importance on that previous interview I had shown her all the cheques to make any necessary comment. The original offender was telling the truth about the cheques not written by her, which we now knew were possibly made out by the company secretary who was sent to prison. It was self-evident a written record of what was said by the accused about her writing of the cheques was of extreme importance, but this was no thanks to Dc GLOVER.

As for accounting to where all the monies had gone, she stated it supported the family income and other luxuries and holidays. She denied her husband had any knowledge but that line of enquiry was now ruined and could not be resurrected, as he was fully aware of what had been said during the interviews.

As I said, I had the last laugh as I had a lift to the Crown Court at the city where the trial was held. Within an hour of the Court starting, she had pleaded guilty to all offences and was given a prison sentence. But Dc GLOVER was unaware of this, especially when he answered the phone whilst in the C.I.D. office. I told him in a firm and demanding manner, "You are wanted in Crown Court immediately to give evidence bring your pocket book and get a move on. Hurry up here the judge is waiting and is losing his patience. He wants to know why you were not in Court at the beginning of the case" Dc GLOVER was lost for words and sputtering in his speech, in a kind of nervous and sensed panic. I put the phone down and just smiled to myself of the mental torture I had just created, being so long overdue and the fact that it could not have happened to a nicer person. Within half an hour after a possible horrendous journey where his mind and thoughts would be in overdrive of all the difficult and embarrassing questions to be asked him, he finally arrived. As he came rushing up the Court steps all in a fluster and totally disorientated. I said, "It is okay, you are not needed now. She pleaded guilty. Take me back to the station." I was fuming inside with intolerable laughter but I dare not give the game away. He never knew the real story but I realised that he would have been panicking and probably needed a change of underwear. I am sure he got his knickers in a twist and paid the price of his failure and fitted completely the description given being dead wood. As much as I wanted to laugh directly into his face, I knew it would create even worse problems for the future. I realised you just had to keep your enemies close especially with a man like him.

Clearing crime can come in many forms and without blowing my own trumpet I had to include this form of a challenge. I was out alone on enquiries. I was just about to leave this shop when a youth aged about 19 years came in asking if they wanted £5 of sixpences in change, this was prior to decimalisation and would be the equivalent of £20 at present day value. Not exactly crime of the century maybe, but just simple curiosity made me approach him. I politely took him to one side away from the building. The shop was unable to fulfil his request and he had the coins with him. I produced identification and asked him where he had the money from. He was a little obstructive and later stated the coins were from his home. He purported that he had collected them, storing them in a bottle under his bed. I asked if he would mind me going back home to check this story out and he objected. Going on the theory a policeman is duty bound to ask questions of any person even if he only, suspects that a crime has taken place. This applies even if later established no crime was committed. I told him if he didn't cooperate I could arrest him. His attitude remained the same and he was arrested on suspicion of committing an arrestable offence. This was a very useful power given to the police and very rarely used, but I was of the view it fitted the criteria perfectly. He was taken to the police station and placed into custody.

Whilst I was completing my pocket book, the jungle drums were already pounding, Dc GLOVER with a couple of other dead beats were revelling in the possibility I had abused my powers and they spent more time being inquisitive about my investigations than getting on with their own work. They clearly thought I had committed professional suicide. I just had to carry on do my job and take no notice. I explained the prisoner had to accompany me to his home address and I needed an assistant to drive us there. A Dc Harold PEGG was nominated, a little loud mouth who gave the impression that he knew it all, but was clearly above his station. Due to his enforced involvement I could see the fear and resentment in his eyes as he felt drawn into this web of insanity, which I am sure he believed was all going to turn out sinister and seriously implicating him into the bargain. Well he need not have worried, we arrived at the address and the young prisoner remained in the car with him. I went to the house and the youth's father answered the door. I showed him identification and he listened to what I had said relating to the circumstances of his sons arrest and invited me inside. We went to the son's bedroom and established full justification for all my actions. There was no bottle under the bed or anywhere in the house. The lad was just plain lazy and as for savings and had not got two pennies to rub together. I produced the bag of coins. The father took me into his bedroom where in the dressing table drawer it was found full of some other 20 plastic bags of the same design, all containing sixpences that he had saved.

Following this I confronted the lad in the presence of his father and Dc PEGG, where he admitted stealing the money from the drawer. His father completely supported my actions and was extremely appreciative. He wanted to prosecute and later I thought a formal caution would be more appropriate, after all it was his son and a crime had been cleared. I was confident from this lad's father's demeanour that he was more than capable of instilling any necessary discipline, to compensate for such criminal behaviour. After all he had not previously come to the notice of the police and this decision proved more positive than any Court action as with the son's remorsefulness it would soon play a major part towards him not reoffending again.

He was returned to the station and paperwork completed and released with the proposed action taken. DI MOUNT, who was very much a disciplinarian and very approachable, heard the full story of my involvement against the backlash of the other officers. He wanted to give me a commendation for my work in pursuing a role many would not have even contemplated. I think this would have been to wind up the dead wood and although in some way a very nice compliment, but it would have been all at my expense. I thanked him for his comments, but refused after all I had enough jealously to contend with. Even the slimy Dc GLOVER shook my hand to congratulate me, but I knew he would rather have seen me fall on my sword. He was losing whatever credibility he had left in his role as detective but I could still use him in a way he did not have the ability to detect, as you will see further in this book. As for Dc PEGG although younger in service, he was to me was also considered dead wood, as the following example clearly shows.

We were working together again one evening and he had to pay a visit to a victim of crime who was not on the telephone. He was investigating the theft of a purse quite a minor but infuriating offence. What he failed to realise was this matter was connected to a series of similar offences in the main town which made it a serious problem where the villains must be caught. After all if you have a purse or wallet stolen not only does it contain items of a sentimental value, money, bank or credit cards, it may include identification, house or car keys. The horrors of such potential for further criminal use of these possessions are a constant worry, in some cases worse than the initial theft itself.

At the house he spoke to the lady who had her purse stolen, which was taken whilst she was having a drink in one of several of the town's licensed premises. This officer who was tall, very fit had five years more service than me and I left him to speak to the victim. He stated, 'I have to see you about your report of crime and inform you I have made enquiries that have met with a negative result. This matter will now be filed pending any further developments'. The lady responded by thanking him for his interest and calling to visit personally.

We were about to walk away I stopped and asked if he minded me asking a question. He looked at me with an element of surprise as I asked the lady did she have any idea who was responsible for taking the purse. Immediately she told me the names of two other women who were acting suspiciously at the time and that she suspected them to be responsible for taking the purse. They were both mother and daughter, who were well known to us in the town centre area. I thanked her for this information stating that I would take positive action and would notify her of any result of my enquiries. We then left the address, but I could not understand why she had not commented during Dc PEGG's conversation. Maybe she had no confidence in the police and if based on the grounds of any previous lack of action by the police, in some past dealings who could possibly blame her. Without my intervention we were utterly defenceless if she had raised any such issue in any accusation of poor police work based on DC PEGG's negative conduct.

Driving back to the station you could have cut the atmosphere with a knife it was that bad. I just could not believe it, he had not even bothered to ask the victim one basic question which is important with any criminal investigation, that being any idea who could have been responsible. Needless to say he had been trained by Dc GLOVER and was his protégée, one of a few disciples still in that circle of dead wood. That said everything. The annoying problem was there were many officers who would have loved his position in C.I.D. who could eat him for breakfast in solving crime. How sad. Never mind Dc PEGG had excellent skills as a football and cricket player and if he had devoted as much time to police work as his sporting activities he might have stood a chance, but from my experiences, I did not think so. He later transferred to a desk job away from front line policing where he remained for the completion of his service.

As for the two female suspects I later arrested them and eventually they admitted being responsible for all the purse thefts over a three month period, well over 30 offences including some not reported to us. They got probation and were fined and had to pay complete compensation to all victims, including the lady who was treated so negatively by Dc PEGG. That was pure job satisfaction and I hope restored a little more faith to those dissolutioned with the police, who have operated with such apathetic approach to their duties and responsibilities in clearing crime.

I remember working one weekend and arrived for the afternoon shift. Walking into the CID office I received a telephone call from an irate man who was a well-known burglar. He was asking where the morning detective was and if he was coming to his address. He had been waiting over an hour and stated he and his cronies had been threatened by a well-known drug dealer who had produced a firearm. This particular man was a renowned criminal, who had an extremely violent background and would easily fit into the category of a potential murderer, as he was completely without any scruples. I advised the caller we would be straight down. No matter what the background of any potential victim, whether a convicted criminal or not, when there is the slightest inclination that a possible murder may be committed, police action must always be positive, no matter what the circumstances. Something this officer clearly was incapable of recognising. This detective officer was a formal golf semi-professional and an advocate of the Superintendent and other senior officers, who had instigated his promotion to CID. Trouble was they did not have to work with him, that's if he actually had any work in him from what I could see. Although likeable enough, all he was to me was a wasted useless addition, more of a liability especially when there were so many other more suitable candidates. I walked into the canteen and there was the alert so-called detective watching sports on television. I thought to myself, I'll teach you. I said to him, "Did you receive a call about an hour ago, over a man allegedly having a gun in his possession making threats." "Oh yea" he replied, as if the issue was of no importance. I said, "Come on then, you will be pleased to know two men have just been shot, ones lying in the street the other has managed to get away on foot believed badly injured." I said, "So what action did you take then." He said, "Nothing yet, I was going to go down later." I said, "That was over an hour ago, so your negative action has resulted in all this mayhem." I told him he was in deep trouble and I kept up this pretence all the way to the scene, where I arrived at the complainant's home address. Upon arrival at the scene, after enlightening this officer to the true facts, I told him let this be a lesson, as it easily could have happened. Somehow he seemed to lose his confidence in realising the huge mistake he had made and could not apologise enough.

Inside the house it was quite invigorating seeing there were around ten people all in the lounge, all serious muggers and burglars, all frightened and afraid to go outside, in turn asking for the protection of the police. How two faced can these people be, dealing in life's double standards where it is okay for them to thieve and rob, but then want protection by the police from other criminals.

All were too scared to make statements, so I asked them how could we prosecute without any of their evidence and if they failed to cooperate there was little we could do. It was a pity the previous scenario hadn't become a reality, then they might have all undergone severe criminal career changes and the detective may have had to take up golfing for a living again. In addition I relished in the idea that he could still come back anytime and give a repeat performance, also guaranteeing we could not give full police protection 24/7, but this did not even change their minds. It was quite an experience watching them all shuddering and in fear, feeling so vulnerable for once they too were tasting the opposite side of criminal behaviour from a normal victims perspective. I could have maintained this pressure for very much longer but we were called away.

The Detective Inspector returned back at the station being on weekend cover, I explained the main offender had been arrested and an imitation firearm found. This gun was surrendered by him and without any witnesses coming forward he got released from custody. It proves the point when you do have evidence you can always use one criminal to put another off the streets all in the name of crime detection and prevention. Sadly on this occasion it did not work but there were always plenty of opportunities during my time in Office.

Discussing later with the Detective Inspector, the subject of this frightened and intimidated group of villains, who had endured such uncomfortable threats of violence, I had the perfect plan to reshape their lives. I just had to smile and see his reaction when I told him I was arranging for the council to rehouse them all and that they were going elsewhere to live, and not on our patch. I told him it's called Crime Prevention in the reallocation of criminals.

He asked where they were moving to and I told him the name of the area I had in mind. He was not amused when he realised it was adjacent to his home address and I cannot repeat any of the language used to express his feelings. Although I was only joking which at the time he did not appreciate, I wished I had explained that's the price you pay if you want to live out in the country, or if you want to take up golf as a sport and meet to recruit future police detectives. However in the circumstances for once, I think I had said enough and did not wish to push my luck.

So here we were several years later after sorting out all the dead wood and they started transferring officers of this calibre to CID. One might think to one's self does nothing ever change in life as history clearly repeats itself.

CHAPTER 03

NIGHT DETECTIVE

Several times throughout the year I had to perform a week of nights, seven days without sleep that was my problem. I covered all four stations on the division, being the highest ranking Detective on duty, where your talent and ability was tested and often called into question. There were so many interesting cases I could write forever.

We had a warehouse on the one area where five men were involved in loading a lorry. They had broken into the building and were in the process of removing electrical items including televisions, microwaves, computers or anything else they could get their hands on. The police were called and one young dedicated uniform constable attended. Upon arrival he had disturbed them. Three were from one family all hardened criminals, who were with two other known offenders. They all drove off and the officer was able to circulate the number of their vehicle. The lorry and stolen goods had been abandoned. With combined efforts of the shift they were all arrested at their home address, in a cul-de-sac where they lived opposite each other. They were all violent upon arrest and had to be restrained and were taken to the police station with each of them denying any involvement.

It was 3.00am and one of the men in custody had just half a beard as he was in the process of shaving when suddenly apprehended. He was not allowed to continue and later photographed for evidence. I was summoned to attend and in turn I interviewed each and every one of them under caution. All I did was just listen to their lies which were just pathetic, but enough for them to lose their credibility. Especially the man with half a beard it was just so funny, he even went to Court where I am sure he was a laughing stock with many other spectators, something today which would cause criticism from Human Rights supporters.

We were then interviewing under tape recording facilities this was an excellent step forward in detecting and investigating offenders. The down side we had to write up the interview ourselves if you wanted everything to be included, otherwise the typists would only do a short precise which sometimes was not enough. Some police stations however were still awaiting tape recorder interview facilities and in these cases we had to revert to taking down questions and answers in the form of contemporaneous notes. This was an arduous and tiring experience compared with interviewing by tape and video recorder which was a great improvement to everyday policing. Their Hans Christian Anderson fairy tales, combined with forensic evidence found at the scene and the arresting officers descriptions of what he discovered upon arrival, cooked their goose. There was more than enough work for the daytime staff to continue with to complete the enquiry. All were later charged with Burglary and Theft involving an incredible amount of high value property and were remanded into custody. They eventually all pleaded guilty and received substantial prison sentences.

One of my main promises that I had made prior being in C.I.D. was that I would never take the glory for other officer's good work, uniform or plain clothes. I remembered back when in uniform, like when I arrested three persons for stealing cash from the public house and had no recognition for my work with C.I.D. taking the glory. This time I was determined to write up a full report relating to the excellent good work and involvement in clearing the crime. Quite rightly all officers involved received commendations.

One other occasion again on nights I attended another station where a prolific burglar was in custody. This offender together with another had been seen running away from attacked shop premises where jewellery had been stolen. The other man was still at large. The man in custody had a reputation for being difficult and awkward who was denying responsibility. Aware of this, the uniform Sergeant asked specifically that he and I conduct the interview together anticipating a hard confrontation where we would have to dig deep for the truth.

In between time I was able to have a quick word with the prisoner who was well known as a drinking buddy with Dc GLOVER. I falsely told him I had spoken to this officer and that he advised him to come clean tell the truth about everything, and he would call to see him later in the day. It worked when we did the interview the uniform Sergeant nearly fell out of his seat when he admitted straight away what he had done and even implicated his accomplice. The uniform officers then went to this other man's address and he too was arrested. All the stolen property was found and together both of the men were later charged where they later both pleaded guilty receiving prison sentences.

I don't think Dc GLOVER ever realised this had taken place, but it was good to see that he did have some uses, even if he was in my view, more on the side of the criminal. Eventually Dc GLOVER had lost all his sponsors and instead of being returned to uniform duties which in my view was long overdue, he was side moved into an intelligence role. At least he was in a position where he could again attempt to creep around gaffers. Even from his new role he would still have a dig and for all the small drawers in and around his desk in the Intelligence Office he would leave cards showing the words, Fuck off - LUNN being my surname. I think he went to his grave hating me, quite sad really.

Later in my service I started working with a woman Detective Constable Shirley MYLES who had transferred from the city. She was in her late twenties, attractive and well-presented who was always smartly dressed. Initially no one wanted to work with her so I volunteered and did not regret it for one minute. She was a lovely genuine hard working person. She was extremely dedicated and proved all her critics wrong. In the end we were the envy of the office and they tried to split us up in order to reflect some of our hard working ability on others.

We had received information that heavy plant equipment valued at £100.000 was going to be stolen from a building site. It was to be driven onto a heavy goods vehicle and sold. That was all we knew, but all these types of property were exported through the black market worldwide and sold on to undeveloped countries which proved to be an extremely lucrative crime.

A call was made to confirm it was on and at about 6.00pm on this Friday night we staked the area out together with a team of other officers, all being fully prepared to work throughout the night. We established the vehicle taking the plant equipment was in place. It had been reversed back into the side of an embankment and exactly in line with the ground level for it to be driven into place. Further sightings in the distance showed another person was driving the plant towards our direction. When it arrived, both men communicated with each other, whilst the plant was guided into place onto the vehicle. It was time to strike, as we did they split up running off in different directions but eventually were each arrested.

All were taken back to the station. It was late Friday night and just about midnight and my female colleague and I were on duty all that weekend, with both men in custody we had more than our fair share of work. This was not including anything else that would happen or could have been reported to us. Of course no one wanted to assist and work with us once the arrests had been made. I suppose you could not blame them really after all it was weekend, so it was down to Shirley and me. We had a Detective Inspector Sidney ATKINSON who was close to retirement, with certain qualities which he could have used more often. He was in his late fifties and had black hair with signs of grey which I believe he dyed regularly. He stated he was on weekend cover and if we needed any advice he was available on the phone. How admirable.

I suppose it sounds a little bitter but when you are working your socks off and others are just in the background earning higher wages and not doing anything it just goes against the grain. In any case we were better off working alone. Morale was never high in the office when he was in charge as there were so many better senior officers who were the complete opposite and extremely harder working and professional. As we worked into the night and the following day, both men went on the basis that they did not know each other and were both totally unconnected with any crime. The one man stated just prior to his arrest he had phoned his wife to say he was calling at the chip shop and would bring home some supper, as he had gone to meet his mate in the pub, but he had not arrived.

I always carried two important documents with me whilst on duty, [1] Witness statement Forms, and [2] Consent to Search Premises Forms. They proved so invaluable for everyday police work and their uses feature in a further story. It was necessary to search both home addresses using a uniform Inspectors authority. At the home of the one man we had interviewed, we spoke to his wife who was a genuine smart lady. She told a completely different story to that of her husband and I thought this has to be committed in writing before she colluded with him and changed her mind, thus the importance of having a witness statement with you at all times. During a search I discovered a photograph of both men together and the wife stated it was her husband and brother in law. That was it, the connection was established.

Back at the station we continued interviewing and both men tried to blame each other before finally coming clean. All their clothing was seized and sent off to forensics and scenes of crime examined both vehicles. Fingerprints were found for one of the offenders. We had assistance from other staff and both were charged, they later pleaded guilty, both were sent to prison.

As for D.I. ATKINSON needless to say was busy in a supervisory capacity and left us alone to deal. He was not far from retirement but thought he was God's gift to women, always combing his black dyed hair in the mirror. He had been out most of the afternoon this one day and when he returned back into the station I told him another detective officer had tried to speak to him. I just extracted the urine in other words, took the pee out of him and tongue in cheek said, "Don't worry Boss, I just told the caller Elvis had left the building." I was obviously referring to him fitting the description of Elvis. With a look of utter disgust from him and at frustration with what to say in reply, I was waiting for his reaction. If he had criticised me I simply would have explained Elvis was a good looking bloke and I was paying him a compliment. Either way he didn't address the issue, I just smiled thinking to myself I had upset him for that moment, had he lost his sense of humour, that's what you get with moody people, an attitude which mostly attributed to his character. He always liked to dish it out, but when it came to him taking a joke well that was a different story. His pedigree was always using excess authority to cause mainly policewomen to cry, in other words having the actions of a bully. To me regardless of any rank these people deserve no respect whatsoever and were a disgrace to the job. He just walked off and made no comment possibly thinking how he could put the knife in or try to get me back. I could live with that as deep down I had no time for these vindictive kinds of individuals.

Again I was on nights and sent to a nasty indecent assault, bordering attempted rape upon a female. A young uniform constable attended the scene, together with other officers. Due to good positive action by this young officer he had searched the area and had detained a middle aged man fitting the description whom he subsequently arrested.

Upon arrival, together with this same Officer we conducted an interview. The man was denying any involvement and the interview document was completed. All his clothing had been seized and we also had him medically examined by the police surgeon.

At a separate part of the station a policewoman interviewed the female, who was with her parents and she too was seen by the police surgeon. Altogether all the various specimens were taken and logged correctly for both victim and offender, then placed into police storage for sending off to forensics, together with all the seized clothing. I left a full report covering all action taken for the early C.I.D. shift and the offender remained in custody in order further investigation could be continued. I remained present at the station until the morning detectives arrived. I spoke with two officers a constable and sergeant, completely covering all the aspects of the cases and each and every action undertaken, which was all included in a full typed report which I also handed to them for reference. So then I left and headed for my own station to debrief officers there of events taking place that night before finally booking off duty.

Due to it being busy, I did not hear anything about the case and about 6 weeks later and phoned up in curiosity and spoke to the officer in charge. I spoke to the Detective Sergeant who was near retirement, who had taken over the case from me finishing the night shift. He was a close associate of Dc GLOVER. Although I could not prove it, I thought here we go again behind my back the poison had been put about running down my ability. Enquiring about the case he explained the offender was allowed police bail, and in view of no further evidence the charge was refused. I was gob smacked, what was going on, this I did not believe.

I asked about the results of any forensic examination and he did not know what I was talking about. Retrieving a copy of my report left with him at the end of that night shift, I reminded him of all the issues and pointed out again all that we had done including the taking of specimens.

He too was flabbergasted in that he had overlooked the issue of all the forensic evidence which was still in the fridge and storage area. It just was not good enough I believed he was more credible than this, I told him exactly my views, which were justifiably severely critical comments and the fact that I had shown gross disappointment in his lack of actions. He apologised profusely and finally sent off all exhibits for analysis. I thought if you just did your job instead of listening to jealous tickle tackle, you might just be a better policeman.

Finally the result came back positive, connecting the offender to the victim, through clothing and intimate samples. He then re-arrested the offender who was duly charged and pleaded guilty, where he was sent to prison. I raised this issue with a senior Officer at that Station, but it did not make any difference, the same Sergeant remained in C.I.D until his retirement a few months later. He was just lucky that the man had not offended previously, or whilst out on bail, as the type of offence he had committed was partial ingredients for being a potential killer. More importantly the victim in the case deserved better and fortunately she never knew of this poor police work. At least in the end the offender was punished and finally sent to prison. I would have hated to have thought of the consequences if I had not telephoned for an update of the case. The forensic specimens and clothing could have been there for time immemorial. It just goes to show you should never ever take your finger off the pulse.

It does not matter what rank you are, in police work you have to always cover the basic principles and leave no stone unturned. Either I was becoming more professional, or the job was changing. Sadly it was the latter and I found after that, you could not ever take things for granted you had to ensure yourself the job in all aspects had been done properly. Where as in the old days this would hopefully never of happened. There is no accounting for thoroughness which is always a complete must.

CHAPTER 04

MINOR CRIMES LEADING TO SERIOUS OFFENCES

With WDC MYLES we had another menacing form of deception, this time committed by a man who was from an eastern country who was married to a lady from the Caribbean Islands, both had immigrated and they owned their own property on a neighbouring division.

He had entered our country legally some 15 years previous and upon marriage became a British citizen. She had lived here three years before. Unfortunately a short time, of being here due to an injury he became disabled. Eventually he was in receipt of full benefits and was being paid not only for the interest, but all payments against his capital on his mortgage as well and had received such payments for a least a five to ten year period.

Not being allegedly capable or able to work, he would tour round various DIY stores of a well-known national retailer, creating a nuisance in the pursuance of obtaining property by deception. He would find expensive tools and switch price labels to a lower amount. Taking the goods for payment at the till, when the price did not match the correct value for the goods he would argue in a menacing manner that he would only pay for the goods at the amount displayed. He stated if the mistake was the sellers tough, he demanded to buy the goods for the amount shown, which unknown to them, he himself had instigated in a thoroughly corrupt and dishonest way. Then not happy with this selfish crime, he would take the goods to another store a couple of days later stating they were inferior and not suitable for purpose and asked for a refund. He claimed he had lost the receipt, but some documentation was still attached to the item showing they were sold by this national chain. He was refunded twice the amount he had paid for it. This he did not once but several times when visiting at least four different branches of their stores throughout the country. The chief Security Officer for the Company was a former serving police officer and had formulated the evidence, which all lead to the same offender. His frustrations were endless as he could not get the matter deal with on a one to one basis, as other police divisions in our force area would only deal with their own incidents. This was minimising the actions and deceit of the man responsible. Surely if he was capable of this kind of criminal activity, he was also able to work as he could drive and walk.

With two locations of crime on our sub-division and the remainder within our force area, I took on board the enquiry in the interest of justice and although not exactly crime of the century, the matter needed to be dealt with collectively and correctly.

Together with a uniform presence, we both attended the offender's home address. I explained the nature of our enquiry, to which he denied all knowledge. He was duly arrested for criminal deception and informed a full thorough search would be made of his home address. During the search various receipts and incriminating evidence were found. His wife remained calm during this period, but his behaviour was getting restless and in a menacing manner he was shouting obscenities towards us all. He was suddenly aware his previous escapades were finally catching up with him. I saw he had what appeared to be a small metal object, a blade exposed from his one hand. He was immediately restrained and a metal Stanley knife was taken from him, he was handcuffed then placed into a police vehicle outside. He was later taken back to our area, and interviewed at length in the presence of a solicitor.

Throughout questioning he still maintained his innocence, saying he had bought the goods in good faith, but just changed them for a refund. He knew exactly what he had been doing making over £100 with each transaction, but the worst experience was all the nasty incidents Staff had to tolerate, in his committing of the offences. He was extremely arrogant and abusive when demanding refunds, the experience for them in some cases was unforgettable and that was also his downfall, which helped Staff remember him clearly. He pleaded not guilty at Court but was found responsible and fined. Upon him being convicted the firm in question was so relieved that it was hopefully the end of his reign of terror in committing such nuisance offences. It was also pleasing and refreshing for WDC MYLES and I to receive a letter of praise sent via the Chief Constables Office, for the hard work and determination in finally prosecuting this culprit. I still have a copy of such letter in my possession today. It was a pity the Court did not contemplate making an order for him to be medically examined, where he would have most certainly been found eligible for work and capable of getting employment. Then like everyone else he would have to work honestly for a living. In my view he had a clear and dishonest streak about his character as soon as he realised he could always get something for nothing.

Another amusing story which I recall was the arrest of a notorious family member who was always violent in his actions or approach to police officers. We received information he was responsible for obtaining goods by deception and with support of uniform we visited is home early one morning. True to form he was violent and a forced entry was made. He was arrested for criminal deception and informed the house was going to be searched.

During the search in a vase on the dressing table I saw a British driving licence. It was not the current computer type with a photograph we have today, as these documents then had not been invented, but the green type licence in a plastic holder. Immediately I saw that the name and address related to some other person. This was the document I was looking for which was involved in the deceptions. I said to him, "What about this licence then, why is it here?" He replied, "Well I am glad you found that Officer, you have saved me a visit to your local nick. I was outside the house a couple of days ago and I saw it lying on the pavement, so I picked it up. I thought being the good honest citizen that I am, I would hand this found property into the police. Now you have saved me all the time and trouble. You can take it with you."

He could not have said a worse thing, as you will find out during the interview. So he was duly arrested for Deception offences and back at the station he had his Solicitor there holding his hand, I mean representing him. We went through the formalities and he reiterated the circumstances and the story given over the finding of the licence. I then showed him over 20 documents all relating to several high value items of plant equipment, amounting to several hundreds of pounds. They had each been hired at numerous locations during a two year period, by a person purporting to be the holder of this licence, which had been stolen. No property hired was ever found, and was obviously sold.

As I showed him each document individually, he gave the same reply, "No Sir, never seen that ever before in my life." I then couldn't resist saying to him, "Well let me put it to you straight, you are clearly not the honest good citizen that you purport to be Mr Jones." This being a false name to protect his identity. "In fact nothing could be further from the truth." It was then pointed out that majority of the documents shown had been forensically examined and that his fingerprints had been identified as being present on the surface of each, proving without doubt they had been handled by him. It was suggested this occurred during the time he signed for the goods hired by him and that he had obviously been lying to us from the very start about his full involvement.

His immediate answer, for which I wished I had at least a £20 note for every time I had heard it said, was, "No Comment." He could have been a parrot from then on, for that was his answer to every other question for remainder of the interview. That was fine, but it had the right effect his cockiness was deflated and the smile removed from his face. He was charged with all the offences and later made an appearance before a Judge at Crown Court where he pleaded guilty. This Judge was not impressed or amused with his rendition of being a good honest citizen character and this reflected in the worthy sentence of imprisonment that was given to him.

One of the most incredible crimes we detected was due to the activities of a dishonest lorry driver. He was travelling throughout most regions of our country and was clearly very much an opportunist thief. He had his own modest home, but the back garden was something else, he had six large purpose built garden sheds for the storage and disposal of a varying amounts of stolen property. You would have thought for this man who was in his early sixties and a grandfather he could have set a better example. One who would have been satisfied being in a secure regularly paid job and a role for which he had held for many years. He clearly was in it for greed as when we looked into his background this life of crime was all unnecessary. We also had to think how long had he gotten away with such activities before being apprehended.

He was caught red handed driving off in a lorry without authority laden with television sets, during the daytime from a warehouse, resulting in several people being arrested. He was well away from home and during his stay in custody it became apparent he was no innocent person. It was decided to accompany the man back home whilst in custody where a thorough search was made of his home address.

The house was clean but the purpose built garden sheds revealed that it was a complete thief's paradise. He was so well organised he treated his criminal profession either as a business or a major boost to his pension funding. For a man of his age he quite frankly should have been ashamed of himself. All sheds were found full to capacity, all with stolen goods which he had received at some time previous which were under his care or protection. A large amount of confectionary was discovered well over a hundred single boxes of classic chocolates made specifically for wealthy organisations, including the Royal Family and the House of Commons the names of which were printed on the packaging. In addition there were numerous electrical items, drills, sanders, all still in original boxes and a varied selection of other expensive DIY tools.

He was selling all items to increase his income, and kids were walking the streets eating the described chocolates sold at £1-00 a box when in fact they were valued to be each worth a minimum of £10 at cost value then, yet alone compared to today's prices. All this with expensive packaging of the highest standard especially made for the chosen few. The remaining stolen property was sold through newspapers, or in local pubs. In addition he also sold tools and electrical goods which he advertised in local newspapers and had a thriving enterprise. He admitted responsibility for varying offences of theft and handling stolen property, yet despite his age quite rightly was sentenced to imprisonment.

Life moves in mysterious ways and one weekend I went into work and as always, my first visit would be to the cells, where I would see who had been arrested overnight. To my amazement I recognised one person whom I had not seen for over 20 odd years. I had to look twice as I could not believe it he was a distant relative who was in custody. He was a mature sensible man, an Accountant by trade and close to his late forties. Speaking to the arresting officer, a young uniformed sergeant who advised me there had been a party at a semi-detached property on a private housing estate. This man had invited both neighbours from either side and all those in close proximity as gesture of good will to come and join his girlfriend and close friends in a birthday celebration. He advised everyone who did not wish to attend that it would be going on until sometime before midnight, which my colleagues and I thought was quite reasonable.

The evening went well except for the one neighbour next door, who complained to the police about the noise around 10.00pm. Upon arrival of the uniformed police everyone confirmed the actions of the party organiser had been fair and sensible. The complainant was advised the party was finishing at 11.00pm and they informed him this was a special occasion and perfectly reasonable. As he was advised, at that appropriate time everything closed down and eventually all left quietly as initially promised.

For some reason this was not good enough for this man's neighbour, as all he had on his mind was revenge and obviously bore a grudge. At 4.00am the following morning to demonstrate his objections this man decided to turn on his stereo full blast to the annoyance of everyone in the neighbourhood, in a pathetic attempt to have his own back. This was going on for some time and the man who had held the party awoke, went downstairs and outside. He found this persons garage door open and went inside using a torch. He found a fuse box and turned off the power, thus stopping the noise of the stereo. As he started to walk out he accidentally kicked over a full bottle of milk which was broken. At this point the owner who had made his way also into the garage confronted him for being in his property and punched him to the face with the man retaliating also punching him in the chest.

As a result the neighbour called the police, who upon arrival arrested this alleged criminal intruder. No problem with this, but there always two sides to a story. This young sergeant advised the neighbour had also been arrested for assault as well who had been charged and bailed. As for the man in the cells he had been charged with burglary with intent, theft of milk, criminal damage to the fuse box, and assault. Talk about an overkill. He had never been in trouble in his life and could have ended up with criminal convictions due to this unfortunate incident all because of this man's antics.

Not that my relative was anyway correct in his actions, although some people might have thought otherwise, he should have waited for the authorities to deal rather than take the law into his own hands. He had the right to elect trial by a jury at Crown Court. Whether he was a distant relative to me or not was immaterial, I would have helped anyone in that kind of situation. I told him to seek the advice of a Solicitor and plead not guilty.

All this man was really guilty of in the circumstances, as with the neighbour was conduct likely to cause a breach of the peace, which is no conviction and both had to agree to be bound over to be of good order and keep the peace for a period of 12 months. It was a job well done, all due to simple common sense in an awkward neighbourly incident.

Earlier in this book I always raised the importance of where minor issues lead to serious ones and sometimes it is good to follow up a small lead with what appears a petty offence. We had one such an example which proves the very point. We had information from a fairly reliable source that this man had bought a brand new settee for cash and information was that it might have been stolen.

This kind of sale goes on all the time as a man has a friend of a friend who can get something at half price. That maybe genuine if he has access to a Company's Discount System, or not if he is selling stolen property. We started off making routine enquiries and visited the home address of the purchaser, who was obviously concerned but also cooperative. In fairness he bought the settee in good faith believing the person was entitled to sell it. He had paid a fair price in cash without receipt and gave the name of the contact. We obtained a witness statement from him, together with details of the model and manufacturer of the furniture, which was trading within our sub-division, being a fairly major concern employing a good workforce.

Our next move was to trace the source and after visiting several addresses we finally located this man who actually used to work at the same factory. He was taken to the police station and placed into custody. He put forward the name of the person who could get the settees, implicating they were off the back of a lorry. It was obvious things were underhanded, as this other man he had been sacked some 12 months previous from the same factory. It was beginning to appear also that more than one person was involved. In pursuit of this other person named we established his home address where we called. He was present on arrival and also taken into custody. He was panicking and straight away admitted selling over 50 settees all since he had left the firm. It transpired when the firms van was loaded with orders, an extra settee was added which had been stolen. This item was dropped off at this offender's home for storage in his garage until he had a seller.

He implicated altogether half a dozen staff who was involved. In addition he took us out showing us different premises where he had access and we recovered 3 three piece settees, each with a retail value of £1000 each.

We then visited the firm, and went down with several colleagues and spoke with the Manager. As a result of enquiries a further six men were taken into custody, which accounted for about one third of the workforce. It just mushroomed with everyone shopping everyone and even the Manager was later implicated. It was necessary to fetch in the Area Manager who took over the running of the business whilst our investigation continued.

We could not prove offences against everyone but it was a good crime prevention exercise for the future with the company, albeit after the event. The main offenders were charged and appeared at Court, where they pleaded guilty to theft and handling stolen property. They received varying sentences. All this from a suggestion someone had bought a dodgy settee, which might have amounted to nothing but gave the opposite result. If only we had the same luck with all of our enquiries.

CHAPTER 05

CASES WORTHY OF
FULL INVESTIGATION

An interesting case that I dealt with involved a young man in his early twenties employed in the town as a butcher. The Manager of the shop entrusted this man to take the end of week takings on a Saturday evening to the bank and deposit money in the leather bag provided into the night safe. Not a problem after all the same person had being doing this for well over a year and there was no reason to suspect he had done anything wrong.

However when the Manager called to the bank on the following Monday, the night safe wallet was not to be found. This caused major worries for him as in access of £2,000 was inside, all in bank notes of various denominations. In the late 1970's this was of course an extremely large amount of money and for some still is today. I was in C.I.D. when this Manager came into the police station with the problem. I stated before I consider any action we need the bank to ensure the night safe system was not flawed in any way, in that the leather cash bag may not have inadvertently become lodged in the mechanism, or elsewhere.

We needed to be completely sure the bag was still not in the possession of the bank and stuck in an isolated position in the night safe, before any police enquiry could commence. As always this establishment cooperated and engineers later stripped the whole apparatus completely, the bag was not found, which concluded with the inference that a theft had taken place.

With all this knowledge in mind, a couple of days later, I invited the young man who had banked the money to meet me at the same branch just before he finished work. He did and I asked him to show me what had taken place. He went through the procedure and got to the point where the bag containing cash was placed in the night safe. I asked him what happened then, he stated he pulled the shutter back and he heard it drop inside the machine. That was precisely the answer I was looking for, as this reply sealed his fate and he was now in a more incriminating position. With a little hindsight this young man if he had had the presence of mind to state that the bag had been left there without dropping down, the next customer could have been blamed which would have involved an even more complex enquiry. Thankfully he didn't come up with this alternative answer.

At that very point I informed him he was under arrest on suspicion of theft and he was taken into custody. Later under interview he denied completely any involvement, sticking to his story. Each time he tried to give an answer which did not make sense and the main issue just kept bouncing back. He had taken the money and unless he gave it someone else he was the only person accountable as the bank so far had been exonerated. It took a while and eventually he came clean and admitted the theft.

He was asked what he had done with the money and he stated he had stayed with his grandmother over the weekend, and it was hidden at her home. With an escort we went with him to the address. In his bedroom there he showed me his transistor radio. He unscrewed the back and there it all was minus £50 which he had spent on himself. He was full of remorse and I thanked him for finally telling the truth. He clearly had put some planning into the whole issue and if not for him finally telling the truth he may have gotten away with it at Court. These days confronted with the same situation, in giving different answers, he may have said absolutely nothing and got away with the theft completely and this is so sad. I gave the young man a strict talking to about changing himself around. He was obviously going to be dismissed and had this impending court case against him. I told him to come clean when he tried to get work, which takes courage, telling any prospective employer you wish to be given another chance. If he was lucky and got another job, stay on the right side of the law. He ended up with a fine and probation.

Some five years later I was out with my wife in another town when this same man approached us. He identified himself as the person who had stolen the night safe wallet, which naturally I had forgotten all about. He thanked me for all I had done in giving him good advice, in that he had never re-offended and was now settled and with a wife and child. Job satisfaction just doesn't come any better than that.

One weekend we had an incident where a man in his mid-twenties had possession of a hand gun and ammunition. He was a habitual criminal for such a young person, with several serious previous convictions for house burglary and robbery and had no respect for anyone, friend or otherwise.

I had arrested him a few years before when he was a juvenile, if you recall having a lift and being late for work to save being disciplined by the uniform shift Inspector. He still had a nasty streak and we suspected possibly this was drug related due to the number of times he had been inside. He was drinking at the main local watering hole in the centre of a run-down housing estate and fell into an argument with one of the locals. This resulted in him brandishing his weapon which was loaded and in the public bar in front of a room full of people fired several shots. Most missed hitting anyone, except for one bullet that hit this one man and creased the side of his head. He was stunned but apart from that unhurt, but it easily could have been far worse. The offender got into a vehicle and drove off. He stopped at a friend's house and had a fight inside where again he produced the gun firing shots causing injuries to a man he wanted money from. He was shot in the shoulder and had to be hospitalised. He also fired the gun out in the street at passers-by but missed whereupon he left the area. As a result the identity of the man responsible together with his vehicle were circulated throughout the force area and also elsewhere.

We had a woman well known on the estate who worked the bar and she assisted the police, giving an incredible statement to a frame by frame account of exactly what had taken place. This included incriminating evidence where the offender was seen in the act of shooting at the man's head, and at other people whom she knew and identified. It just showed the importance of taking time and letting the witness recall all that happened from memory committing it in writing.

Eventually the man was found and arrested and charged quite rightly with several counts of attempted murder. With the man in custody and a future trial impending this sadly placed the female witness under enormous pressure as the local jungle drums were pounding. Living in the close proximity, the accused had many friends and supporters and clearly she was experiencing problems, with several threats and intimidation by the defendant, his friends and family. Despite declining protection from the courts she stated that she would not give evidence and went into hiding. It was so serious a crime that the Judge ordered the issue of an arrest warrant for the woman. Finally she was found and placed into custody for her own safety and to ensure her attendance at court. The case was then listed to go ahead.

When the trial was re-listed she was produced at court and gave her evidence openly and freely, as competent as one could be recalling exactly everything as portrayed in her statement. This evidence played a crucial part of the case. The defendant was found guilty on several charges for which he was given a life imprisonment sentence on each, all to run concurrently with each other.

The woman and her family were relocated and I believe they were given new identities, the least of what they deserved.

Sometimes today, the wrong people get this all too easily, as the costs involved are extremely expensive and where their involvement may be exaggerated, owing to the Human Rights Act.

Even the detective constable in charge of the case responsible for interviewing and bringing this dangerous offender to court did not escape the threats and intimidation. He was the subject of threats made to the CID office by unknown criminals all supporting the man facing justice, where they stated their intention to cause this officer physical harm and injury. In addition this officer also had abuse from people in the public gallery, whilst giving evidence along with all the other brave civilian witnesses. These people were removed from the court on the instructions of the Judge and were lucky not to have been imprisoned for contempt of court. This man served several years in prison for these offences and some years later also had his sentence extended by several more years for grievous bodily harm inflicted by him, on another prison inmate causing life threatening injuries. He clearly was a very dangerous man who had not learned his lesson.

This sadly happens far too often in all parts of the country where very dangerous criminals are at large for extremely serious offences such as Murder, Rape and Armed Robbery, Certain detectives of all ranks, having led an industrious career chasing such villains naturally locking up the same criminals time and time again as they clearly know the modus operandi, of the person and how their minds tick and the way they conduct their activities in crime. It is not a case of being vindictive other than being a conscientious crime fighter. Many an offender of such serious crimes when serving a lengthy prison term is determined to make the detective or uniform officer responsible for his incarceration to pay the price when he is eventually released and puts into place his own personal agenda for retribution against the officer, his family and colleagues whenever the opportunity arises.

That is why careless talk is so dangerous at any time. Whether out socially or answering the door, or telephone, family and friends are all too naïve and can and do give out personal information without realising it. Just by saying what their uncle, aunt, sibling, cousin or mate innocently does for a living. Where they work, where they live and what car they own, plus where their relatives work. Not that this issue should become paranoid but best to advise family and friends not to talk out of turn with people they do not really know. This actually happened to me personally with a close in law relative, where she was out in my presence and being sociable in a public house. She became engaged in conversation with a man whose family had an awful reputation for serious crime and violence, not that he himself was a bad person but not knowing what she was discussing it was necessary to make an excuse and leave. In fact my sister was out at a dance venue and became involved in conversation with others. It was not until some weeks later I had locked up this habitual criminal whom I had had many dealings with. We were searching his home and his mother blurted out, I had a sister she had met at a function and that I was in the CID, and obviously she too had spoken out of turn. What else she had spoken about my sister never said, just too embarrassed being confronted by me over her stupidity. One thing being proud of me but clearly she did not understand how dangerous talk can lead to all kinds of problems and she too had a strict talking to. Trouble is you never know what silly talk can lead to, even by people you do not establish are responsible.

Like in all criminal investigations all people charged are innocent until proven guilty and yet sadly even serving police officers can be rightly or wrongly implicated all kinds of serious offences. No different to armed officers adjudged to have a case to answer in allegedly using a firearm or laser gun, a spray for incapacitating a person where a person has been shot or seriously wounded. Apart from being suspended from duty pending a court appearance, the officer has to face a torrid line of press publicity and in certain cases has had his home address identified by the media. This kind of unnecessary action although only happening on rare isolated occasions still leaves the officer and his family, vulnerable to all kinds of dangerous implications from people he has dealt with. The job is dangerous itself in the nature of the work without inviting unnecessary problems, at home or work due to carelessness and thoughtlessness.

Another interesting case involved a nasty armed robbery during the early hours of the morning at an all-night petrol station. A young man who regularly worked nights always working alone was the victim. Two girls were enquiring about certain goods on display but out of view, within the small shop area of the garage. Against policy he allowed both to enter the main door which he opened instead of passing goods via the serving hatch.

To his surprise as soon as he opened the door for the girls two men appeared from hiding and burst inside and confronted him. Both men had balaclavas to hide their faces and brandished iron bars and struck him about his face, arms and shoulders making threats that they wanted all the cash on the premises. The cashier was badly injured as he fell to the floor whilst being attacked and was also kicked to various parts of his body. Only a nominal amount was available and as he had no access to the floor safe and he was left beaten quite badly.

The men took what money was present just under fifty pounds in cash, but cleaned the shop out completely of cigarettes before leaving at the same time as the two girls. It was obvious they were the decoy into him opening the shop up where he was just trying to be helpful. Eventually he was able to raise the alarm and call the Police and he was later admitted to hospital and the garage was closed. Unbelievably at the time of the robbery there was no surveillance cameras anywhere within the garage or the forecourt and it looked as if it was going to be one of those unsolved crimes as no forensic evidence was found.

I made initial enquiries but owing to the time of day there were no witnesses around and it was basically down to the cashier to recall as much as possible about the incident. He remained in hospital for a couple of days and returned to work the following week. The only thing of significance that I later would realise would assist the investigation was the installation of camera equipment albeit after the event.

About four weeks had passed and still there was no further information coming to light to assist enquiries despite maintaining full contact with this witness. Within a couple of weeks I received a call to attend the garage where there had been a slight but helpful development. During the early busy part of the night shift the man recognised one of the girls who had entered the garage at the time of the robbery. She was alone and called into the shop to make a purchase and unknown to her he was able to get a couple of photographs taken of her through the new garage security system. Both photographs were seized and blown up to a better view at our Technical Department which was circulated to neighbouring divisions within the force area. In addition I used them in everyday enquiries with various contacts until eventually I had a name and was able to track her down. Together with a colleague I visited her address where she was found and to be identical with her photograph. She was arrested on suspicion of her involvement in the robbery. It wasn't long under interview she admitted her part, implicating the other persons who were responsible. Later that same day further arrests were made until all were in custody. Each one of them admitted responsibility and were charged and bailed. At Crown Court all pleaded guilty and each received lengthy custodial sentences and each had to pay quite rightly compensation to their victim. It was always rewarding to get a positive result especially when someone is seriously hurt in a cowardly act, which made all the hard work completely worthwhile.

CHAPTER 06

ARSON

Arson is a vindictive offence which can involve murder, or attempt to cover up a murder which has been committed. It can be a jealous act by one business man to another, in sabotaging a successful competitor's company or enterprise. It can be simply down to a builder in order to get rid of an unwanted listed building, to reuse the land, or down to basic insurance fraud to recoup sufficient funds to restart an ailing business.

Claims against house cover are all treated with suspicion until proved otherwise. It also comes under the realms of the delinquent who just wishes to see havoc caused, or the frustrated fire fighter who gets a kick from seeing the fire brigade in action. This includes the thief who has burgled or stolen a vehicle covering his tracks by fire.

Whatever the reason it is extremely serious, especially when accompanied with sinister overtones such as with intent to endanger life, with explosions from power sources, or acts of terrorism. All these scenes are depicted every day in television programmes and films, all giving ideas to the offenders. Sadly majority of cases are just simply plain accidents which we all know have devastating consequences, resulting in the loss of life which in most cases like any accident can be preventable.

Most of the scenes of suspected arson I have attended are always proved forensically involving fire and police scenes of crime investigations. Photographic evidence in these cases is of a major importance. It is made easier when an offender is in custody as normally the intent can be established. The presence of accelerants on an offenders hands or clothing or burn injuries no matter how slight, even when denying being at the scene can all be circumstantial, but very incriminating evidence. I have visited numerous fire incidents throughout majority of my career, both in uniform and CID involving sudden death and autopsies which mainly have resulted in accidental death. It is an area where an open mind is essential where there maybe evidence sometimes to the contrary. This is sometimes where the cause of death cannot be truly established and an 'Open Verdict' is recorded. Which means where further evidence later comes to light, can result in a body being exhumed, or an Inquest into the case being re-opened.

Examples of this is where someone terminally ill or in custody for other serious matters, decides to come clean about his past involving fire which has contributed to the death of a person whether caused by accident or otherwise. Some people hide away from the truth but in the end cannot live with their conscience and have to face the course of their own actions.

I was working with Dc Mike GREEN on one occasion when we had a young man in his late teens in custody. He had been arrested for quite minor offences involving theft from motor vehicles. He had never been in trouble previously and we were going through his criminal activities so he could move on with his life and go straight.

When asking him what else he had done, he stated the worst thing he committed was breaking into a well-known Supermarket and stealing bottles of drink. He could not give an exact date other than it was some 3 or 4 years previous. He stated within a short time of gaining entry by smashing a rear window and climbing inside, the burglar alarms had activated. To cover his tracks he used cooking oil combined with paper bags and newspapers, to burn the areas where he had been so as not to leave his fingerprints. He left the scene and hid nearby seeing the police arrive. At this stage the fire was taking grip quite aggressively and by the time the fire brigade arrived, the whole of the Store was in flames, with stock completely damaged by smoke and fumes.

We later checked our records for the location and could not find any record of burglary. At a loss on which way to go we suddenly decided to contact Scenes of Crime Department and one of the officers a true professional, recalled exactly visiting the premises even after so long a period, the morning after. No evidence was gained to assist us, as the cause of the fire was only recorded as doubtful origin, by the Fire Service and ourselves. He did have a record of the Force Police Photographer having attended and we eventually we able to resurrect an album of pictures which showed the full devastation that fire caused.

The final cost of the damage caused was in excess of £250.000, and that was 25 years ago. Can you imagine the cost of this kind of damage if caused today it would possibly run close to a million pounds. The young man was put before the court and received a Probation Order, which normally would always have been a custodial sentence if not for his honesty in admitting the offence, which otherwise would have remained undetected.

I remember when I was a teenager we had a young couple running a local public house close to where we lived. Things were not going well with the marriage, his wife was attractive and flirtatious with the male customers. She eventually left him. The husband was drinking heavily and this obviously affected his stocks and to cover his losses he foolishly set fire to the premises. I remember speaking to him the morning after, as he was sitting on the outside steps. The whole of the building had been gutted and later had to be demolished. I asked him what had happened and all he would confirm was that there had been a fire. That was the last time I saw him. He was a man in his mid-twenties, polite well-mannered and inoffensive, the last person you would believe capable of such behaviour. He obviously acted out of desperation and losing his wife his world was crumbling apart. Fortunately no one was injured in the fire. It was 1962 and he later pleaded guilty to committing arson. You could not help but feel sorry for him, but he knew what he was doing and what the penalty would have been. He was sent to prison for the maximum period of 7 years and he would have served that sentence at that time without remission or luxuries afforded to inmates in present day. He certainly paid the ultimate price for his crime.

One of the extremely rare occasions that I saw the comical side of Dc GLOVER was when we went to a local village church hall that had been gutted by fire. The cause was that again of doubtful origin and I recall Dc GLOVER speaking to the local Vicar subtly uttering the phrase 'Well God knows who done it.' Even the Vicar could not resist smiling. It's a pity this side of Dc GLOVER did not surface more often but you cannot change a person's real inward character overnight, if at all.

I remember being called out to a neighbouring division where there was an incident room set up for a potential murder enquiry. This involving a fire started within a high rise block of flats, where on the fifteenth floor a middle aged lady was frightened to evacuate, until it was too late and she eventually could not leave. She suffocated and when the Fire Service eventually recovered the body, it was as if she had been microwaved due to the constant heat rising from premises below. Fortunately she had died through fume and smoke inhalation and well before the fire had taken hold. Someone in a lower flat had set fire to rubbish as a prank, not realising the fire would eventually spread to the whole of the upper building.

No one was found responsible, so another case that one day sometime in the future, it might twang someone's conscience to come forward with the truth, but that takes moral courage some people will never have. It's a pity the offenders of this crime are not made to attend autopsies to see for themselves the awful sights and devastation of human life that is caused, which is dealt with daily by brave fire fighters, paramedics and police throughout the country.

Majority of offenders for arson were juveniles, either for burning down Schools or other buildings blaming boredom as the main excuse. If only they could realise how lucky they are in society where they have every facility, compared to so many poor people all over the world of similar age.

The amount of officers who attend such crimes and write down names given of suspects, without failing to take any action used to baffle me. I know they can be busy but by acting on their own initiative and following leads can clear serious crimes, where suspects can be apprehended with evidence of accelerants on clothing can be detected. I had many cases clearing these kinds of offences, which could have been cleared at the time and not a few days after the event, which makes the job so very much harder. It is extremely frustrating having to make enquiries where the trail has gone cold, but with skilful questioning it used to be possible to get to the truth of the matter. This especially true when you find witnesses who can build up a picture of how things took place, where the main perpetrator suddenly becomes implicated.

In many cases it is not always necessary to arrest just conduct a formal interview at the police station, this mainly applied to juveniles and young persons if they have not previously come to the notice of the police. Naturally the same rules apply that the suspect is afforded legal representation at every opportunity and that persons rights are adhered to. If required a parent or an Appropriate Adult is present. I was able to clear many offences in this manner, but you have to be fair and rather than charge, you have to report such people for summons to appear at court, where bail conditions do not apply. Either way you may look at the circumstances, this crime is still detected and in most cases, the cooperation of the accused voluntarily attending the police station, without any need to be locked up in custody to assist with enquiries is taken into account by the sentencing Court.

Sadly in present time there are far too many murders today where the main instigator has either injured or killed his spouse or children for something that happened in the past, or present with issues affecting everyday life which they cannot face up to.

One of the cruellest methods of killing is where they are trapped having been locked up in a property or attacked, then they set the building deliberately on fire, regardless of the consequences that all too often result in tragedy with one or even more deaths. This type of offence is occurring far too often in society and is on the increase.

Events leading up to these incidents can involve facing up to unwanted bankruptcy with debts spiralling out of control, or through gambling or bad business or redundancy or simple acts of infidelity. This can also be jealousy, where the relationship between the man or woman, or common law marriage has irretrievably broken down and there is a new girlfriend or boyfriend on the scene. All these issues coming to the surface all that the individual cannot face up to. In other words taking the coward's way out, rather than accepting and facing up to the problems that exist and dealing with them. If they are desperate to take their own lives that is sad enough but to kill or seriously injure anyone else for whatever reason is really unforgivable. With people bottling life's problems it is not always easy to get to these people to help them, as sometimes the warning signals are not always apparent.

I recall working with Dc WATSON again when we were both involved in investigating a burglary of a nightclub that had gone wrong. Two men had broken in and were looking for the takings. Fortunately the Manager was not staying in the living quarters at the time otherwise it could have resulted in possibly a murder scene. It was later established that both men being frustrated in not finding the main prize, decided to burn the place down anyway just through pure madness on their part. As they left the premises the burglar alarms had activated and a public spirited neighbour had been able to take the registration number as it drove past her address. She had gone outside in her dressing gown, hearing the alarms, and as the vehicle drove from the night club car park.

She had the presence of mind to write the car number down on the pavement with a stone that was there for all to see. Brilliant, I made sure she was one lady who received a letter from our Chief of Police in gratitude. I always made sure these remarkable people did not go unnoticed and orchestrated many such letters during my service.

Eventually we made enquires and the two men involved were arrested. It appeared they had been at the premises for several weeks, sizing the place out, but had chosen the wrong night as the money had already been banked. They admitted burglary and arson and we each given custodial sentences.

The Management were ecstatic with our result and promised us free tickets with our wives, to an evening of entertainment with a major celebrity, for the re-opening of the Night Club when the building had been refurbished. I thought no more about it, but it was not often these little treats came along and made the job even more worthwhile. With Dc GLOVER now moved, and Dc PEGG in an Admin role, I was quite annoyed when behind the scenes the lazy police excelled themselves in working hard for their own reward. Basically their job was to take the odd additional statements to complete the file which was requested by the prosecution, after we had submitted the main bulk of evidence. In addition to prepare cases for Crown Court and where additional witnesses had been traced obtain relevant statements. This was sometime used to their own benefit especially when there was the smell of a free evening floor show initially offered to those whose hard work detected the offence in the first place. It was a pity the same hard work by these staff was not put to good use on other more important occasions.

This was pursued by a former detective sergeant, who was now PC WHITE, who was a close friend also working with Dc PEGG. He had been reduced to the rank of Constable under discipline action and had been transferred under a cloud to our division, where in fact he was lucky not to have been sacked.

His demise came when on duty in plain clothes he with another officer, had taken an inmate out of prison to detect offences he was suspected of and as a result of his short time of freedom had taken him to licensed premises for a drink. Undoubtedly the man returned to the prison the worse for wear and under the influence resulting in the prison Governor making a formal complaint to the Chief Constable. In addition, this same officer then tried to gain entrance to a horse racing sporting event using a false pass to avoid paying the normal entrance fee. What possesses a police officer of whatever rank to even think they could get away with such actions. Surely there was no need to fall to such poor standards after all he only had himself to blame for his fall from grace.

Although we had cleared the crime and submitted the main file of evidence, a short updated statement was needed from the management of the night club regarding final value of damage caused. Realising the generosity of management offering free tickets to the re-opening night, this officer could not help using the situation to try and better himself purporting he possibly was one of the main officers involved in the case. Unknown to me he had invited the Superintendent, Chief Inspector and himself to the function with each of their respective wives, in an attempt to lure himself back into the good books. He did not realise I was sent a ticket independently together with Dc WATSON who had since left. After all we were the officers who had detected the crime in the first place. I could not resist telling Pc WHITE that I had received an invite and asked if he had as well. He sheepishly agreed he had, so I stated we could go together.

That put the cat amongst the pigeons he now was in a dilemma in how to explain the bosses were invited and also bring his wife along at the same time. I kept him in suspense until the very end, when all four couples were allowed to attend. I had spoken to the management and offered to pay, but numbers were down and they were only too happy to make us welcome. It turned out to be a very good floor show, but I made it clear to the bosses that I nearly was not included. It just shows that some people will do anything behind your back, to try and take the glory to try to justify their existence. It was like that back then, but I would imagine things like this have not changed in this respect and have probably got worse.

Not being content in staying in the job he used every opportunity to creep round bosses in an attempt to try and get back into CID. What a liability I have known officers sacked for far less. Who would want to work with him anyway, after all there were far better candidates waiting in the wings for a future transfer to CID.

Despite this the demoted sergeant now Pc White could not resist sitting down in our main CID office chatting in a friendly way and creeping round our Detective Inspector. Continually hinting how invaluable he would be in our office and detecting crime. With all his obvious bad points and pedigree of never learning by his mistakes, he was nothing more than a person untrustworthy who would most definitely give a repeat performance of his shady dealings. In addition placing his colleagues in total jeopardy and possibly embarrassing this time the whole department if his antics resurfaced bordering criminal activities. A risk too great to even consider. I could not help myself during his intimate conversions with the boss purporting himself to being God's gift the world of detectives. I just loudly asked him the question in front of all present, 'Have you been to the races lately Pc white?' He shouted back in angry words, 'Just you mind your own bloody business'. This resulted in bellows of laughter and he got up and stormed out of the office. I was told well done. After all we had worked with enough dead wood over the years and this officer was well beyond his sell by date.

When it comes to modern technology with breeding I hope they never clone people in the future, especially all the annoying ones that I have referred to. It was bad enough working with them once in a lifetime, but please no more than that, and never ever again.

CHAPTER 07

BURGLARY

Like in most police forces throughout the country, every area had their own prolific burglar who was active and always regularly believed he was one step ahead of the police. We had one such person who had previous for house burglaries with his wife, who actually went with him breaking into homes and attacking the old or infirm or anyone who got in his way. This pathetic excuse for a lady even attacked the police officer who attempted to arrest her whilst caught almost red handed leaving the attacked premises, causing him injury and even made good her escape. Later when arrested this woman went on an Identity Parade and more surprisingly he could not even identify her, he was not one of the best motivated officers.

Later the couple were caught breaking into another house, and charged with several other similar offences having found stolen property from several attacked premises. The husband received a long prison sentence, but his wife who was very attractive with a horrible nature fleeced the Judge into believing she was coerced into breaking into houses, how pathetic. Her convictions were nearly as long as her spouses and she was just as evil. Not considering for one minute the devastating fear and trauma imposed on their elderly victims. The woman offender got probation which confirms all that is wrong in our society where a real punishment should come first and fit the crime. She was actually more ruthless and vindictive than her husband and richly deserved a custodial sentence.

House burglary is one of the most heinous of crimes in my book, in the western world and now there is hardly a deterrent in some parts of the country as sentences fluctuate so much where the punishment should always be prison invading people's privacy. Many victims have nightmares and feel utterly insecure for a long time after the event resulting in many families moving home. Some courts seem to show pity for the offender's and do not have a clue of the consequences caused to the victim by the offender's dishonest actions. You break into a burglar's home and I always found that they were the worst victims full of hate and tantrums what double standards.

Upon release this man went back into his lucrative career living from crime, although he avoided house breaking as his sentence put him away for 3 years even with remission. I had dealt with this man right from when he was a juvenile and now he was in his thirties and was still much an active villain despite all the talks and advice given to him by his father who was the complete opposite, an honest and hardworking individual. I think in the end he just washed his hands of his son's activities completely, having nothing more to do with him. In fact there was no reason as far as I could see why this person should have pursued such a criminal career, but he had big chip on his shoulder against society for no real reason, like so many others in the same walk of life. Despite being on licence from prison he could not stop breaking into shops, public houses or any building where he could steal cash, drink and cigarettes anything he could exchange for cash which gave a modest income topping up his dole or spending money.

We had three such premises broken into the one night and he had been arrested by uniform for officers for the offence of - going equipped to steal. In other words he had implements with him such as screwdrivers and chisels when not at his place of abode this being a much lesser offence than burglary. He was amenable to interview and confident we had nothing on him and always careful not to leave his fingerprints at any unlawfully entered premises. I had done my ground work before interview as I had spoken with Scenes of Crime officers. They had an excellent foot print from a boot, left on the floor in one of the attacked buildings.

Whilst in the police cells his boots were left outside the cell door. This was an accepted practice rather than removing laces which could be used to cause injury. I took them to scenes of crime office and on initial examination they matched perfectly. That was good enough for me. I placed the boots back and when he came into the Interview room he was wearing them. I went through his movements during the night and other evidence and he denied having anything to do with any of the attacked premises. All of a sudden as a kind of distraction, I quickly asked him, the question "Are those your boots." He said," Yes." I said," They are not stolen are they", and he said, "No." I said, "Since you have owned them who else has worn them" He said, "No one. " That was it. It was too late for him as he had opened his mouth without even thinking.

He never suspected for one moment what I was going on about, but it was too late. When I told him about a footprint being found at the scene, the interview continued on a no comment basis. He was informed it appeared all burglaries were interlinked and he was later charged with all of them. The footprint impression which had been photographed was sent off to forensic for examination and proved categorically it was his boot at the scene. He was unanimously found guilty despite advice to the contrary from his Barrister and went off to jail. He would not make that mistake again leaving his footprints behind to incriminate him.

As you will appreciate in various stories throughout this book there were very many clumsy criminals who were just jail bait, but equally so some very clever criminals and with those kind you always had to think one step ahead and plan your actions properly.

A couple of years later I received information from a reliable source that the same man who was now out again, was up to his old tricks. I was informed at his address the one bedroom was full of several boxes containing thousands of cigarettes, together with an excessive amount of bottles of spirits. I went straight up to the Magistrates Court and swore out grounds for a search warrant for his address and the one below. He lived in accommodation situated on the top floor of a multi storey block of flats. Yes, he was a modern day Spiderman, as previously I knew he had evaded escape by climbing over the balcony of his flat to the one below and I knew of no reason why this time he would not risk this action again. He was either brave or very stupid, as one slip and death would have been instantaneous especially from 14 floors up.

We went to both addresses simultaneously and when knocking the door he refused to answer. Force was used and he was seen climbing over the balcony as we went into the lounge. Meanwhile downstairs he was arrested, as everything went according to plan. His wife too came into custody. We filled an entire large van with property including boxes and boxes containing cigarettes and others with bottles of spirits. They both pleaded guilty to theft and burglary and the man went back to prison. She again, surprise, surprise, was treated more leniently.

I remember we had this man coming from gypsy background living in a house on our area. He was hard working and had a wife and children. One day when they were all out the house was broken into and a large amount of jewellery had been stolen, some sentimental, all being given to him and his wife over the years. We circulated a description of the property, but as to who was responsible we had no idea. Enquiries with neighbours also met with a negative result. He mixed in dubious circles and the names of many of these people were known to us. This man also had connections with other established detectives in the force, some high ranking officers and he was using them against our credibility. Then one day he came up with the names of three family members who he was adamant were responsible. He could not back this up with any evidence, but due to the background of the persons named and the fact they associated with his family we treated it as being as reliable as we could, or was he just clutching at straws to blame anyone. One of the best ways of catching someone is if they continue committing offences of a similar nature they might just slip up, but even this idea did not match up with any new reports of crime coming in.

We decided to arrest the named persons on suspicion of the burglary but, a couple of weeks had gone by, the trail had gone cold and we were skating on thin ice. Unless we were lucky and anything was found to give us a bonus we had nothing. Despite all our skills in fetching these persons into custody, searching their homes, leaving no stone unturned we were still facing a mystery as to who the real culprits were. We had drawn a blank and in fairness they might not have done it anyway. This man I believe expected us perhaps to get some blow torch and vinegar and torture them to get the truth and break every rule in the book. He called up to see me at least 2 or 3 times a week at the station to ask how the enquiry was going. Enough was enough. I felt sorry, but we had taken the matter as far as we could and I had to tell him face to face no further action would be taken unless there was positive and direct evidence leading to those responsible. Just imagine if every victim behaved like this, you just have to be realistic, and be up front with the truth letting them know who was in charge. After all some you win, some you lose.

Later that month I was away on holiday together with my wife and children, on a well-earned break. This was our first holiday for some time and just a week away was just what the doctor ordered. We travelled just over 100 miles to a popular holiday destination and stayed in a mobile home at an established holiday site and the weather was glorious. We were one day into it and the wife received terrible news that her father had died unexpectedly. We were in the social club on the evening arranging her return home, where the boys and I would follow later in the week.

If that wasn't bad enough, a man came up to me and tapped me on the shoulder, I looked round and it was him, the victim from the burglary. I told him we had just received very bad news but still that did not stop him. Having the knowledge of what I had just told him, he even had the audacity to ask how the enquiries were developing with his burglary which was now old crime and filed pending any further developments. His comments were without any thought or care for my wife's feelings and although she was present, she received no condolences or any words of sympathy from him whatsoever. He was given the most despicable look from me it was possible to give and told him to have some compassion. I am sure I was paying for sins I must have committed in the past. Whoever had said to me enjoy your holiday had thrown me a jinx, we all have bad times in our life and that certainly was one bad experience and we certainly did not need any unsympathetic approach from a person like him.

When people say that being a policeman working hard to clear crime must be frustrating when after all the offenders just get a slap on the wrist. This particular case could have hardly been truer. We had a prolific burglar who was always in and out of prison. It annoys me without being political, but why should legal aid be treated as a business benefit for a career criminal. I believe the line should be drawn whenever this kind of abuse of the system is detected and used only in clear cases of innocence. Yes everyone has human rights and is entitled to legal aid for one mistake, but two mistakes I think not. Obviously who am I to say, after all it's only my own opinion but I am sure there are many who would not disagree with my comments. Since the country was thrown into deep recession a couple of years or so back and austerity measures were introduced, legal aid has incurred many changes. Close monitoring of allocation of funds affecting payment to solicitors and barristers and to whom those they represent, a policy in my view which has been so long overdue for the reasons already given.

This man had recently been released from prison and within two weeks was again on bail for burglaries elsewhere. His vehicle was seen leaving the scene of a factory and office burglary where a number of computers had been stolen. He had a unique cabriolet motor vehicle with a private number plate and two separate witnesses to the incident between them were able to come up with the registration number. He was locked up and eventually he admitted being responsible. He was charged and remanded into custody, only to be released by a Judge in chambers.

Then again whilst on bail he was arrested again, this time a short distance from a garage where boxes of brand new tools were taken. His footprints were found inside the premises at a place he would never have been allowed access, so again he was charged and remanded into custody. Surprise, surprise again a bail hearing and the same Judge released him again albeit it was the second time of committing offences whilst on bail.

I hate being cynical and I am not making it up, but again in less than a month he was caught again committing burglary at a warehouse and found in possession of cigarettes which he was loading into his car. I was dealing with him again and this time Hooray, he was kept in custody as he was being committed to Crown Court for trial, finally facing justice.

Not in this country anymore, how things had changed. Whist waiting to appear at Crown Court he was produced elsewhere in relation to his first offence committed on bail. As the Crown Prosecution had failed to link all matters together, he was sentenced separately to six months for burglary, with our offences all fairly serious matters being left to lie on the file and not be proceeded without leave of the Court. In other words he had got off completely scot free, unless the Judge in his wisdom decided he would not have given any additional punishment anyway for these other offences all committed on bail. Where on earth was the sense in that? What message did that send out to these people committing crime on bail and to some criminals it contains the hidden belief that all bail given comes with a licence to continue re-offending, as you will not get punished any more for this gross breach of trust. I think as a society this is where things started to go horribly wrong, but that is only my view. How do you explain that to companies whose business has been suffering and not helped by the activities of one such person, plus all the time and effort by everyone having dealings which all cost a fortune to implement. Unfortunately as time went on later in my service these situations became more of an accepted practice, than that of facing real justice.

Back in the mid-eighties any person who had been to prison for a set period of time, which was three years or more, and upon release had re-offended in similar serious crimes would fall into this special ruling. When again appearing at Crown Court upon a finding of guilt, a 'Notice of an Extended Sentence', would be served, to the detriment of the accused in the dock. Meaning he would receive a sentence of imprisonment of no less than five years.

One such person who was a recipient of such an order was this prolific offender who just could not stop breaking into houses, causing so much misery to many innocent people stealing sentimental items which were irreplaceable and trashing properties into the bargain. He just did not care one iota about the feelings of these poor victims. As soon as he was released from a prison sentence he was at it again causing more misery breaking into more properties upsetting people's lives and continued on a regular basis with his criminal lifestyle right up until his past finally caught up with him. He was found guilty of several dwelling house burglaries and served with an extended sentence where he received 5 years imprisonment. Through this on top of his usual sentence he received an extra 2 years, something he was aware of that would happen if he carried on re-offending.

He was 50 years old on eventual release from this last period of being housed at H.M. Prison. His first few steps of freedom were sadly to be short lived and only consisted of walking across the forecourt of the entrance to the prison gates, where he suddenly dropped down dead onto the ground. Whether this was fate or not or the pressures of experiencing his forthcoming liberty. In fairness he had paid for his crimes and whether he would have gone straight had he lived we would never know. Without being too critical or judgemental I suppose we can at least state he went to heaven with a clean slate.

I remember another set of circumstances in a similar vein where another burglar had made a career out of stealing. He had been released after serving three years for aggravated burglary, either entering with a weapon of offence or using violence when inside. In this case he had tied up the occupants whilst ransacking their home, so he was a nasty piece of work. So there we were he was out again and not long before he was committing house burglaries, on one of our local housing estates.

We had several house burglaries with fingerprints of the offender being identified from a couple of houses. We made enquiries and traced the person to another area and arrested him at a lodging house where he occupied a couple of rooms. We made a full search with other property recovered he was returned back to our station. He admitted responsibility and was charged with various offences. He was remanded into custody by the Magistrates, but allowed bail by a Judge in Chambers hearing.

As soon as he was released he was back at it breaking into even more houses. He sneaked into one house whilst the occupants were watching television. The back door had been accidentally left open and there he was rifling through the bedroom drawers stealing money and jewellery. He placed a gent's watch on his wrist not realising on the back plate there was an inscription in the name of the householder for 25 years good service. He left the house making good his escape before any discovery was made.

During the same evening he broke into another two properties and at the last address was disturbed. With police already in the area he was chased on foot and eventually arrested. Property he had thrown was recovered and at the police station they removed the stolen watch from his possession which he was wearing on his wrist. On the reverse of the watch on the back plate was the owner's name and the words for 25 year's loyal service.

You could not get better evidence that that against him. He was duly interviewed and charged with three house burglaries and remanded into custody.

Some people say that prison is not a deterrent maybe, some people will never change so the lesson is simple as if you cannot do the time do not do the crime. At least they cannot harm anyone while inside, which is where they deserve to be. Guess what happened he got bail. Where he would have gone straight to Crown Court at one time and served with a notice to implement an Extended Sentence, he would have received a minimum of five years imprisonment. Yet again he re-offended committing more and more house burglaries until he was finally kept in custody until his appearance at court.

He was at Crown Court and had pleaded guilty to the first series of burglaries, based on the fingerprint evidence submitted. However to all other charges some eight other indictments of house burglary he had pleaded not guilty. The Judge selected for the trial was basically a County Court Judge who was excellent relating to civil matters, as for criminal Courts his experience was limited to procedure only. The defence Barrister was aware of this and used this opportunity to his own clever advantage.

The first part of the evidence relating to the watch with identification thereon, found in the prisoners recent possession soon after the burglary, however was never heard. Hard to imagine, but the barrister played an issue of attacking a member of the jury, whom he objected to for various grounds causing the first trial to fold. A new jury had to be sworn in and so we now started a second trial after various legal arguments. It was clear this Barrister was using every trick in the book and the Judge who was only at this court session for one week clearly stated the trial could not run longer than for the next two days as he was otherwise committed.

We were in the second day of this new trial and through various legal arguments put forward again by the same defence Barrister, we still had not heard a shred of evidence. A new jury was sworn in and again for the remaining day he found flaws in that jury as well and raised several leading arguments all which were time consuming. At one point the Judge made a decision only to have the Barrister persuade him to look at it from a different perspective and made the Judge change his mind with a completely opposite decision to that initially made.

He then submitted in fairness to the defendant we have another trial. It just made a complete mockery of justice and that is where the Barrister defending saw the opportunity to run rings around him, which was exactly what he did. This possibly would never have happened with an experienced Judge, who would not have tolerated any miss trial in the first place. So here we were with the first three days of the week already used up and starting our third trial, swearing in a third jury. So whatever happened next was completely out of our hands and for the first time ever I was disgusted with the whole British Justice system which I had seen at its complete worst.

The Barrister for the defence again took the floor and with still further legal arguments, before we eventually started. We were through to the afternoon and although the opening had been commenced by the prosecution, we still had not heard evidence from all witnesses. It came to the point that the Judge had to stop the trial as he was not in a position to complete the proceedings due to all the complications, in other words he had run out of time. So the jury for the third time was dismissed and we were back to square one. In any case the real reason he was not there the following week, was due also to the fact he had to fly out abroad on his pre-booked holiday. The case was adjourned for the following day.

The final day of the week came and slotted in was a proper criminal Judge and no one would mess around with him. However it was all too late, the same defence Barrister who had pursued three trials all of them collapsing, then put forward that his client if faced with a fourth jury, it would be unfair and an abuse of process so all indictments laid against him were dismissed. A scenario which he himself had created using all his skills in out witting the former Judge who was totally inexperienced for such cases. You would think a burglar found in possession of identifiable property shortly after a burglary there would be justice, not anymore there wasn't and I was just a hard working detective doing my job. It's a pity the job was not done that day in Court.

I remember walking over to the defence Barrister looking him in the face and saying, 'Have a nice Christmas Mr SMITH' 'You have a nice Christmas.' He looked at me with anger in his eyes because from the manner and tone it was said, he knew what was behind my comments. My statement portrayed the complete opposite, in other words 'Have a horrible Christmas'. Naturally the name Mr SMITH is fictitious to ensure protection of identity. This barrister had done his job and had ensured the freedom of his client, whose sentence for the offences he initially pleaded guilty to, had balanced out with his time in custody. He was free again to commit more burglaries and might just as well had been given like most offenders today a free pass or automatic right to bail, where they can continue their profession uninterrupted.

It is a shame when these things happen, but human nature sadly played a part, as the Barrister was just using a situation before him to his own advantage. Who could blame him, but I don't think the Judge in this case had been chosen properly. He was obviously a very clever man who excelled in civil law and although it was not only my view, that it was unfair for him to be put in charge of a criminal trial without background of the shrewd and cunning activities of some Barristers. No different in my view to putting a Criminal Judge in charge of a complex civil litigation case, or a traffic Superintendent in charge of a murder enquiry, or allowing a Heart Surgeon to perform a Hip Replacement, when they have no experience in these areas. After all Barristers, Solicitors and Judges are extremely clever people who quite often deal professionally with serious and complex cases involving fairness and honesty with all kinds of people.

No one ever wishes to criticise any person in authority, but let's get real we do get bad examples in our lifetime, take an American President who was kicked out of the White House, more than one Member of Parliament over the years sentenced to prison for blatant offences of perjury, Members of the House of Lords for fiddling expenses and struck off as a barrister, plus many from the legal profession committing criminal offences and suffering the same fate. Even up to present day with false accusations of war crimes committed by our brave troops investigated by corrupt solicitors. After all no-one is above the law and all deserve a day of reckoning facing justice for their crimes.

In addition sadly, over the years we have had too many real miscarriages of justice where the wrong Judge has failed the community in ridiculous sentencing. This matter only being rectified, where on appeal at the cost of the taxpayer the proper penalty was imposed which should have been given in the first place. Many who are not up to the job should in my view simply be sacked or pensioned off. If let to some people or politicians, we would have no prisons at all. Many who have crossed the line and paid for their mistakes with serving prison sentences have gone on to lead better lives and full credit to them. You will never stop those who wish to live their lives as professional criminals as they know the rules and must laugh in the face of such ridiculous judges who impose soft sentences, where the only deterrent is a sentence of imprisonment that fits the nature of the crime. We can never have a safe society if dangerous or persistent criminals go unpunished for serious criminal offences.

Back at the station, I had to face the wrath of another victim. This juvenile had broken into a Launderette where he committed damage stole a bunch of expensive and unusual keys to the washers and dryers, which he had thrown away. Not only had this caused him to be out of business for two weeks losing regular customers, but the horrid offender had excreted into a couple of the machines which had to be fumigated at further expense. This in addition to higher insurance premiums it was easy to have sympathy for an honest man just trying to make a living. The offending youth had pleaded guilty at Court and was given probation. The Probation Officer wanted to make an appointment with the proprietor in order the juvenile would have the opportunity to apologise. Possibly a sound gesture on behalf of the probation service, but they were not taking the feelings of the victim fully into account. The victim stated if he bought the youth anywhere near his premises he would not be responsible for his actions.

In which direction can you go with these suggestions, after all is the offender sincere or is the victim unforgiving. I know we have to start somewhere to make amends but it is very hard satisfy some of the victims. This is especially true when a person has got off very lightly with no redress to costs or compensation and the victim ends up losing out through loss of trade and earnings. It appears discipline is now only a word and that its meaning should be instilled by parents and teachers at a very early age and maintained as they grow older so they fully understand the meaning between right and wrong. If not they will grow up and become out of control ignoring life's values and principles which sadly happens all too often. Fortunately not every young person pursues a criminal career and we have examples everyday of encouragement from all kinds of young people who excel themselves in life and education, from whatever kind of background they are born.

CHAPTER 08

PROFESSIONAL MOTOR CAR THIEVES

Throughout the whole of my police career I had dealt with absolutely loads of thefts of motor vehicles when in uniform and on the beat and in my role in CID. I had many investigations involving several teams who were stealing cars to order. Some gangs were very professional in changing the identity of different vehicles. The offenders in most cases would find a plausible business, in an area not too well known, where a small proportion of the trading is straight, under the cover of highly active criminal on goings. Either selling or repairing the odd genuine vehicle masking a remaining full garage containing stolen motor cars all in the process of having their identity changed. This would mean swapping engines with other vehicles and removing identifying features also respraying some in different colours and using with stolen or forged documentation.

In these circumstances active thieves would steal to order and target high class vehicles. These would be stolen either by way of house burglary where keys to the vehicle were found easily accessible and allowed the offender to drive off away from the scene with virtually little or no damage caused so any change would just be cosmetic with just a single respray.

Other thefts would occur as part of a robbery known as carjacking where the driver normally a lone female, or vulnerable adult who would be attacked when parked momentarily or when stationary in traffic. They would be threatened with violence resulting in surrender of the vehicle to escape physical harm. This would prove to be all quite disturbing and repulsive crimes for some victims to experience, leaving many with traumatic nightmares. Although no substitute for what they had endured, at least they would be covered by insurance.

As a result of information received, a tip off from a reliable source, we went to such an address in a remote part of our area, where two men were working on vehicles in the garage. Altogether there were approximately ten vehicles inside the premises, with a further similar amount at the back in an adjoining compound. Two or three of the motor cars were less than a year old. We made a quick search and found on initial inspection that one vehicle was without number plates and was prepared ready for respray. Steering lock mechanism was found to be broken. As a result of this both men were taken into custody.

Photographs were later taken of our findings and with assistance of the Stolen Vehicle Squad we identified some 20 stolen vehicles, some being high value cars. We saw all kinds of property strewn all over the floor and in piles, which was suspected as having come from inside some of the vehicles, from either the boot or hand luggage compartments. All these items were seized, especially where there was a chance of identification, which did link some of the owners to individual motor cars, which also proved very useful.

Forged documents were still easy to obtain back then with criminals having the right connections. Today this still goes on but with computer technology is more intricate due to number plate recognition linking this with insurance and M.O.T details. However retaining the excise licence as covered in an earlier chapter, is a document which in my view should never have been stopped, as it had so many uses assisting in the detection of this kind of offence.

Eventually a total of three men were charged and later received substantial prison sentences which was expected back in those days for such serious crimes.

We had a burglary at Garage premises on our area where a complete book of blank M.O.T. Certificates, over a hundred in number had been stolen together with a printing pad and kit used for authenticating the certificates. As entries back then were made in biro ink, and stamped manually after vehicle inspection it was easy to see how popular they were with the criminal fraternity.

This kind of stolen property was always circulated nationwide in the event a driver was stopped and produced such a document to any Constable. It was then down to the individual Officers discretion as to how far he goes with his enquiries in checking out the background of such issue. Unless serious doubt is raised the offending documents would go unchecked. Today the driver would find it almost impossible to get away with such production, especially if all of the documentation was scrutinised against records held on computer. The information was received that it was believed some garage in a remote part of the UK had possession of such stolen property. We liaised with the local police and a search warrant was issued. With assistance I went with a colleague and at the garage executed the warrant. Two foreigners were working there having leased the garage and needless to say the search for stolen M.O.T. certificates resulted negative.

What we did find was a garage full of some fifteen stolen vehicles all of high value. They were examined and the same actions carried out, proving they were all stolen from different parts of the country. With the location quiet and out of the way it was the perfect place to work unchallenged, where vehicles were in the process of being ringed and having their identity changed. For the area in question the local police experienced a new learning curve, as it was for some, the first time they had ever had dealings with this kind of offence. Both offenders were dealt with, and received heavy prison sentences.

Over the years security has been a number one priority for car owners and this is despite the fact manufacturers have always tried to keep a step ahead of the evermore experienced vehicle thieves. Going from a forced quarter light in the sixties which was access to an open door for criminals, with no steering locks or other mechanism to tackle other than wire crossing to start the engine. In more recent times manufacturers introduced central locking systems, car alarms and vehicle tracking systems serving as a new deterrent in the fight against crime, thus lowering insurance costs if for only a brief time.

Without telling anyone how to suck eggs it is well worth having any vehicle checked professionally prior to purchasing either as a result of an eBay website or private sale. I would suggest drawing up two identical contracts for the sale, one to retain, the other for the new owner. Most important is to record accurately full details of the seller, buyer and vehicle. All details shown on registration document, exact mileage at time of sale and details of excise licence, including number date issued and expiry. An absolute must is the time of sale including the date, with details showing method of payment. If the new owner commits any offence it is a safeguard to prove you had no involvement at any material time after the sale. Well worth doing just for peace of mind.

With the influx of many Eastern European criminal gangs entering the U.K. along with those already in existence there are now many bogus claims for medical injuries arising from so-called staged road accidents. These gangs have been highly successful in fictionally orchestrated scenarios clever faking pretend injuries, such as concussion and neck injuries resulting in claims against the insurances companies. With false evidence from alleged witnesses, these criminals have deliberately braked without warning, stopped and reversed unnecessarily into innocent motorists and with false evidence against them have been unable to rebuke any of the sham taking place and pay-outs have been substantial causing premiums for many drivers to escalate.

As time went on with an escalation of these offences, as a result of excellent co-ordination of police forces and sophisticated surveillance equipment, in addition evidence gained also from individual motorists own on-board video cameras many teams have been rounded up and sentenced quite rightly to heavy terms of imprisonment. These individuals clearly are the scum of society and where applicable they should be deported forthwith, possibly without costs to the taxpayer. In addition claims of such injury are now very often contested and for those considering false clams a very good deterrent indeed.

With the introduction of modern technology involving new motor vehicles in the form of computer generated vehicles using electronic keys or keyless car entry systems, one might think that the average motorist is again safe from the ever persistent car thief. The only sad reality is that the Eastern European gangs have also moved on also with such advanced technology.

The gang member involved in such illegal activities obtains a device on the black market and waits in any location such as where a new type vehicle is stationary. As the owner is monitored parking and securing his vehicle with their wireless key fob, unknown to them at the same time the offender with his device blocks the signal between the fob and vehicle, where unknown to them if not checked, the vehicle is left insecure and unlocked. As the member of the gang gets inside the un-protected motor car, they are able to activate a blank key against the vehicles computer system with this illegal device they are able to start and drive away without any effort whatsoever. In most cases it will be the top of the range Mercedes, Range Rover, Lexus, BMW or Audi or any other suitable high powered vehicle. It goes to show that even with modern technology basic common sense principals in crime prevention are an absolute must. Always park your car if possible, where it is monitored by close circuit television cameras, public or home fitted devices or hidden in a building or flanked by a less expensive car. Just as simple, do not have any of the features of this keyless facility fitted if able to in the first place.

Other scams can involve the use of cloned keys, or breaking into houses just to steal high value vehicle keys. An extremely violent theft of taking a vehicle if known as vehicle hijacking, which really is basic robbery and this violent type of crime is easily committed and on the increase. When the opportunity presents itself try to lock all doors from the inside, which may prevent this type of crime, except when direct force or threat is made with a weapon or instrument against the windscreen or side window.

A vulnerable driver of any age can be forced out of their vehicle without notice, usually waiting in a line of traffic where escape can easily be made, or by distracting the driver to open the door where they are forcibly removed with violence assault or threats and intimidation. The offender takes the role of driver and steals the vehicle, horrifyingly in some cases driving off with a small child on-board alone. Usually they are abandoned a safe place away from the scene, but the consequences of additionally abducting the child at risk of injury with erratic driving attempting to escape, especially if involved in a subsequent chase or serious road accident.

Just like all the expensive heavy plant equipment that is stolen all over the UK, these heavy vehicles including JCB's will end up driven out of the country or hidden in massive containers and shipped out and bound usually for third world countries or wherever there is a market for quick sale with high rewards for those involved. These gangs are a scourge on our society and are the very worst part of un-vetted people coming to our country. They sadly cause disgrace to other valuable, talented and honest countrymen of their nations, who themselves do not wish to be associated with.

CHAPTER 09

TERRIFYING CRIMES OF VIOLENCE SOME WITH APPALLING CONSEQUENCES

Today we live in a modern country which is relatively peaceful compared to other places in the world, where law and order is enforced within strict budgets creating a very much unfair society depending where you live. With mass immigration of so many races and many Muslim people, all from different countries, with many good people, and sadly many the opposite, when we already have enough of our own bad people. Perhaps that is the reason why we are all here in the first place, so we can improve with age and maturity and help others who are so much in need. Over the years I have seen sights of injured victims who might well ask if the offenders are actually part of the human race.

As for victims taking the law into their own hands, although it was not a case I was involved in, I recall some men slightly the worse for drink, were making a nuisance of themselves at an eastern style restaurant. This resulted in the police being called where they were ejected from the premises and told to go home away from the location. They walked off but later returned making verbal threats and this resulted in one of the chefs running out towards the men carrying a wok full of boiling oil which he threw directly at all of them. Two had slight burns but the one man received horrendous injuries to his face and neck, being taken to the burns unit of the main city hospital. He survived but was scarred and disfigured for life. The chef ran off and later left the country and I believe was never traced. As a result, news of this outrageous attack spread amongst the local people and eventually the business collapsed, resulting in the premises closing for good. No matter what the reason no one can ever justify this kind of retaliation and it is where taking the law into your own hands becomes an act of vengeance. Even more disgusting was the fact the man was never brought to justice.

As horrific as the last incident was today we still see too many evil cases where one might think parts of society are inhuman. We have had cases were couples have broken up where the male ex-partner in particular has held a despicable grudge where he has hounded his former girlfriend or wife and in an act of vengeance deliberately thrown a large amount of toxic acid over the victims face. With this resulting in terrible consequences involving many operations to correct disfigurement with plastic surgery involving tremendous courage and bravery on the part of the person concerned.

One case I also dealt with was where this husband was having domestic problems with his common law wife and for no reason attacked her to a terrifying crime of violence. He knocked to the floor in the lounge of their home and got astride her. Then with his knuckles, using one bent finger with both hands continually hit his wife in the eyes again and again. As her eyes became more swollen the cruel subject suffered his wife to even more pain due to him alternatively flicking his fingers into her eye balls, for what must have been an alarming period of time. The consequence of his actions was that his wife passed out, and her eyes had swollen to the size of tennis balls which were also completely bloodshot. Each eyeball had the appearance of looking like two beetroots protruding from the eye sockets, an absolutely appalling and horrendous injury. Although it was too late to prevent what had taken place it was believed a neighbour had called the emergency service, ambulance and police and the husband was arrested and taken into custody. He was interviewed, admitted responsibility and was charged and placed on remand. The injuries were photographed and although at one stage it was thought the woman may have lost her sight. Miraculously after much care and treatment detained in the Eye Hospital her eyes returned to normal, although she had extreme bouts of blurred vision. He received a substantial period of imprisonment, pity he was not subjected to the same horrible fate.

You may think that story was bad enough but then in the national press was another example of extreme brutality where a former girlfriend was being attacked by an ex-boyfriend. This despicable object purporting to be a man, held the victim down and whilst she was powerless, gouged out both her eyes, leaving her totally blind and unable to ever see her children ever again. Then more recently in present day in the Canary Isles we had the savage attack upon an innocent woman who was stabbed and in the process decapitated with the offender running round carrying her head by the hair. This is where mental illness appears to take over any prosecution, but nothing can condone this evil behaviour.

These incidents are just totally unbelievable but actually did take place. Whether this offender was mentally ill or not, or those who committed all other such attacks it is hard to believe that they form part of the human race. During my time in service I have seen many despicable attacks involving deplorable injuries but at least then, especially in my earlier days there was a deterrent in place when punishment was given out. How do we as a society rid the world of these evil people from committing such crimes, I am sorry but in my view, this is not a time to listen to the do-gooders who have in many ways contributed to falling standards especially supporting those who continually commit crime. Another serious issue which is on the increase in modern society is the amount of offenders who punish their families in committing murder of their spouses and children and then selfishly commit suicide. If they wish to harm themselves so be it if they cannot live with their sins, but why take out innocent loving people as a sacrifice to their own epitaph of crime or misbehaviour.

Sadly the next story involves the fall from grace of one of my colleagues, DC WATSON whom I worked with on many criminal cases both in part of CID and uniform duties. As I have previously described he was hard working and dedicated officer, whom I always had great respect. He was married with four children all young and lived with his family and mother who financed a granny flat next door to his property. Whatever was wrong with his marriage I do not know but this officer unknown to me was seeing other women prior to us working together. He was very popular in the office, but clearly something else was ruling his head and it was not connected with crime detection. No-one is perfect in life, including myself and he was heading for utter disaster both professionally at work and within his family domestic situation.

Whether it was a mid-life crisis or not, but it certainly was self-inflicted.

All this culminated with DC WATSON one day being admitted to the Burns Unit of a major city hospital, where his condition was critical and life threatening. He had been viciously attacked and received serious burns all over the front of his body from his neck down to both ankles. The contents equivalent to a large container of cellulose thinners apparently had covered him and had been set alight and Dc WATSON was claiming a nasty accident had taken place. He was lucky to be alive and apart from this alleged accident it was more likely to be nearer the truth of a case of attempted murder. This explanation at the time was clearly not accepted by him and he was under full investigation by senior officers for having an intimate relationship with a female who had serious previous convictions.

In addition residing at a place not authorised by the police, the home of a criminal family. Later I was sent to the hospital to see him in an effort to establish as much as the truth as possible. The more knowledge that came to light Dc WATSON clearly was the author of his own destiny.

He was very good at mixing within all areas of society, especially the criminal fraternity which is essential for any good police officer uniform or CID. Only trouble was with DC WATSON he always just got too involved crossing the line between being professional and outright dangerous. Either letting off some criminals he had knowledge of committing offences in reward for information of more serious offences, whereby my philosophy was, the victim of any crime came first. The example a bird in the hand was worth two in the bush and rather than making any deal or closing his eyes to what he had discovered, was crossing the line in my book as he had no such authority to allow this to take place. Far better to deal with the issue, arrest and charge the individual for the crime, then the wheeling and dealing can take place where he can have all kinds of help legally, where he would be even more useful in giving information where we would remain in control. Such as letting the powers that be, become aware that he was extremely helpful to the police and that may help reduce any future sentence given.

We used to visit this household where this notorious criminal family resided, virtually all of the occupants were involved in some serious crime or another and had numerous criminal associates. During our joint visits nothing untoward ever took place, but as always I sensed here we go again he was getting too personally involved with them, no more so than with a young 21 years old single female whose brother was into all kinds of nasty and violent crime. There was always friendly banter between them all and I often wondered where is all this going and where would it end up.

Apparently I did not realise but away from work this officer was calling round to see the family off-duty and had developed a relationship with the young lady and had started taking her out. Not only did this again breach police rules, but even more unbellevable he had fallen for a female who had convictions for grievous bodily harm. A couple of years before she had glassed another female in the neck causing life threatening injuries, for which she received a custodial sentence. What an unstable and unpredictable woman she was, and my colleague was now her boyfriend.

I was off duty when Dc WATSON had been involved in a road accident in the area we policed, a direct result him driving his vehicle with his new gorgeous girlfriend as passenger. Whist driving they had an almighty domestic, it seemed a very volatile relationship and she began fighting with him whilst he was driving, causing him to crash the car, in the middle of the town, whereby the uniform police were called to the scene. That let the cat out of the bag and Dc WATSON was hauled before the bosses and removed from his post as detective. He was lucky not to have been suspended or sacked for bringing the police force into disrepute and was taken off operational duties and employed within a custody block on another division.

The one day he had to attend our station to be interviewed under discipline and I was able to make arrangement to see him later in the day away from work when I was off duty. Not that I ever condoned any of his behaviour far from it, but he had been a good friend over the years as well as a work colleague. His family were lovely from his wife, mother and all of his four children, what on earth was going on and how could I get things back on track to either save his marriage, or from him committing himself to all future ambitions for policing roles ending up as professional suicide or in total disgrace being sacked or forced to resign. No matter how good you have been in the past, when you fall from grace not many people take this into account.

However he stuck to his guns, I went out to meet him, and my wife was aware my main mission was to try and help this individual try and get his life back. We had a quiet drink and I spent a long time going through all that he was losing, and he stated he was going back to sort things out with his family. I could do no more hoping he would accept and stick to the advice that was given. I later learned he did visit his wife and have a talk but the criminal family turned up and took him away with his girlfriend who by then was expecting his baby. All future contact was worthless as he was always guarded by all of these unsavoury characters. Eventually his wife divorced him and they lost the house along with his mother who had to be put up by the local authority. If he had got back with her she would have stood by him, but sadly it was not to be.

As the story enfolded there were strong rumours banding about from various sources he had become too involved with the family, had fallen for the daughter and he had to prove himself worthy of membership. It is not known if truthful or not but suspicions were that he went along with them on some criminal escapades and either played an incriminating role, where they had a hold over him. There was even a house burglary where a former colleague also suspected that Dc WATSON was involved possibly with this family, as from the method of entry was unique and only known by close contacts, he being one of them. The occupants, both police officers were convinced their former friend was behind this too and several items were stolen. How low if true, can someone once their closest friend finally stoop. If ever the trust was broken with this criminal family he would be shopped and possible facing further ruin even prison, which if true he would have fully deserved. He had been seeing another girl before all this association developed and again he had become too involved. The woman was pregnant by him, so he had to some degree chosen his destiny, how irresponsible. He had sorted arrangements with the mother unknown to us all in the office and we thought he had learned by his mistakes. When that relationship finished, within a month he was seeing this other girl who we all suspected was behind the vicious attack causing the severe burn injuries. So not only did he get out of one relationship smelling of roses, he then decided to get himself into a worse predicament which was exactly what he did. Not only did he jump out of the frying pan into the fire but actually dived in. He had hardly any friends and who can wonder and sadly that then included myself for other personal reasons.

With a couple of weeks Dc WATSON became well enough to be visited and had begun the slow painful experience of recovery. He had already had two or three major skin grafts, with more operations to follow. I was sent to see him with a view to trying to establish the truth and report back to senior officers. Bearing in mind he was the future father of the child he was expecting, from a girlfriend who had serious criminal convictions and clearly had an unstable and dangerous background. He stated he was in the garden of their family home and burning rubbish and was using cellulose thinners and accidently tripped dropping the liquid over him which ignited, and totally insisted it was nothing more than an unfortunate accident. He stated his girlfriend was present and called the emergency service. However throughout the local criminal fraternity many were aware of this relationship and the pedigree of both of their volatile behaviour towards each other. Rumours were circulating that they were in the garden she approached him after an argument and shook the container of cellulose thinners all over him until the container was empty then threw a lighted match at him when he became engulfed in flames. This allegation was put to him, which he adamantly denied had taken place. In addition the injuries he sustained were more consistent to the latter description of circumstances other than just an accident as put forward by himself. It was explained no way would the burns be so extensive if it was just an accident, but despite every avenue challenged he would not change his story. No witnesses ever came forward and the initial scene was well cleared by the time the police became aware of the incident. I reported back fully my findings to senior officers, as nothing would have given me greater pleasure in charging this dear lady with Attempted Murder, for which if true she greatly deserved but with no evidence substantiated she was not charged.

Dc WATSON was disciplined for certain matters and was reduced to permanent uniform duties spending the remainder of his service as jailer in the custody block. His initial excellent previous service saved him from dismissal, but it so easily could have turned out into a very different ending, if any evidence had materialised and was proved against him. On the other hand, was he simply telling the truth and not involved in anything wrong besides having an ex-marital affair and was unfairly judged to be guilty by association and falling in love with a woman he could not handle. We will never know. I never saw him after that and when he retired he later went to live abroad.

CHAPTER 10

INDECENCY WITH CHILDREN

Like with majority of crime to write individual stories about all of them the book would become endless and possibly extend to even 3 or 4 volumes. Indecency offences were also sadly very common place in the area I worked.

I cannot believe the amount of cases over the years I have dealt with which have involved people of high standing in the community. These offences have involved schoolteachers, scout Masters, road safety officials, driving instructors and many more men coming from all walks of life. All men having jobs of position and trust that should have known better and have crossed the line in there lust for interfering with underage girls.

No thought is given by the offenders as to the consequences of their actions. Who apart from tearing their own families apart, through loss of employment, or a marriage ending in divorce cause endless grief to their victims. We must not forget either all the victim's families who also experience the after effects of the crime, in having to come to terms with their close relative reliving the consequences of such an ordeal.

The strange thing is when these matters come to light and the person is arrested, the amount of eccentric behaviour that follows the guilty person. Some respond with an overkill of public confession directly aimed at putting this right with their wife or family and others just moving out of their home and leaving altogether, others denying all to the bitter end.

In addition with male schoolteachers falling for pupils under 16, or vice versa, they just do not see it as being jail bait. They go ahead and build up a sexual relationship thinking they will never be caught. Sometimes it can be the attractive young mature pupil, who is not so mature in reality, who has a crush on her teacher, or may even be vindictive just through jealousy of another. Whoever is responsible for starting such a path of destruction, should realise the law is there for a reason and the line should not be crossed under any circumstances.

In some countries elsewhere in the world the age for consent of the female is lower, which is the same for marriage, but if you are living in the United Kingdom you have to live by the law of the land in this country and not that of any previous place of residence. If only offenders showed restraint and maturity and could see this coming beforehand and the consequences of their actions, they would not commit the offences in the first place.

One of the worst cases I had ever seen, which I myself were not personally involved in made my skin crawl. We had a team of petty criminals breaking into cars stealing property. A stolen video camera was the one item that blew this disgusting offence to the surface. It was viewed by the offenders as it contained offences of indecency involving a man in his early sixties committing gross indecency with his 8 month old granddaughter. All having a criminal background they all decided they could use this to their advantage and blackmail the man into departing with his money. Realising his game was up, he confessed to the police and all were finally arrested and subsequently charged. What frustrated me was prior to this, in the office the incriminating evidence on the video camera was being repeatedly viewed by some of the officers. Not as a sideshow far from it. We were all appalled and disgusted, but I had to point out to them and to DI CLINTON that if they wanted the perverted man to get away with it at court, you are nearly giving any defence lawyer a possible bonus on a plate. They all looked in bewilderment as I said bluntly to them. One touch of the wrong button on this video recorder where its records, even for a second in any part of this CID Office which is recorded and the evidence is then contaminated.

It needed to be switched off immediately and taken to police Headquarters and the actual tape authenticated, in other words preserving the original as untouched and a proper working copy issued in its place. We all live and learn and they heeded my advice, otherwise if the unimaginable had of happened, they would never have forgiven themselves. I often wondered really if I was liked for those actions, or given credit, but I never had any compliment from anyone, including D.I. CLINTON perhaps they were all surprised at how stupid they had been. I just could not let the inevitable happen, that would have played on my conscience should the man have got away with such a disgusting offence.

One incident I experienced close to home happened when I took my dog for a walk into parkland whilst officially off duty. I walked towards this stream and at a bridge I saw this man in his mid-fifties sitting close to two young girls who were both no older than 14 years. All of a sudden I saw this girl kissing the man full on the lips which in itself in my book was indecent assault. I confronted the man about his behaviour and he stated he was doing nothing wrong that he was a friend of the family. I had pen and paper with me but no identification. I spoke to all and took names and descriptions stating I was to call the local police to attend and to walk to the other side of the area in the direction of their home. I kept them in view then quickly returned home where from my lounge window I could see them in the distance. I contacted the police and gave full details and asked them to meet the three as they walked in the direction of the opposite park entrance. This they did and confirmed to me all were to be taken back to the home address of the parents. A full written record of the incident was recorded into my police notebook, including the names of all involved. I invited the mother of the one girl who I saw kissing the man, to visit me the following day at the C.I.D. Office.

When I finally had chance to see this lady she was adamant the man was a sincere person and a good family friend. Even though I advised her he had seriously crossed the line in kissing the girl full on the lips, she decided that she wanted no action taken. This was despite me raising my suspicions in that her daughter may have been under abuse from this man. I made a full record of the actual incident and recorded details of our conversation, as instinct told me this matter could easily raise its ugly head again.

Needless to say in less than 12 months I received a telephone call from another police station where the same man was being held in custody. Apparently the girl had finally confided in her mother as to what had been taking place and the man since being seen kissing the girl had developed a relationship ending in sexual abuse. He was charged and appeared at Court. He initially denied all offences but pleaded guilty before I was called to give evidence. He was sent to prison which is the only sentence anyone accused of these types of offences can expect. The mother eventually apologised for failing to listen to the initial advice I had given and applauded my intervention.

Although the area where I lived had memories of where many ancestors once lived, we eventually after retirement moved to another area. At the time we lived there and still in the same CID office the neighbour in our adjoining property never really came to our attention. He had moved in upon marriage with the house paid for by his mother. Later he had two girls and although he kept to himself, he did speak and pass the time of day. It seemed a funny relationship all we ever saw the girls eating as they grew up were small bowls of cooked spaghetti without any other sauces or ingredients. We often commented that they could have done with eating proper food and gaining some weight, but they were not under nourished after all they were not our children. There was never any suggestion of neglect and other than that we did not take much notice. He always gave the impression he was a law abiding citizen.

During my retirement one of my old neighbours telephoned me to look at the local newspaper which I did online. There he was our ex-neighbour with his full picture on the front page, charged with numerous offences of having photographs of child pornography in his possession on his laptop. He was currently out on bail and required to live away from the family home in a Bail Hostel and was awaiting committal to Crown Court.

Reading further into his acts of depravity I saw that he also faced additional charges of taking indecent and pornographic pictures of children. This obviously put an entirely different reflection on his behaviour which indeed was very sinister, especially when the victims were his own two children. Although not completely sure of their ages they were certainly around 6 and 8 years old and would remember all events taking place. How degrading and utterly disgusting and I shuddered to think that when this was happening his wife did not find out either from comments by the two young girls, or even play a part in the whole sad affair.

What was even more amazing he appeared at Crown Court where he had pleaded guilty to all offences. He received a non-custodial, suspended prison sentence. This I could have accepted if just for downloading pornographic pictures. Surely not to be given an immediate sentence of imprisonment for grooming his girls and taking indecent photographs and publishing them on the internet for money, this was nothing more in my book that a total miss-carriage of justice no matter what the reason given by the Judge. If prisons were full at a time of cuts, which may have swayed the decision, they surely had got it so wrong. He fully deserved to be put away, what a danger not only to his own children, who would forever live with the consequences of his actions, but all other children as well.

Although the internet is a marvellous addition to the modern world, giving great pleasure to all ages, sadly like everything in society it is shared with criminals. Today we have sexual grooming by paedophiles purporting to be chatting up young girls, when in actual fact these evil men are years older and all they have on their warped mind is sexual abuse. They gain the trust of vulnerable teenagers, then meet on a blind date unknown to friends and family. Sometimes they are successful and abuse the victim without them realising it, others are scared and tell their parents. Fortunately due to excellent police work some of this people are monitored and when they start the grooming process with online chat it is clear what they have on their mind, knowing full well the alleged victim is under age. Then when they feel the opportunity is right they set up their meeting which of cause is a legitimate police trap. Although this achieves positive results this is very consuming for the police on limited resources.

In addition there are other evil monsters who obtain indecent photographs of young females in the same scenario, which they then circulate online send them to the friends and relatives, causing all kinds of depressive problems for the victims some sadly who commit suicide. Then the ex-boyfriend who is either violent or jealous or just unsuitable and the girl finishes with him for the right reasons. Having taken some indecent personal private photographs or videos during their relationship, he then resorts to criminal activities. With sometimes blackmail on his mind or other threats if not met, he sends the material online to employers, friends and family with the same tragic consequences.

It is a nightmare for police to have to investigate, not all related to sex offences, but along with all other material which relates to numerous other offences of a sinister nature. The Courts are now imposing strict sentences for all these kinds of offences and quite rightly so with many offender getting sent to prison.

In the UK we have always welcomed the right people coming into our country and settling down from all parts of the world. Especially when they commit serious crime when given a chance and allowed to stay, sadly these people have abused their privilege and many are deported, sadly not enough as appeal after appeal by Human Rights Lawyers preventing this from taking place sometimes makes a mockery of our present laws imposed on us by Europe. Due to the policies of previous Governments and the European Union in a relatively short period of time we have been subject to an influx of mass immigration, in addition to those entering illegally. That is fine so long as the right people are allowed in, learn the British way of life and do not spread racial hatred to our citizens. Many live friendly, industrious lives and settle down integrating well into society. After all we have more than enough trouble makers, serious criminals of our own without adding to that with the wrong people from abroad. This has changed many communities, with these people not even monitored or checked by authorities when entering our country.

In many northern towns there have been hundreds of serious criminal offences committed by foreign criminals, where young girls have been groomed and abused for sexual rewards resulting in serious rapes and extreme gross indecencies. It is believed many of these incidents were covered up by the authorities which is under continual investigation and if true deserve the full force of the law in being prosecuted regardless of the excuses.

CHAPTER 11

INFORMANTS – A POLICEMAN'S BEST FRIEND BUT ALWAYS TREAD CAREFULLY

I n those days C.I.D. to some people gave the impression they were always in the pub and some uniform officers used to frown upon this. It was a perk of the job okay, but later in my service some naive senior officers who were not involved in crime just did not understand or appreciate the advantages. If you did your job right you mainly went into premises where you would speak to criminals and in some cases cultivate them as informants. You learned who was associating socially with who and where, all important intelligence when needed.

The most important issue was, when a fresh face appeared on the scene, it in most cases meant he had met his mate when inside prison and they met up and joined each other to commit crime and were active again. The unknown person was your next burglar, or robber or handler of stolen property. In some cases that happened and when any occasion came for him to be arrested or interviewed, we knew where to possibly find him and any future contact barrier had been broken.

The golden rule was to put the job first in dealing with positive police work and when any arrest and subsequent dealings with any prisoner had been finalised then was the time to go out for a couple of half pints towards the latter part of the shift.

We would select the trouble public houses where we knew most of the cliental that would frequent the main bars. In most cases we all knew each other and there was friendly banter or the opposite where they felt uncomfortable or our presence was possibly pricking their conscience over something they thought we were aware of. Other occasions it was sometimes essential just to let off steam and relax, especially when hard work together with your colleagues materialised in a successful result.

Over the years, however it was abused, some younger officers went to trendier pubs to look up the women, rather than places active criminals frequented. Then there were other posers who went for nice food and one armed bandits where they would spend most of their time talking to no one just feeding their gambling addiction and nothing to do with accumulating intelligence. Hand on heart those officers never learned anything beneficial to the job.

From experience when you visit these premises with determination to cultivate criminals in turning to informants, it's amazing how the odd drink or cigarettes could get their loose tongues wagging, especially when over a period of time they could obtain your trust in a positive way.

One interesting evening I was out with a well-known and good experienced detective Sergeant. There were several middle aged men drinking in the bar of a local public house who had enough convictions between them collectively to have spent 25 years in prison. The one was loud mouthed and got well out of order. He was uttering snide remarks, the fuzz are here, always drinking on duty, but the more he spoke the more stupid he appeared. The sergeant went up to him in front of all his mates and stuffed a £10 note into his front top coat pocket. It was there for all to see and he just said to him, "Thanks for the info. It worked a treat, keep it coming" He was completely demoralised, lost for words. From the looks that he got he was well stitched, as the room fell to an eerie silence. I bet his mates treated him differently after that. When together in a group they are always brave but in reality their character is the opposite. There's always more than one way of skinning a cat.

As time went on and we had some less dedicated staff, I remember one detective sergeant who was qualified for years and not actually promoted to any higher rank, in the last year of service was temporary promoted to acting detective Inspector. This also applied to similar uniform and CID postings of all ranks. This was another perk that senior staff enjoyed as this last year of service counted to their pension which was increased to that of the last rank they had served, which involved quite a serious amount of money. Despite being in receipt of his increased salary in the acting rank, this officer used to come out for the last hour of the evening to do our round of visiting licensed premises. He was so money incensed watching his every penny, that I soon detected his clever moves. When we went out on each and every occasion over quite some period of time, he never bought a round of drinks even though each time he accepted free drinks from everyone else.

To his embarrassment we all went out this one night and on the steps of the entrance to this public house bar, before going inside I just told everyone to stand still. I said to him, "You can go in first as it's now your time to pay for a round of drinks, we are not stupid stop sponging off all of us and pay your way." He denied this was the case and I clearly pointed out that he had not bought anyone a drink during the previous three months and all present agreed. How stingy can anyone become most of us realise when we miss a turn, we are the first to precipitate without any hesitation. He knew exactly what he was doing and from there on he always paid his turn. Just a pity we did not say anything to him earlier.

Throughout the criminal fraternity no one can stand a grasser or police informant. It goes against the grain and to them, no one should ever shop a friend, relative or accomplice, to some it is just morally wrong. In their misguided and false standing in society that the world owes them a living, it breaches their code of honour. Experience has shown that every criminal has the potential to inform, even the most hardened. Normally those you would least expect will cross the line, even those who hit the headlines for serious offences and get sentenced to long prison terms have their price.

Whether it is revenge against a previous grasser to get them back, or for reward or reduction of sentence but everyone believe me will or can turn at some time through their dishonest career.

Police can be clever and if it is done right play one villain against another. It can be done with subtlety, by just inadvertently dropping out an innuendo enough to trigger suspicion in the criminals mind, or just by blatantly telling him he has been grassed either by one villain or more.

This was particularly true one day. We had a man in his mid-twenties who came from a family of several brothers, all prolific house burglars. This family was well known to me, as I had dealt with them all at one time or another. I was dealing with the one son who was in custody for five house burglaries who did not care a damn for his victims. His principles were just greed to steal rather than work for a living.

When I did my job I would not offer these kinds of people any favours, but whilst I was fingerprinting this one individual I asked him if he would like to know who had grassed him up. His curiosity was magnetic and he listened with intent. I stated he had been grassing up everyone on their housing estate and none more so than his own family. That did it I had his undivided attention and I told him if he repeated anything it would be denied, that he must keep it to himself. He fell for it and could not wait to hear me say the name and immediately I told him that it was his brother Tony. I advised him keep all this close to his chest and when the time was right and he was able to get his own back, that was the time to visit me again, not to mention it to anyone else otherwise I could not protect him. Of course it was all completely made up in the interests of justice.

I recall telling him to say nothing just bide his time and come back to me whether it be next week, or six months' time. Grass him like he has grassed you. His elder brother was a nasty hardened burglar who you would not like to confront anytime, yet alone in the middle of the night. He had previous for attacking people in their homes to aid escape or complete the job, which he did without a hint of remorse.

As time went on I thought no more about it and several weeks had gone by. One day this person came to the station to see me. He told me Tony's girlfriend's name and where she was living together with his brother. I was told all the property from over a dozen house burglaries he had done over the previous few days, was still at their address. It was spot on, he was arrested and all property recovered. Subsequently the brother was charged and sent off to prison which he richly deserved. It was as simple as that, what an easy way to clear burglaries, recover property and send the offender direct to prison. Who says there is no honour amongst thieves, just proves the opposite.

In my book the general but well established rule, was one informant to one officer that way you could build up trust in both directions. Some officers including sometimes fairly senior officers would be over zealous in anyone who attempted to muscle in on their territory in having access to their informant. This sometimes turned out nasty and I remember one incident involving two detective Chief Inspectors was close to being resolved with discipline action, being taken against one or both of them in running the same informant, especially where the issue of professionalism was concerned. At the end of the day the police force would always argue that informants were owned by no one and were in fact police property which in my view was the positive way in stemming any inter-colleague misunderstandings. Although informants are an essential tool in the investigation of crime in my view they never ruled the law enforcer as many thought they were allowed to do. If this ever came close I would lock them up as I always retained something in their past which would come back to haunt them should they decide to cross the line.

In one of my earlier chapters I related the story where I cleared up an armed robbery, all from stopping a motorist who came back with the information necessary to secure arrests. Later when in CID he came to see me providing information about several burglaries which I looked into. I went back to see him, things just did not ring true, was he making it all up, or trying to falsely accuse or set up some innocent person due to a personal grievance. Talking to him at length he became very insecure and stated he had fallen on hard times and had made things up in the event he would be rewarded. Feeling sorry for him, I bought him twenty cigarettes and gave him a fiver, hopefully sowing seeds for the future but in the end nothing ever materialised information wise again. Possibly he was too embarrassed, but clearly if he had supplied information in the future I would look at it with interest but also scrutinise every detail before acting upon it.

This is where informants can be so dangerous. No different to spies in the world of espionage, informants can say one thing to the police, at the same time get involved playing a serious and more important role in the crime that they were informing on. When deceiving the police and implying they were only playing a very small part on the fringe to gain the information and confident of his associates. For example double crossing the officer's trust and going against the rules, playing a major part being one of the robbers or attackers in a robbery that clearly is agent-provocateur and would put him on the same level as all those involved and criminally responsible. The danger then is when they incriminate the police as having full knowledge implying they were encouraged to get more involved. That is why more than ever informants must be held on a tight leach and fully controlled, always protecting yourself and corroborating your actions, protecting yourself against false claims. No wonder I always trod carefully and remained in control with these people at all times.

So the rules are clear and in place for a reason to protect everyone, perhaps created over past issues well before I had joined the police where certain police activities needed to be addressed. Whenever mistakes occur either in the legal profession or police procedures that is when the rules are changed to prevent repeat mistakes happening again in the future and quite rightly to. With DC GLOVER moved to an intelligence type role, his former younger colleague a protégé of his decided to transfer working with a crime squad.

This officer had worked with Dc GLOVER for a couple of years upon transfer to the department and allowed me to escape from his clutches to work with someone on the same level as myself. The young detective working with him was the complete opposite in nature to me, whereas I was dis-liked intensely by Dc GLOVER, this officer felt privileged to be able to work with such an experienced old fashioned type of copper. In fairness this young detective had no idea of my background, did not really know me or anything of my pedigree. He was certainly influenced and sadly brainwashed by Dc GLOVER whose peevish anger uttered in many daily conversations with him whenever my name cropped up. I just lived with it, I could tell in the sheepishness approach whenever this younger officer had dealings with me, and his reticent behaviour.

Whist working on the crime squad Dc GLOVER introduced his former protégé to a well-known informant of his, who was well into organised crime in various areas of the country. This informant although not known to me, especially knowing Dc GLOVER's pedigree fitted entirely into the category of very dangerous and untrustworthy. This younger detective was left alone to control the informant and source of the information he was acting upon. Not having any of the rapport that previously existed with DC GLOVER the informant was behaving well outside the rules on his own agenda. In actual fact although I only got the truth of the story after the bubble burst which I overheard in the office, from Dc GLOVER the informant appeared to have double crossed the young officer. No different to the scenario such as in spy films where the man giving the information was a double agent.

Clearly such an informant should have been in control of a senior officer, where every part and parcel of the ongoing operation should have been reported back immediately to him. Whether this happened or not I do not know, but knowing Dc Glover's pedigree I very much doubt it and the young officer was vulnerable to the untrustworthy informant's actions. It was feared that this informant was implicating the young detective in that he was falsely giving him permission to get too involved with the other criminals he was grassing on and possible playing the role of agent provocateur. All the time hoping he would benefit from the job at the same time seeking anonymity from prosecution, a very dangerous scenario indeed.

With pressures from home as he faced a divorce, the young officer was sliding down the road to obscurity with no brakes and was drinking heavily. One evening he became involved in a nasty argument with a uniform officer at another police station and it was apparent he had been drinking. They just waited the opportunity to stop him driving and he was breath tested positive and charged with drink driving.

He appeared before the Chief Constable some short time later and as he was found to be on duty at the time of being over the limit, it meant instant dismissal and he was duly sacked as a police officer. At the time those involved in the operation in which the officer had been running with the informant clearly all fell apart and if he had remained in the job he would have in any case faced serious disciplinary offences with possibly the same result, or even allegations of criminal misconduct which would have been one word against another. Dc GLOVER certainly did no favours in giving this young officer such a dangerous informant to handle for which he was clearly out of his depth with no senior officer involvement to even protect him. Dc GLOVER policing skills certainly remained in the past and even though he associated with the young man now a civilian, everyone around him knew he did this officer and his career a great dis-service. After a period of time he eventually established a new career and got his life back on track and formed better relations with his ex-wife and child, no thanks to Dc GLOVER.

One of the better ways of receiving information was through the Crime Stoppers or Crime Watch which was introduced towards the last few years of my service and was extremely valuable and still is today. Another extremely good source of information would be created due to marital breakdown where one of the ex-partners in the relationship would eventually give very accurate tell-tale stories of sordid issues which were believed buried but finally resurrected to the offending party to be brought to justice.

Sadly this next story involved the wife of a well-respected policeman who had a rural beat in one of the forces where I was stationed. He had the respect of the community and the sort of chap where butter would never melt in his mouth, until he finally divorced his wife for the love of another woman.

She immediately grassed him up for being responsible for several high class dwelling house burglaries in the village where he patrolled. In most of the cases he had allegedly discovered the burglaries as back then there was a system in place for monitoring homes whilst people were away on vacation, when in actual fact he was the burglar.

His ex-wife stated she was unaware of his criminal activities but having some suspicion over his past behaviour, gave information of where valuable property went, with some items left by him at his then current marital home. When I refer to this being sad, it is to reflect that it is a very black day for the police. To think that an officer fell from grace and bought shame and discredit to the police force, every individual officer took this personally from Constable, right to the top of the tree. The officer responsible had achieved some 15 years' service and turned out thoroughly corrupt, why and how can anyone in his position behave like that. There was just no excuse.

I suppose credit must be given to his wife for coming forward, but for how long had she been aware of his behaviour and was she in some way an accessory to crime. I am sure even if this was an issue, she would have been dealt with in exchange for putting away one really rotten and bad egg.

No one ever complained that he was given five years imprisonment, as if many officers had a choice or opportunity they would have doubled his sentence. That was in mid-1970 so at least he would have paid for his crime with such a well-deserved harsh sentence. Public trust in the police is always a must and of utter major importance where any breach should be thoroughly investigated and the source responsible to be brought to justice.

CHAPTER 12

FRAUD

In those days I found only a limited numbers of Officers in C.I.D. would investigate fraud, as it was time consuming and hard work, especially when on one hand they allowed you time to complete enquiries and on the other hand still continued to give you more and more work. The work was not balanced throughout the office and those lazy could talk their way out of situations without any senior officer being aware, it was just easier to let the volunteers take over. I was happy with that the more I dealt with, the more experienced I became.

Over the years I had several of these types of cases, nearly always committed by female staff as it was a role many girls initially took on as office clerk. A fraud always appeared easier to commit with smaller companies, as there was less supervision and a bond between staff which when breached usually resulted in theft and false accounting.

In most cases the offenders had been with the firm in question for several years and as previously stated would start to dip into the petty cash, so much to a point it could not be replaced. When confronted, usually with over whelming evidence, the person would admit full responsibility which always ended in a Court case and sometimes imprisonment. Theft from an Employer was always treated seriously in those days. I would advise the offender if charged with such an offence to tell her next of kin, normally husband or boyfriend, and offered to do this for them, but in nearly every case the answer would be they would sort it themselves. It did not always work out that way, as I remember one young woman promised me faithfully she would confide in her husband over the dishonesty and impending Court action.

I received a complaint from a firm that the issue of petty cash had discovered discrepancies of two thousand pounds. The lady arrested was polite friendly but clearly had some financial worries back at home. She was responsible for handling the petty cash and started dipping into it borrowing and later putting it back. When she reached the point she had taken too much and could not replace it. The next step was to cook the books. Which was exactly what she did. She back tracked former weeks and covered entries made with ink with a correction fluid which when dry could be re-written over in the same ink pen and would be hardly recognisable under the naked eye. Trouble is figures had to balance and when you paged back over weeks into months it became easy to see where it all started and work out exactly what was missing. This lady denied responsibility at first out of fear, but broke down telling the truth and went through all the ledgers explaining how it happened and what she had done. Even so, the courts always looked harshly at any crime like this and although it was her first offence, the court did not always show mercy or sympathy.

Several weeks later out of the blue his wife went out one day and failed to return. The husband attended the police station to report her missing and the station sergeant recalled her being dealt with by me and I was contacted. I made enquires, and earlier that day I established his wife had been given six months imprisonment by the Magistrates Court and so she was in custody.

I had the task of breaking the tragic news to him and explaining fully what had taken place. It's a fine line we cannot cross, as if a person of age is determined to sort out her own domestic issues we cannot interfere. Occasionally some women would be vulnerable and we would get a close friend into the police station, so some kind of confidentiality would take place in coming to terms with the issue.

In other cases to go against a person's wishes is also incorrect, but I always remembered the sad consequences of the man who committed suicide in an earlier chapter when he could not face telling his wife. Either way a person can be pushed in the wrong direction and must play a part in coming clean to a friend or loved one, which is part of the process in getting their life on the correct path in learning by their mistake.

One appalling catalogue of deceptions related to a man who was collecting for local charity. He was unemployed and would visit local firms over a 20 mile radius and ask various companies if they would sponsor his local sports teams, with proceeds going to charity. A fine proposal one might think, but not in his case the football team did exist, but had disbanded some 12 months before, same as the cricket team due to lack of interest. He would ask for a monthly contribution of about seven pounds, which he asked be paid by cheque and made out to himself, also naming him as organiser of a local football and cricket team. This was not a problem in those days, so long as he had the name on the cheque he could pay the funds into his bank account. He would provide letters to the firms in question stating certain amounts had been paid to charity. He had built up a large round and each day would travel to different firms who in some cases had prepared a cheque ready, from a prearranged phone call. On this basis he would collect several cheques each month, which all amounted to hundreds of pounds, providing quite a substantial annual income which he used to buy a car and travel on holidays. Absolutely no proceeds going to charity accept his own.

All came to light like so many of these issues, when his wife had thrown him out of the family home and had started divorce proceedings, all as a result of his criminal activities. He was arrested and pain staking enquiries tracing each sponsor revealed deceptions totalling £5,000 over a twelve month period. One might have thought someone would have smelt a rat, but the offender was so convincing in his approach to all of the companies. Needless to say he was given a lengthy prison sentence, as with theft from employer Judges do not like involving theft of monies belonging to such organisations. Donations to charities can be seriously jeopardised through criminal actions such as this, against the generosity given by so many honest and helpful members of the public.

Sadly today some charities leave a lot to be desired with many so called Chief Executives receiving annual incomes between £100.00 to £200.00, or even much higher salaries. An insult when so many volunteers work for absolutely nothing and the proceeds actually going to charity becoming less and less. Indeed some charities have been completely bogus and this is straight forward serious criminal fraud. There have been sadly other charities funding terrorism. I know of one such Chief Executive in charge of a Hospice, a multi-millionaire who only worked 2 or 3 days a week and still fell into the category of being very well paid. He spent most of his leisure time on the golf course and going on cruises and foreign holidays. He owned two racehorses, why did he even need this kind of job, just pure utter greed, as he did not have a clue of the workings of the place and how so many people young and old suffered. In addition he disregarded the hard work and dedication of experienced, auxiliary staff and volunteers, who were there 24/7 and often went that extra mile for caring and giving the ill terminal patient final dignity in what short time was left in their lives. All he was noted for whilst working there was recognition that he spent a fortune refurbishing his office and spent £800 acquiring a new mahogany desk. What an insult to all staff and especially the poor patients to whom the monies were donated in the first place. I bet this hypocrite never donated a penny to charity so full of greed and a professional miser.

The trouble is all this sad news about bad practice involving greed and fraud is not often the case and the examples I have given do little to protect the very good charities and workers who do it for really sad and deserving causes. Many work extremely hard and are dedicated to projects in the local community and are not even main stream and fully in the public eye. National charities have the advantage of full media advertising and have head offices in major cities all from donations, which had become a multi- million pound empire and classed as a business, sometimes losing the thread of what the real causes are in the first place. Some are doing very good work, but with hundreds of charities all ongoing concerns I am sure some areas are not fully monitored and the opportunity for fraud is inevitable.

We had a series of deceptions involving goods being purchased at various stores throughout a major Shopping Mall, where they would be returned and a cash refund requested. It is quite disturbing the amount of theft by shoplifting and fraud that is committed against lawful businesses, who are trying to keep people in work, and also to run shops or stores successfully and keeping within profit. As time in my career moved on, it seemed that the deterrent to commit crime, especially fraud had become less and less.

Although I have now been retired over ten years, this situation has not got better, in fact is has totally deteriorated. With instances of shoplifting or fraud associated with it, even when committed by organised gangs, they just get their hands slapped and told not to be naughty again. That's if they are even apprehended, one might ask why things in society have and policing got so bad. Still we must not forget all the good work that is still performed by many dedicated officers, who are working a dangerous role with morale low due to staffing shortages. Where it all will end I have no idea, but justice does not seem to matter anymore and this is sad as people do learn from their mistakes especially when accompanied with a suitable punishment.

One disturbing feature of the modern world of technology is Internet Fraud, in so many different ways of conning innocent users of all ages, is also extremely despicable. Even worse where extremely large amounts of money are stolen, never recovered and often the offenders who could be anywhere in the world are never apprehended. I would have loved to have had a go at catching these devious criminals as combined with all the technical resources, a good experienced criminal investigative mind is always essential.

In the latter years I was in the job and still today most transactions are with either a debit or credit card and any refund is not given in cash but paid back directly into the appropriate account which has proved a positive step against fraud. In this one case we had a man with a female acquaintance return to a national store for a refund on clothing, which had been paid by cheque using a payment guarantee card. On the insistence of the customer, a cash refund was given and they both left. Subsequent enquiries later caused the security to contact the police, as it was established a stolen cheque book had been used. I made enquiries and checked CCTV and established both travelling in the same vehicle some 20 miles from the scene of the crime. I placed an interest on the vehicle and a few days later it was sighted at the same shopping mall in our area. I arranged for observations to take place and the man was caught walking along the Car Park. He was arrested and it was found he did not have possession of any keys to the vehicle, as it had been driven by another female person.

Later at the police station a search was made of the man's personal belongings and a Filofax folder was found in his possession. It transpired that his girlfriend was to have met him on the car park and we allowed him to call her on a mobile to give details he was in custody. She eventually came to the police station where she was also arrested and her motor vehicle was searched. A stolen cheque book was retrieved with a banker's card. Both were interviewed and denied all knowledge.

I arranged for two of my colleagues to travel to his home address, in order a thorough authorised search could be made. Albeit they had to travel around trip of some 40 miles it proved extremely worthwhile. Both officers were meticulous and leaving no stone unturned found stolen cheque books in cushions within a lounge. In the kitchen and inside the fridge they found opened cans of beans and chutney where banker's cards had been secluded. All items were seized for further investigation.

Meanwhile both of the people in custody denied all knowledge and agreed to give fingerprints and hand writing specimens for elimination purposes. They were each bailed pending further enquiries. As for the Filofax this contained details of several acquaintances mostly female of which some six other women were located.

All were invited to attend the police station and denied being responsible in any conspiracy to defraud. All provided fingerprints and handwriting samples also for illumination. Upon a full search being made against this material altogether a total of 12 stolen cheque books were found to be connected between them all which had been used with matching valid banker's cards. Eventually all stolen cheques were retrieved and together with all fingerprints and handwriting specimens they formed the case against them. Today DNA would be available if authorised where considered necessary. Some 200 hundred cheques had been encashed, with each transaction up to £50. It was established all the women named in the Filofax were involved in the organised fraud involving this man who used all the women to cash stolen cheques, most who had never been in trouble before. Finally all were re-arrested and charged with conspiracy to defraud. This engulfed all the offences and the circumstances involving all concerned which was a joint operation to deceive the public.

It clearly needed in my view to be treated seriously. The case finally went to Crown Court, and they dropped the conspiracy to defraud and carved up the whole file into far lesser criminal deception offences. In my view it was a travesty of justice but who am I to say, I had done my job correctly and had to accept the findings of the court. Needless to say they were all treated with kid gloves and had all received varying non-custodial sentences, with no prison sentence or suspended sentence served upon any of them.

During the enquiry the man was driven into our area by different women involved. It was found he was a banned driver and I discreetly sent his photo and home details to the division where he was living and within a very short time he was caught driving whilst disqualified. He never went to prison for that either my how times have changed.

CHAPTER 13

ABUSE OF TRUST

We had one case involving a large steelworks where lorries delivered scrap metal for the furnaces. Nothing wrong with that I suppose, just a natural thing to happen with a large nationalised steel manufacturing company. It was established security throughout the premises was a joke and it transpired that drivers were taking in loads of scrap metal and getting paid in cash. It was established that this happened between six to eight times each day. The only problem was no one clocked that it was the same load being driven into the area each time, the same lorry left via another entrance again unchecked and after reasonable break it returned again with the same load. It was suspected that this had been going on for a considerable time with collusion of some security staff involving numerous vehicles.

The matter was investigated but records had either been destroyed or had not been accurately recorded making it difficult to obtain all the necessary evidence. The one driver was caught as a result of police observations and enquiries, and he together with two security staff were eventually charged with obtaining monies by deception and sent to prison. By this time the damage was done and it was suspected the tip of the iceberg had only been touched. As a result of this scam, and possibly others not known about, security was greatly improved with majority of staff being replaced with another more honest and efficient team, but it was just too late for these premises to survive. Naturally the business suffered major losses and a few years later the premises closed completely. As always due to a small minority of criminal minded individuals and lack of positive action in the first place regarding security by management, several hundred people lost their jobs, some never being able to find work again.

I remember attending a course connected with my job and asked a Union Representative why it was in certain parts of the country, car firms came out on strike for no real reason. I was referring to when someone is either arrested or charged with stealing vehicle components or accessories when they are stop checked leaving the premises. I recall he gave a valid but plausible answer in dealing with incidents of dishonesty.

He stated that the workforce were not all treated equally. A white collared worker classed as being higher in position or in authority being staff members often having benefits as sick pay, free health care, free car parking and bonuses unlike shop floor staff. He stated many of these staff can be found to have say wheels and tyres fitted to their vehicles, which in fact were stolen and unpaid for. When under any investigation receipts are suddenly and conveniently produced. Other workers would not be able to have this escape facility, not that they were entitled to.

He explained this was an abuse to the company an unfair privilege, amongst some higher dishonest staff that also had many accomplices. Difficult to detect and even as or more serious a theft than committed by the ground floor staff. There might have been some truth in these issues, but we all had to tread carefully over these kinds of allegations as police officers we had a duty to investigate all incidents of crime providing there was evidence of such in the first place. He did make a valid point which was open for discussion, but it was up to the unions also to ensure there was better security within the company workplace to detect staff at all levels committing crime.

Again it was disturbing to later find that not only vehicle parts were being stolen from this particular car firm, but brand new motor cars coming of the track as the finished product being some of the most expensive were part of a large organised theft racket and never to be traced. How many vehicles were stolen in circumstances like this I do not know, but no business can with stand such losses without some risk to jobs. Eventually several years later due possibly to this problem and other major issues this National Car Industry plant closed for good after years and years of trading. With some profitable sections being salvaged and sold off. Whatever the real cause for closure, some staff sadly never found work again and I hope this included all the criminals involved which sadly were just a small minority of the workforce. Many were never identified, who should not be able to sleep at night for the part played in their deplorable acts of dishonesty. In fact, at one stage the company was taken over and all the pension funds of it workers secretly moved to personal accounts of the Directors. What a horrible scenario and a grim future for many ex-workers or those in retirement with very reduced or non-existent pensions despite having made contributions. Eventually after a general public enquiry it was decided there was insufficient evidence to prosecute. It is occasions like this that the French system of law was not in place - Guilty until proved innocent, instead of our system - Innocent until proved guilty. In my view this was an issue that was in the public interest to prosecute, but those in power suggested otherwise.

We had one disturbing crime in which we all learned a very big lesson. This adds volumes to my previous paragraph where persons are stigmatised by upper Management, who really should know better and keep an open mind. It was only a minor offence involving theft and whenever our force investigated any crime we always took details from the victim and completed a crime report. In my previous force we had a policy where the crime report must always include a written statement of complaint. Due to the volume of crime in our Metropolitan Force it would have been impractical to follow this pattern and sadly that lead us to a downfall in these circumstances.

The Director of this company, who was a personal friend of the Chief Superintendent, called us in to investigate monies that were being stolen from a secure safe in the general office. He was convinced the cleaners were responsible and virtually openly accused them. I ignored completely the unfounded remark, after all it was pure speculation without any evidence to the contrary. In any case instinct always told me to keep an open mind as fate always played a part in revealing the final outcome. It was decided without knowledge of anyone at the firm, other than ourselves and the main Director, special equipment would be concealed in the office. For back then it was extremely sophisticated, only drawback it needed 24/7 cover until the thief was caught and some six officers had to be briefed on action to be taken when this type of alarm was trigged. Altogether we monitored the situation non-stop for a period of some three days, then late one night the signal activated and those on duty had to respond.

The attacked premises were visited almost at once and the offender disturbed in action. Upon arrival the safe had been opened and we discovered the culprit was not any of the cleaners, but an Assistant Director who had been responsible for just helping himself. The main Director was summoned to attend and was completely distraught shaking his head in amazement giving us the final insult that there was no way he could prosecute his friend. If it had been the cleaners they would have stood no chance, without mercy they would have faced court for whatever the sum of monies involved. Just utterly disgraceful, but without a written statement of evidence, there was absolutely nothing we could do. The powers that be would not even contemplate wasting police time, personally I would not have hesitated, but it goes to prove there is one rule for one and another rule for another.

It was a pity the cleaners had not been confronted directly by this pompous so called Director and then I would have encouraged civil proceedings by the cleaners for such terrible defamation of character. This immoral behaviour I am sure still goes on today in some walks of life. I often still shudder at the time wasted when our energies could have been directed to the complaints of other victims, after all everyone deserves the same treatment whether a friend of the Chief Superintendent or not.

This is especially true in many areas of the NHS, especially employing agency staff cleaning contracts thus the work provided was sub-standard. This caused MRSA infections to spread, costing innocent lives which was another type of fraud imposed on the people expecting high standards.

In fact, a friend of my wife sadly lost her son who was admitted to hospital following an injury road accident where the broke his femur. During his short stay receiving treatment he developed MRSA due to infection caused by lack of hygiene and deep cleaning. Sadly in less than two months his health deteriorated and they were unable to save him and he died. He was 21 years old and in the prime of his life with a girlfriend he was due to marry. His mother went to her grave still suffering the loss which was just the same with all the victim relatives and friends throughout the country. Although hard to prove, in a clinical environment employing shoddy staff to save money is a fraud to the public if not actually a criminal offence. The worst issue was sacking hard working cleaners who were efficient and thorough in their work deep cleaning virtually every day, just to save small amounts of money and sacking lower paid staff, when they had to pay agency workers less efficient earning more. These people highly paid themselves never have to answer for their actions no matter if people lose their lives into the bargain. I just hope they can sleep at night.

Finally the powers that be re-instated new highly trained cleaning staff, rectifying the deplorable cost saving exercise of sacking good staff to be taken over by shabby substitutes. Hindsight is something we all learn by and I am sure these mistakes will never be made again.

Even so today in other areas of education, civil service and emergency Services including the police force. When cuts have to be made instead of letting these hard working people retain their jobs the powers that be would rather save their own skins in taking any alternative action such as taking a pay cut or losing higher positioned staff. It was always the lowest hard working people such as cleaners, handymen or couriers who were to go first, where much higher costs could easily have been saved in other circles. How hypocritical. In all major organisations so much funding is wasted or not used to it fullest advantage, where all that was needed was a major efficiency drive to overhaul wastage to keep to a minimum.

CHAPTER 14

GBH, WOUNDING AND ASSAULTS

At this present time we have an increasing violent society where sadly often the lout rules, with abuse of drink, drugs and prostitution where the criminal furthers his career with absolutely less deterrent now, than there was even 20 years ago. All sponsored with free legal aid. With no discipline, love and respect in so many homes, with the use of knives or firearms an everyday event.

With some people living here legally or not, who do not wish to even speak English or integrate at any cost all adds to poor community relations. All these ingredients form the basis for all sorts of public disorder from anti-social behaviour, assault, affray, to wounding or grievous bodily harm or with intent resulting in death from manslaughter or murder. This has caused the Governments from every party to introduce offences involving Racial Hatred, either committed in public or by way of communication by the internet, by email texting Facebook or Twitter, not forgetting via postal communication newspapers and telephone calls. Many in society argue it is not fairly policed and in most cases one-sided with only the real British citizen being punished. With this I keep an open mind, but all police officers have to swear allegiance to the Crown and promise to do they duty without fear or favour to anyone. Sometimes you cannot help thinking politics has taken over every day policing whereas the police should remain neutral at all times. How things have appeared to have changed.

Although in CID at the time of the miner's strike, I felt the role of the police appeared to be somewhat political, after all the miner's striking was their right but run by a greedy and selfish union leader, which only ended up with the miner's losing absolutely everything. You as a human being had to feel so sorry for them. They were doing a job many of us would not relish for a moment, as it was dangerous, risky, with all the breathing problems and illnesses that were associated with it. As a result of this strike action all would lose their livelihoods and communities were devastated by the loss of these and associated jobs, with no future income and lack of future investment.

Again the police were directly in the middle of all this and I am sure some did not like their role given, with others lapping up all the high pay and overtime. I know I did not join the job for this demoralising kind of work. All the damage that was done to community policing, it was a wonder with some of the televised police behaviour we ever gained respect on the streets, as in my view, we were solely used as a political instrument on behalf of the government of the day. Either way the police could not win as violence and general public disorder can never be allowed in any society and law and order must always be maintained.

Yet despite all the anger, when the Black Panther, who was responsible for the grotesque murders of post office proprietors and the awful murder of a young kidnapped girl was finally arrested by the brave actions of two uniformed police officers.

It was ex-miners who rushed from a nearby fish and chip shop to give assistance to the police. The officers who were threatened and injured in the arrest, it may have been far more serious an ending if not for these helpful people doing their public duty in assisting the police to detain and prevent the escape of such a dangerous criminal.

No wonder people with common sense choose not to go out in the late dark evenings, or are careful where they visit making sure they have friends with them at all times. What a society we have sadly become. Thankfully these elements in general life are mainly the minority, as many people live honest and industrious lives and integrate well within communities never offending or causing any problems.

The pressures on the police and security forces are enormous, especially when they are trying to make so many changes. Majority of races come here integrate and do fit in well with society and never try to change our country. However this appears to be the opposite with some of the Muslim population. Many work within all kinds of organisations and businesses and fit in well with the western world especially the younger generation. Sadly in society it does not always feel the same and some of the older generations of people often find it difficult to integrate. Some people make too many demands when living in a western country. All these issues are greatly affecting the old fashioned traditional British way of life and are making the country better or worse. The main priority is living together peacefully and the issue of law and order to be correctly restored so there is a deterrent to committing crime, reclaiming real credibility for the future for everyone. Whatever the reason there should never be areas of No-Go zones and British policing have absolute responsibility for such places. All those committing horrendous crimes against society however do not deserve to live in our country and many are deported for such behaviour, sadly after unnecessary appeals which are costing every hard working citizen in the UK of all races an absolute fortune which could have been spent on far better more essential issues.

Apart from violent demonstrations and incidents of mass fighting in late night clubs or public houses, majority of the isolated incidents arise at special occasions. This can include all kinds of events such as Christenings, Weddings and Bank Holidays, not forgetting New Year Celebrations being the worst evening in my experience by far. In addition, even the innocent victim can lose it, by taking the law into their own hands, inflicting punishment when out of control which was not even necessary. It takes a brave person, but it is always wise to not drop your standard to the level below that of your aggressor. Sadly this has certainly included some isolated police officers who have acted in an overzealous way who deserve no support whatsoever.

I remember coming on duty one New Year's Day and it was nearly always the same, as if the whole sub division at one time or another had been a complete battleground. Where people celebrate a New Year commencing, during that moment it is a time for all to enjoy and spread their happiness with friends and even complete strangers, but sadly quite often the complete opposite happens. It is hard to imagine why there is so much hatred fuelled between so many different people from all walks of life. Yet we only have to go back to the fifties and sixties when New Year was often celebrated at home between friends and families, or in the local public house. I like many other people have fond memories of such events, which were extremely happy events resulting in a friendly sing song with such a great atmosphere between all people strangers and friends alike. What on earth has happened to change or these lovely times when the true British spirit was the envy of the world.

We had a celebration at a local Social Club where for years there was never any hostility and yet this day four people were all in hospital all with severe injuries. One of the victims was without an ear which had been bitten off. All victims had been attacked by just the one same person a young man in his mid-twenties who was a banker, married and with a child. He had never been in trouble in his life but was worse for wear and extremely intoxicated.

Apparently he had gradually got worse as the evening went on and had become abusive and was continually shouting and swearing at other club members resulting in a series of fights taking place in which he was the main instigator. He had smashed a glass into the face of one man and had punched and kicked others. He was finally dragged off his last victim after having bitten off his ear which he had partially chewed and spat out. All being the worst scenario anyone could have witnessed with devastating consequences for all involved, especially in the presence of whole law abiding families who had children with them aged 10 years and older.

It was not hard to investigate as the evidence against him was overwhelming and when the man found responsible was arrested eventually sobered up, he was found to be one of the most polite and sincerest persons imaginable, but it was too late the damage had been done. Surely someone could have stopped him drinking seeing he was getting out of control and removed him from the premises, but no one could have foreseen the carnage that he later would be responsible for. He was the author of his own destiny all because of drink which had bought out the Jackal and Hyde character to the forefront. He paid the ultimate price, lost his job and went off to prison for a substantial period. Whether it cost him his marriage I could not say but what a lesson to learn when he had everything to live for all for the sake of one stupid but costly celebration. Saddest thing was over the years he was not the only law abiding person I had to deal with in similar circumstances who would fall from grace in society.

I could completely fill this entire book with all the incidents I have dealt with under this category, which to me became run of the mill cases fitting whatever degree of violence that was inflicted to the lowest and more serious of offences.

In the most serious of cases clothing was always seized especially when worn at the time of arrest, or discarded with an attempt to avoid detection. In a lot of cases today we have to be thankful for close circuit cameras. No one wants spies in the sky, but when you are the innocent person at the receiving end and want the offender caught this is now a major tool in the detection of such crimes.

The annoying issue is looking through reels and reels of photographic evidence, either through personal video or CCTV cameras, which is extremely time consuming and is a severe restriction on everyday police force manning levels, but an absolute necessity. You just cannot cut corners because if you miss a piece of incriminating evidence showing more blame on one offender than the other, or evidence to support the identity of unknown witnesses the defence will most certainly find it and act accordingly. In any case with defence Solicitors or Barristers they can quite rightly employ every level of staff necessary to form this task on behalf of discovering justice, all under the umbrella of legal aid and we have no argument because it is lawful and very necessary.

Investigations into crime have to be fair and unbiased and on every occasion an open mind must always be kept at all times during your enquiries. We had a crime where a young man in his late teens was working in a popular busy restaurant and he went outside to throw out the trash and suddenly was smacked across the face and threatened for no real reason. A poor vague description was given due to it all happening so quickly. Theft was not the motive and we were struggling to establish any other reason why this could have happened.

I decide to invite the 19 year old to the police station to assist with our enquiries. We asked him to go step by step through the incident which he did, but for this to happen just at the moment he went out with rubbish was unbelievable bad luck. Access at the rear of the premises could have been gained by anyone passing, but it was a fairly respectable neighbourhood. There had been no previous similar incidents at or close to this location.

Without any foreseeable reason or motive, I decided to look into the background of the young man. Treading carefully it was established he had recently fallen out with a long-time girlfriend and although he had still gone to work, I couldn't help sensing there was another side to this story. As we continued he lost his composure and broke down admitting he had injured himself with a blunt piece of wood, hitting himself in the face, making up the whole scenario. My interpretation was that he couldn't cope with his private life experiences and this was just a cry for help.

I had a young conscientious detective with me who asked the alleged victim if he wanted to make a statement, retracting his original complaint of crime. I advised him to hold back and although this young man was an adult, to me he was vulnerable. I requested one of his parents attend the station and although the young man was reluctant, he agreed for his father to visit. Upon arrival I spoke to his dad covering all aspects of the interview and our findings. I asked him to go and speak alone with his son to see if the same story emerged. It did and straight away I could see the relief in both of them and then I asked the young officer to obtain his statement. Both then left the police station and I advised I would submit a report requesting no action be taken as to wasting police time, and the matter be written off as No Crime.

With the younger Detective I explained just imagine if we had taken the statement without an appropriate adult present, even though he was of age and he had gone home stating we did not believe him. He could of alleged we had threatened him to withdraw and were taking no action regarding his complaint of crime, or at the worst, was released and due to depression committed suicide. Whether this advice was appreciated by the detective or not, I am sure in his future career, this incident would be a timely reminder for people being dealt with by him involved in similar circumstances and it is hoped he would take the same sensitive action that I did. These signs are not always obvious but we have a fundamental duty in looking for them. That was an experience we all learn from, including this young man's family who had the privilege of being aware of his unfortunate behaviour. Nothing can ever compensate for this kind of job satisfaction.

Basically unless in self-defence any kind of fighting, assault or attack upon another person is against the law. There are a few exceptions, such as boxing, wrestling, judo and karate providing the sport is carried out within the rules. Whereas if it is your intention to harm a person you commit criminal offences. This I always found extremely useful in getting rubbish off the streets. There are numerous times when thieves or burglars or handlers of stolen property, fall out with each other and although they hate the police we are the first they complain to. This is normally as a result of a visit to hospital, or at the location where it has happened. I would go out of my way to make time to deal and would lock all those up involved and even if they later wished to withdraw action, it was too late they would have already all been charged. They would have to face the music by attending Court even if the assault was dropped, as there was always an ancillary public order offence against them still outstanding. In the worst of cases some would end up being sentenced to prison, so what better way than locking up one criminal attacking another, it always worked in helping clean up society.

At least once every couple of months whilst all my time in CID in the area where I worked there was always a serious incident where many men of all ages were victims of horrendous attacks. Attacks on the old or vulnerable, for little or no reward, with people surviving with a severe disability, such as blindness, deafness or totally incapacitated all through no fault of their own, or just being in the wrong place at the wrong time. In many cases, action either associated with taking of drugs, alcohol, or simply for no reason whatsoever can ignite trouble. Just an innocent glance, or a momentarily stare in the wrong direction, or just the wrong words spoken can lead to or trigger a violent reaction, attitude or jealous streak into an act of violence. This coupled with the possession of a weapon of offence, knife or firearm can result in devastating consequences. Despite this depressing overlook we are still one of the best countries in the world, but it could be so much better. It was either as a result of an argument with another male person on a one to one basis, or just an un-provoked attack against a lone person involving usually a gang of several people.

In most cases where it was one person between another it was nearly always drink related, where the person fighting the other did not know when to stop and if death had occurred the charge would at the very least be manslaughter, or possibly murder depending on the intent. Usually the victim would bang his head on a blunt instrument, or fall and hit the road or pavement causing serious concussion and often unconsciousness sustaining serious damage to the brain which would be life threatening.

Where the attack was made by an un-provoked group of individuals, it was mainly caused by troublemakers bored and looking for excitement. How a group of people albeit youths, girls or grown men who should know better, or those in racial conflict can suddenly surround a lone person and continually kick and strike such an individual until senseless is beyond reason. I suppose they go with the flow without realising the consequences of their actions or the possible outcome, normally through drink or drug fuelled behaviour. All I know is that when the perpetrators are finally rounded up and questioned, whether they remember or not through drink or drug abuse when it comes to law and when arrested had absolutely no reason for the attack and were defenceless when questioned. In many cases they did not even know the victim.

The times we have had a victim taken to the main city hospital where the victim has ended up in neuro surgery and close to deaths door I am afraid there are too many to remember. I have often sat with these patients along with many of my colleagues hoping to glean a snippet of evidence to assist the case, or even take down a dying declaration when they uttered their last words. Those arrested near the scene where witnesses implicate them, together with additional forensic evidence they are in nearly every case found guilty. A nasty attack resulting in serious injury or paralysis or total disablement, can soon become a murder or manslaughter and people have been convicted of such offences not remembering absolutely anything of the incident. How obscene is that. These types of offences were rife in my later days and sadly are on the increase today. What a complete waste of life.

We had a man from a Northern Mediterranean location living in our area. He was in his early twenties and was of dual nationality. He already had previous for extreme violence involving the stabbing in the chest of a man with a stiletto blade resulting in life threatening injuries. On that occasion he left the country and went back home where he was dragged into doing his military service. He was arrested a year later on return through custom and immigration control and received three years imprisonment.

In addition to this he had numerous convictions for assault and public order offences all drink related. When this man was sober, he was the complete opposite friendly and kind. He came from a good home, with strong support of the family. I got to know him well during my service and just knew one day he could have the capability to commit potential murder if he did not seek help or change his ways. How do you stop a person who has all the instincts, or save him from his own self. He was like a time bomb when under the influence and completely unpredictable. When he drank it was if his character changed immediately to an evil, sinister and extremely dangerous person, always using a weapon to attack his enemy.

We had a fight in one of the main bars in the High street, an argument had ensued and the young man had been attacked for no reason, perhaps a glare or the wrong spoken word and that was it. This stranger, a young white man had been bottled in the neck by this young foreigner who despite being well intoxicated had been allowed to get away. Some unknown person believed a friend had taken him away and out of the area, allowing him to escape. No one was coming forward with any information as to his whereabouts, other than stating what the offender did in a nasty complete unprovoked attack. Apparently he had started an argument with him for no reason and just smashed a pint glass, ramming the broken half into his neck just missing the jugular vein. I think deep down they were scared in case the offender later found out, but that did not help the victim who was in Intensive Care and close to deaths door. As a few days went by due to good skills of the surgeon the victim started to pull through and eventually made a complete recovery.

Having good connections with the family I was able to get their trust enough so that their son eventually gave himself up to me. He was utterly remorseful, but I didn't make any promises as to the outcome of his punishment, how could I. He knew later from the evidence exactly what he had done, but also needed in my view some psychological intervention as to his mental state for drink to trigger such a personality change. He went to Court and received five years imprisonment. I never saw him after that, but would never be surprised one day if upon release without the correct treatment he would be capable of reoffending.

If ever there were examples to show drunkenness is no excuse for crime he would certainly fit the bill completely, as do so many others unfortunately who behave just like him. He would sometimes be arrested for just being drunk and disorderly. Whilst in the cells he would constantly bang his head repeatedly against the brick walls which would vibrate echoing completely to the top floor of the 6 story building. This would be continuous for well over an hour and when he sobered up he would have absolutely no recollection of this having took place.

This was a regular practice for many persons who had severe alcohol related problems and other than have padded cells there was little else that could be done in those days. Nearly every serious offence of wounding or grievous bodily harm in most of my service was drink related unless created through someone who was jealous, double crossing through a breach of loyalty or caused through some adulterous relationship. These days sadly most attacks are drugs and firearms related which has turned our country into everything majority of people find revolting and completely against our heritage.

In present day all politicians' clamber together with the UK drink problem and come up with get tough policies. They suggest lets encourage supermarkets and other outlets to refrain from allowing cheap booze to be sold. All offenders get tanked up mainly at weekends before going on the town and hitting the pubs and night clubs where eventually after even more booze and they leave these establishments women and men obscenely fall over each other, throw up in the street, lie on the floor in drunken stupors or fight with anything they can get their hands on.

In my view the question everyone should ask is what exactly are the police doing about these places that continually flout the law. Some police areas are extremely good with licensing laws being strictly enforced, as for other parts of the country they in my view are not policed correctly over this issue or the problems would still not exist. Any proprietor employing a person in licensed premises who sells drink to persons who are drunk or heavily under the influence, or by or on behalf of another person to supply such drunken customer commits an offence. This can have drastic consequences on the future of the licence. The power to close down such licensed premises is a fairly simple procedure and this would go a long way to stopping this embarrassing epidemic mainly involving many younger people.

So why do we keep experiencing these problems just close the offending places down until they learn from their mistakes. Even putting up prices does not solve the issue as like with drugs these kinds of people experiencing addiction will always find the funding from somewhere else. In most of the towns and cities throughout the country according to the press and media, drunkenness is clearly in need of positive action where the issues go unaddressed.

When majority of us back in the sixties went out for a drink, nightclubs were few and far between, and most public houses closed at 10.30pm, whereas dance halls and entertainment venues closed at midnight. We could all drink sufficient at that time acting responsibly and still have a good enjoyable evening, without getting absolutely sloshed as in so many cases today where they lose control completely and become incapacitated. Basically it is always down to the behaviour of the individual.

The main issue is all the hard working majority of people in the country should not have to pay for the minority, in unnecessary raised prices, which some politicians believe is the easy remedy especially another excuse to hide increased taxes, where in Parliament their own bar is subsidised, how hypocritical. Even today Parliament experiences violence between members caused through drinking in its own establishment and they say people in glass houses shouldn't throw stones. They should put their own house in order first and lead by example in putting up their own prices or close down their bars altogether. Better still just leave us alone with the laws that are in place which adequately cater for all circumstances providing they are put into better effect. I suppose only time will tell to see if things improve or not. As for a strain on the NHS with alcohol related matters if all such patients because of their problem were billed like when on holiday abroad, the numbers of outpatients would drop significantly as all drunkards are not only middle class, but also come from privileged backgrounds. As for those not working they should be urged to reform or have their benefit stopped altogether but then we have the human right issue don't we.

Clearly at some time in the very near future, a serious review for having a positive deterrent against those who commit crime will have to be re-introduced, otherwise the law of the jungle will take over. There must be an agenda for total reform of punishment for offenders combined with common sense, taking account the general feelings of the public, after all respect for law and order is always a priority to good and honest people as long as the punishment is fit for purpose.

CHAPTER 15

RAPE, INCEST, INCECENT ASSUALT AND ASSOCIATED OFFENCES

In my early days in CID we were responsible for all types of indecency, with female detectives doing a wonderful job and playing a very important role. This often involved very hard work interviewing the child or female adult victim and completing individual witness statements to the highest standard. Conditions have improved treble fold for the better, as now for all victims of whatever gender or age group, there are comfortable suites with pleasant calming and relaxing facilities. With trained and experienced staff every moment of care is afforded to victims and they are not pressurised to rush in telling their story and are given complete compassion. Medical help is a priority and always readily available. All interviews are recorded both in audio and video and often played to the court who experience first-hand the stress, indignity suffered the state of the victim's composure and suffering. What a very good step towards justice and fairness for the victim.

One of the better senior officers I worked with was a Detective Inspector Alex CLINTON. He was about five years younger than me, always smart in appearance with a good sense of humour, being very experienced in this role these factors always demanded respect which was regularly shown. Unlike some he always made sure he paid his round when out socially and was a very friendly approachable boss firm when needed and utterly professional, who knew his job having gone through all the CID ranks. He just did not suffer fools or lazy policemen at any cost.

One sad case we both worked together on involved the offence of incest. The woman was in her mid-twenties and her parents separated. She was married and pregnant with her first child, which should be a magical time for any young woman, but this forthcoming event trigged all the horrendous memories from the past, secrets she had kept only to herself, which finally erupted to the surface. The poor victim from the age of thirteen had gone through so many years being tormented by guilt of being subjected to acts of sex performed upon her by her disgusting father, which had continued right up into her late teens. Only at this time in her life she could not live with concealing the truth any longer and confided all to her mother. After talking at length with her daughter, both eventually attended the police station where a formal complaint was made. She was skilfully interviewed by selected professionals, who delicately unfolded the full story.

This horrible man had completely manipulated the one person in his life whom he should have loved as a proper father and stole God's gift for his own gratification. He took away her years of innocence and made her promise never to reveal his disgusting and despicable nature. Finally she was speaking but I feel in my own mind she would never deep down be rid of this ordeal and would need ongoing counselling.

Her witness statement was obtained and we arranged to arrest the father. He was a habitual criminal, always in and out of prison for most of his career, all for various forms of stealing. He was a local hero to his criminal friends and feared by many, a jack the lad type of character and extremely nasty with it.

Working with DI CLINTON was an utmost privilege he was a highly respected policeman and a good gaffer all in one and I was proud that he chose me to assist him, but furthermore he allowed me to take charge of the case. I always spoke to him as a good friend and colleague and we had a wonderful rapport between us. If only there had been more staff like him.

Despite this we had a serious case to deal with and we had to use all our skills in attempting to get to the truth which was certainly no mean task. He declined not to have a solicitor and was interviewed under caution by way of tape recording. Every time we asked a question, he would answer trying to change the subject giving a rigmarole of nonsense all with an attempt to avoid the issue. I recall at one point asking him what he would say to a Psychiatrist in these circumstances which baffled him completely and he came very close to spilling the beans, but just couldn't. He made no admissions of guilt surrounding the offences but not any denials either. He was charged with various counts of Incest and remanded in custody. During this period he wrote various letters to his daughter and enclosed in this documentation were admissions in his own handwriting to the awful offences that he had committed with her together with several apologies, but all were in vain. She finally gave them all to us to use in evidence against him.

For a reason I never understood, he was finally allowed bail, whether or not denying the offences played any part I did not know, but later we were to realise it was all to cheat his way out of facing up to his guilt. Whilst obtaining his freedom, he was able to commit suicide by hanging himself outside the home address of his former wife. In other words he was a complete coward and nothing like the Macho Hero he portrayed to his criminal world buddies. Even criminals have principals, he had crossed the line and knew it and could expect retribution from all sides whether he went to prison or not.

It doesn't matter what happened to him, it was the poor young lady and future mother who was the main priority. She had to live with this ordeal all over again because of him and certainly not for one moment should she have attributed any of her actions in being blamed for his death. She was the poor innocence party in all of this tragedy. I cannot think of any person who deserved proper care and important counselling to help convince her of this and that it was all completely out of her control. Not an easy thing for her to accept but after all, it was he who was the author of his own destiny being the instigator of such abuse and some would say he paid for the crime in his own way.

I will never forget identifying him in the mortuary as the same person I had interviewed, so the Court could lawfully finalise the case. It was eerie looking down at the face of a man you have interviewed, which had so many horrible secrets, which he took to the grave alone. Not a thing I would like to experience too often.

On another occasion I was with Dc WATSON again, who I had also worked with in uniform and CID for several years. We always had good relations with majority of the press who would phone up daily asking if anything of importance had happened. Not that this is the appropriate chapter but I recall we both used to give the reply if quiet, there are No Rapes or Pillages to report today.

We always had to be mindful of our conversations, but the press together with Radio and Television were extremely good media outlets to circulate so many of our requests for help. I had to smile we had one reporter who was a good friend who also had a sense of humour, wherever we appeared in the press he always addressed us as Defective Constables a deliberate typing error which we personally knew he was responsible for. In any case we always took it in good spirit after all he was probably right in his reporting expertise assumptions.

This was not the only offence of incest that I had dealt with. It was several years before we had a case where this divorced man had access to his daughter at weekends and she with her friend would go to stay with him. Both girls were 14 years old and he would ply them with drink, the result being he would sleep with them in turn having full sexual intercourse. He would corrupt them both into believing they were doing nothing wrong and it was all part of being in adulthood. Fortunately it was not long before the ex-wife discovered the truth and a complaint was made.

We arrested the offender, who denied all to begin with. He eventually told the truth and we could not believe he was just laughing it all off, until reality set in and he was crying uncontrollably. He received several years, quite rightly behind bars. Whatever the offence is under this category as detectives we learned to be patient to get to the truth. You have to empathise with the offender and not show any feelings of revulsion in determination to getting to the complete truth, in being open and fair to all parties, especially where the evidence was flimsy and possibly exaggerated or made up.

When evidence was clear and corroborated we would persevere lengthy interviews to finally get the truth, always hoping the offender would tell his side of the story in admitting the guilt of what took place. For younger witnesses who sadly but bravely have to give evidence, the Courts now regularly use video evidence, which is a welcome improvement and major step forward.

More importantly with all victims we would do our utmost to obtain a full and frank confession so as to avoid a not guilty plea, to save the witness the ordeal of standing in open Court, facing cross examination, having to answer questions involving the most embarrassing and intimate issues in their personal life. Should the inevitable have to take place where the victim had to give evidence in open Court, in the face of overwhelming evidence against the accused, this was always taking into account by a Judge on a finding of guilt by the jury, before any sentence was passed.

We had one offender who just did not learn, quite a nasty individual who had at least three pages of previous all for blackmail and robbery all following a continual pattern of crime. Altogether this 40 years old man had spent fifteen years of his life in prison at various intervals for exactly the same offences, and his latest experience was no exception.

He would frequently visit commons and parks where he would witness the sexual activities of two men meeting together. As a result He would cleverly follow one of them to their home and establish that he was in a family relationship, having a wife and possibly children. When the opportunity arose he would wait his chance for the next encounter. After taking photographs, he would then follow the same man again driving his own vehicle. When possible he would approach the man when the vehicle had stopped and tell him his findings where he would subject him to threats of exposing his behaviour to his wife and family. He would blackmail him into parting with his money in exchange for photographs which he promised to later hand over. He would then follow the man to a nearby cash point and ask for a minimum of £200 which in this case was paid out to him and he would hand over the pictures stating he would not trouble him again.

A couple of days later the victim eventually came clean with his wife as to what had happened, as she queried the withdrawal of the monies. The victim with his wife then started to tour the same area where the man had been and a few nights later the offender was seen in his car. The police were called and attended the location, where the man responsible was found and arrested following good work from the uniform officers.

When he was initially interviewed he did not admit everything to begin with, but like most others he finally came to the terms of the truth in the end. It was discovered he was already on bail again for similar offences and was remanded into custody. He received another severe prison sentence adding to his memorabilia which he more than deserved, in preying on the vulnerability of those men having problems identifying their own sexuality. I do not understand why these kinds of people cannot seek medical help with their problems, or just be honest about their sexuality instead of going to places where they are exposed to threats and intimidation. It is obviously a very sensitive issue and society is a lot more sympathetic today than it used to be back then, which is a good thing in some respects with those people affected.

In addition to the most despicable offences, we also investigated numerous allegations involving sexual assault against women where the offender was an opportunist, either a passer-by in the street who would just grope a woman indecently in the chest or legs area when she was walking alone, or whilst on public transport seated on a bus or travelling in a taxi. All shocking consequences for the poor female who had not caused anything to attract such bad behaviour. In some cases this type of incident would also occur on the trains where the jurisdiction would come under that of the transport police. In these cases whenever we caught an offender, or suspected a person responsible we would liaise with them just in case they were wanted for similar offences, or had a similar pedigree travelling on the trains. After all such a persistent sex offender has no bounds to walking and travelling on all kinds of transport. These offences are normally committed by serial offenders or by stalkers attracted to certain females who have no bounds. All offences really must be reported so a pattern can be built up, as these kind of people can be very dangerous and are all potential rapists or killers.

Normally for indecent assault punishment would reflect in a fine with the more serious incidents attracting a prison sentence. In cases where evidence of rape or attempted rape could not be fully proved the jury can if justified find the offender guilty of indecent assault as an alternative charge, and if guilty majority of cases resulting in a substantial prison sentence. In addition today there appears to be an increase in more offences committed by women of indecent assault, especially where they have developed sexual relationships with under age boys. Upon findings of guilty they too more often than not received substantial periods of imprisonment.

With changes in the law and society we also dealt with cases of male rape and although rare they were just as serious with the same consequences for both victims and offenders. It is interesting to note that in my earlier years these types of incidents were virtually unheard of as any homosexual act was illegal. As with many of my colleagues I have investigated several cases back when two consenting male partners to a sexual act resulted in any complaint being made, would possibly result in offenders being charged with Buggery. I recall one such case involved this man going out with a teenage girl where a relationship formed, the ulterior motive being that the man had his sights on the younger brother. When she discovered the man was having sexual relations with her brother, who was underage, she reported the matter to the police. Both were arrested and interviewed where the truth finally came out and the older male was charged. We dealt with the issue sensitively and he was charged. I think he had a non-custodial sentence as attitudes in society were changing and as we know it later became law for gay relationships, with all old laws being abolished.

Like I stated earlier in one of my first chapters dealing with all kinds of people we were privileged and should never judge anyone for their so called wrong doings, as being such a small world we would never know when we would bump into them again in totally different circumstances. Nothing could have been nearer the truth when we had a murder, involving a man who was gay. This offender played a vital part in giving me information as to the identity of the offender, sadly this information never reached me and was acted upon by a detective who had no scruples or comradeship other than looking out for himself to take all the glory for himself, but fate played a part when he was removed from CID as discussed in a later chapter.

Finally we have seen numerous foreigners quite rightly jailed for lengthy periods who should be deported upon release. Due to the Human Rights Act many are not, when they have raped and murdered people and committed violent crimes with stabbings and armed robberies. They have the audacity to state they face harsh treatment if sent back to their own countries. What about our poor victims many genuine hard working people from all races living in the UK what about their rights. This law is sadly over used by the wrong people and is in urgent need of review. Again as stated we have more than enough of our own criminals involved in serious sexual offences as portrayed so far in this chapter. Sadly the next paragraph supports this comment.

I regret to have to say it but the last two sexual offences I had ever had dealings with, were the worst any man can commit, being rape against a female, of which in one of the cases involved violence.

In the first case, a woman in her fifties, a spinster being a person of quiet disposition and smartly dressed was walking home alone at about 10.00pm. She took a route she always had walked and this night was dragged behind bushes and raped by a young man in his late teens. She did not put up a struggle and calmly called the police as soon as she had the opportunity. She was very brave and tried to keep her dignity but was able to give a full and accurate description.

Together with another experienced detective, DC Ben TRENCH we made full enquires in the local area and each day we were getting closer until we found a man not only fitting the description, but still wearing the same clothes. He was arrested and again later admitted the offence, being completely remorseful. He finally got the punishment he deserved a sentence to match his age, at 17 years old, such a dangerous young man, was at least off the streets.

As for the other offence that was about three months later where a younger woman in her forties was walking home slowly with her dog. Again it was night time when she was attacked. She was partly disabled and wore a metal framed corset, which did not deter him. He attacked her punching her and subjected this poor lady to various acts of gross of indecency in between raping her more than once. She screamed and he ran off, but fortunately she was heard and the offender chased and stopped and the police were called and arrested, thus taking a very dangerous individual off the streets.

He was interviewed by me and again Dc Ben TRENCH. He was another loyal and hardworking detective officer who had spent twenty plus years in CID who had attained 30 years at the age of fifty and wanted to stay on another five years. That was acceptable, but because of tenure of post it could only be served in uniform, where he would work under several less experienced officers of various ranks who he could eat for breakfast.

This was the same experienced detective officer as referred to in Chapter 05 responsible for the conviction of that dangerous man who received 5 life sentences. What a complete waste of such an experienced officer, officers of such calibre that less than five years later they had to bring back into service to support the thin police line in a civilian role, as the people responsible for such decision had caused so many good officers to resign or retire under health grounds. He had seen and done even far more than myself and would never fit into the category of being dead wood as he was the complete opposite and an unrecognised credit to the police service. Such a talent that was soon zapped by defence lawyers who offered him a job immediately against ever employing the wasters that created the rules in the first place. Tenure of Post was introduced all because some detectives and other uniform police officers in various roles at lower rank had more practical experience than themselves being in higher rank.

We had both dealt with the previous offence of rape. This time the circumstances were too horrible to write truthfully and were really shocking that the poor lady would never forget. He admitted responsibility for everything and actually got Life Imprisonment, which in my view he deserved to spend, every minute of, in prison.

It is sad to see more and more cases coming before the courts where women have falsely made up allegations of rape or have wrongly implicated offenders who are completely innocent. I am positive all law abiding people find this horrendous as not only does it send out the wrong messages, it can cause heartbreak, divorce, mental break down, loss of character and many other problems for the accused who should receive public sympathy and compensation.

In all cases the offender should expect the full weight of the law in receiving adequate punishment for their wrong doing. It makes very real concerns and problems in proving difficult genuine cases where victims courageously give their evidence having their honesty tested in open court. These cases where the guilty offenders prey on the vulnerable and if caught try to lie using normally that consent was given, as their way out of it.

The most satisfying side of police work is the enormous amount of detections emulating from DNA. Complaints involving a variety of sexual offences where specimens were taken and stored, which were committed several years ago continue to be relooked at.

I remember when I was in uniform, some 15 – 20 years previously in my career. We had a very nasty and serious rape in the grounds of a local main hospital. A young Nurse who had finished a long shift at work was walking across the grounds to her residential block. She was in full uniform wearing her blue cape, so it was clear that the attacker knew who his subject was. She was knocked to the floor and received nasty injuries and raped repeatedly in the gardens of the hospital, before the monster ran off and made good his escape.

The nurse finally managed to get herself back into the main hospital area where she received help from her colleagues. She was extremely distressed and could only give a limited description of the offender. Eventually she was medically examined and a full statement of complaint taken. As a uniform officer I joined a team of other officers and we did a meticulous house to house check in all the surrounding areas, hoping we could gain the slightest amount of evidence to assist the enquiry, with the main target being sightings of an offender. Due to the offence happening during the early hours of the morning, sadly we drew a blank and were not able to find any clues. Years went by, with no news and even since retiring I just hope one day after a case review due to D.N.A. the offender was identified even better if arrested, convicted and punished. It is amazing that the offenders who committed such despicable crimes thinking they had escaped detection some 15 to 20 years or more, after the crime, are finally being brought to justice. They deserve full weight of the law as if the crime was recent, after all memories of these horrible serious sexual offences never go away and haunt the poor victim the remainder of their lives.

CHAPTER 16

THE LUXURY OF AIRLINE TRAVEL

In the first year of my CID probation working in the office, I received information a prisoner was in custody in one of the main Cities in Scotland. He was wanted for serious fraud involving stolen cheques accumulating to several hundreds of pounds. The law was different to that in England, being across the border we needed an arrest warrant before we could have him returned. It was decided that I together with a Detective Sergeant, with whom I had the utmost respect for, travel the journey by train. It was for us to return him back and deal with him accordingly.

This made a complete change of scenery, but it was not to be, as the day the warrant was to be issued there was a train strike meaning our journey was cancelled. I was then selected to go alone by airline transport, so I was booked for the following day on a scheduled flight to Glasgow and to return him later the same day in custody back to our station. You can imagine the jealousy with some of them, but I had been selected, tough get on with it, I certainly did. I was picked up the following morning and arrived at my destination.

Detective Chief Inspector MOUNT had formulated a report that I had to sign of which he kept a copy, stating I was to collect and return the prisoner then interview and prepare all necessary paperwork. Fine no problem but I had a rude awakening. I arrived at the airport and upon being met by a member of their force, I was taken to the city central police station. During the morning the staff in the C.I.D. office in Glasgow were busy, I had to remain there in the city for nearly 10 hours before leaving on the return flight. They suggested I do some sightseeing and then return shortly after midday where we could go out have lunch and a social drink. Within a short time of walking out I came across the Sheriffs High Court building equivalent to our Crown Court which I thought would prove interesting. It certainly was there were 12 men all stood in the dock charged with Conspiracy to Murder. It revolved around a riot in which a man was killed and no one was admitting responsibility. I could not stay long but I recall the court in question was of some eighteenth century design, cold with a feeling of justice and deterrent.

The Judge was high up, as were the jury and the dock. One man giving evidence went into the witness box, walking up the steps, where he was on the same level as all the others. For some reason each defendant had two barristers, so after giving his evidence in full, he had a sea of some 24 barristers who were popping up and down like flies each asking questions. I thought how do they ever get people to come forward to fulfil this role, you had to give them respect after all if it was not for the likes of them the police force would not be able to do its job. The witness was perfect and full of confidence answering each question without hesitation, one after the other. I wished I could have stayed longer, it was very interesting and I was frustrated in not knowing the verdict, but it was certainly an experience I would never forget.

Back to the station I met up with several police colleagues and we enjoyed a good afternoon on the town, unlike England back then licensing laws were all day in that part of the country. I was not drunk, but well-oiled as they were determined to make my short stay enjoyable. I collected the prisoner and we had a good flight back. I established it was his third flight back over some years for committing the same kind of offences. Who says crime does not pay, only problem is when you get caught and he was facing another lengthy sentence. Upon arrival back at the airport on my return, I was joined with a colleague who kindly volunteered to deal with the prisoner on my behalf as he could see I had a very long day, and for this I certainly owed him. So much for the instruction of Detective Inspector MOUNT who was none the wiser and knew when I had to be I was a hard worker. I thought I was privileged to have been allowed the experience of escorting a prisoner during an airplane flight, but later in my service I was asked again to perform such a duty.

This time it was from Belfast in Northern Ireland, needless to say jealousy struck in with immediate effect. I just went along and continued to fuel the fire rubbing it in to all my enemies, not failing one minute to miss out with Dc GLOVER and rub his nose in it. This time it was fairly straightforward in that the man was wanted on a crime warrant and had to be escorted by a detective and taken into English custody. It was all over in half a day. He had already been interviewed and charged previously so it was just a formality presenting him back before the court where he had failed to answer his bail. Back at the station different civilian staff, uniform and plain clothes officers all asked inquisitively how I had got on.

At the time of my visit to Northern Ireland there were still problems with the I.R.A. I just couldn't resist with the select few of those extremely gullible pretending I went with an army patrol, up to the Falls Road and stormed into a house under military escort and detained the man. They just stood there in bewilderment not knowing if there was any truth in it or not. A couple of my friends smiled secretively knowing my pedigree leaving the others to absorb the fantasy. I just had to have a laugh which I certainly did. I never knew if they had fallen for it or not as I never raised the issue with them again.

I recall Dc WATSON was working in the office and we had a detective sergeant transfer from another sub-division. He was a likeable man married to the daughter of a Chief Constable from another force. I am sure it was his personality that won him over with the family and his wife was a lovely lady, whom we met at various social functions. The only trouble was this officer had more qualities in his character than he did in police experience. This showed him to be very naïve and limited often drawing on the benefit of more experienced detectives, which was admirable. However, this became very irritating when then pulled rank which was totally unnecessary in a good industrious operational CID office. If only he used common sense, but this behaviour clearly showed his insecurity and the fact he was over promoted, possibly due to his high office connections.

This officer received a request from the Jersey police to interview a local man for a series of frauds, conduct a formal interview. With the evidence strong against him formulate charges and hold him in custody where they would arrange an escort to return him back to the main Jersey High Court.

I was off duty and my colleague Dc WATSON was soon hijacked by this officer to assist in the enquiry. The only trouble was there was bitter rivalry between them both. They were a little like chalk and cheese, both very outspoken and often at loggerheads and we had some very explosive funny moments when their personalities clashed. A very capable experienced officer working with a complete opposite, the perfect recipe for disaster waiting to happen.

So off they went and together they arrested the subject who was placed in custody at our police station. The man was formerly interviewed and partially admitted being responsible and but the blame on others who were still living in Jersey. Back then there was no requirement for contemporaneous notes and tape recording facilities had not been introduced. Notes were generally made immediately after the interview whilst the facts were fresh in the officer's mind. Dc WATSON the more cunning of the two, suggested while making the notes together he would write them in his notebook and the detective sergeant could sign the entry in his book as being correct. This was agreed. The man was charged Jersey informed and an escort arranged to take the man back there.

A couple of months later the detective Sergeant received a Court warning from Jersey for him to attend the trial and give evidence. However he had to explain that it was necessary for both interviewing officers to be present, as the evidence had to be given from Dc WATSON's notebook. This shrewd move guaranteed both had a visit to Jersey for at least a couple of days, with all paid expenses courtesy of Jersey police. As the date of the trial arrived both officers were dropped off at the airport to begin their journey.

Dc WATSON was on true form as he stated they arrived the day before the trial and booked into the nearby hotel and headed directly to the bar. I had to smile when he told me he drunk the detective sergeant under the table and had to virtually carry him to the lift and to his room. Awake early he went to ensure his so called friend was all getting up. After a while the door was opened and his colleague looked like a bridegroom who had been on a boozing stag weekend, in need of emergency action to get him prepared for court. Black coffee and cold showers eventually aroused him somewhat then downstairs into the dining room for breakfast. Both were a little noisy and unable to find their place and some residents who were smirking pointed to them in the direction of their table. After breakfast he helped get him dressed into his shirt and tie and eventually he appeared dressed to kill in his suit for court.

Both officers remarkably gave their evidence to a decent standard and were thanked by the judge, who was unaware of their night on the tiles. The man before the court was found guilty and sentenced accordingly. Dc WATSON stated it was like going back in a time zone as they were about 10 years behind the UK in their court procedures, being quite independent in these issues from the mainland. The Police and Criminal evidence Act had not even yet been implemented, despite being law in the UK. Within a couple of days all was over and they arrived back in the UK. Both appeared to be unhurt, no bruises or scratches or medical dressings, because unbelievably they held a truce between each other for the whole of the time they were together. However within a couple of days things were back to normal as the banter between them both soon returned with snide comments and remarks. What characters these were.

CHAPTER 17

CLEVER CRIMINALS

It is appropriate to mention that over the years some of the criminals clearly are very clever in planning their activities in committing serious crime and although you may feel they deserved some credit there was no way anyone should condone such actions.

One of the principal offenders and main organiser involved in committing the giro-cheque thefts a few years later was eventually released from prison. It certainly did not take him long to re-offend and this time the offence was even more sinister. With another man they committed an even more despicable theft against an old age pensioner, a man in his late seventies.

I had become well established at that time in the same office and I had a wide knowledge of the criminal fraternity. One day I saw this same man walking in an area to which he had no reason to be and instinct told me he was up to no good, but I had no idea of what was taking place. He was looking around furtively before calling at one of the houses in that same road. I made the relevant entry into my notebook which was always good practice.

Bearing this in mind I had an appointment with a known inmate at a local adult prison close to our police area. He was being interviewed in connection with some outstanding offences. I soon learned that seeing offenders who had been sent to prison was a very useful exercise. Not just for clearing up offences committed previously by them, but the intelligence they provided as to what was happening inside and at home was nearly always bang up to date. This time it worked I asked the inmate if he knew the man in question who I named. He stated he had dealings with him but never liked him. I asked if he had any idea what he was up to,and described seeing him in a strange circumstances and gave the location where. Straight away without any effort he revealed he and his accomplice were both ripping off an old man and stealing his money.

Back at the station it was not long before I found out the details. Both had purported to be from Social Services and had called round visiting the old man, stating they would be able to get him some home help. They had spent a considerable amount of time in his property, where one would have kept him occupied whilst the other rummaged through his belongings. They found his banking details and stole his cheque book. They left promising to call back and help him.

They did go back but not to help him, but just themselves. Having prepared pre-written letters for him to sign and the relevant part of the pages where the signature was to have been made had been cut out, where beneath that, they inserted blank bank cheques. Altogether some 12 letters had been prepared over several weeks, where the same amount of cheques were signed and altogether a total sum amounting to £25,000 had been stolen unknown to the man, wiping out completely all his life savings.

As stated before, banking rules were extremely lax back then and any cheque could be encashed by being paid into a third party account. This practice has since been totally abolished and today only cheques in the names of account holders can be paid into any bank account. This action was taken to prevent money laundering. What the main offender did in this case was produce the cheques to a local business man well outside the area with whom he had done previous legitimate construction work. When the full circumstances of this heinous crime were outlined, the person cashing the cheques on behalf of the offender cooperated at once.

This case was being dealt with by Dc Harrold PEGG the protégée trained by DC GLOVER who was at the time working with shrewd younger uniform sergeant attached to CID. Not being un-kind, they were 2 to 3 weeks into the case but they were struggling to find the main culprits and really had no idea as to who was responsible even after arresting other people who were nothing to do with the fraud. From that sighting of the offender, I made placing him well him out of his area and in the vicinity of the old man's address, together with the information gained from the prison visit it was clear I had far more evidence for the case than they had. It was a matter of protocol that really I could not pull the rug from their feet and take over the enquiry, so I did the honourable thing and put everything on a plate for them, something DC PEGG would not have been capable of doing. Giving them total cooperation, they devised a plan of action and a witness was able to identify the offender, confirming by enquiries and actions were bang on. They later arrested the man and soon after being confronted an accomplice too was apprehended. Both men were eventually charged, however none of the money was recovered as he blamed bad gambling debts. They both received five years imprisonment. Sadly the victim in this case died possibly from the shock of what had taken place being too much to overcome. Whenever anyone ever passed me information, I would most certainly of mentioned them in conversation and not have dismissed their actions. I later found out they had taken the glory for the detection but omitted to tell anyone where the real information had been obtained, otherwise without my information this case would have been another filed pending further developments.

In addition to this, I later gave the same officers information of a photograph I had of their principal offender who was quite distinctive in character. He had a curly hairstyle moustache and wore glasses. I then showed them an entry of a suspect circulated in a police internal magazine of wanted criminals in a regional area covering several police forces including our own force. It was for the sale of a stolen motor vehicle made at a car auction in a neighbouring force. Unknown to him the picture had been taken when he was paid the full sale price for the stolen vehicle in cash. Without a shadow of doubt it was definitely the same man, the moustache, hairstyle and glasses matched exactly. I was extremely busy at that time and owing to the fact they had cleared the job up on the information I had supplied, I thought if they had some kind of rapport with the man now serving a lengthy prison sentence, they were in the best advantage to clear this matter up as well. However they visited the man in prison, who denied all responsibility. No mention of liaison with the other police force, seeing what evidence they had possession of and no mention of any forensic comparison of the photographs, which in my view would have been a positive result. Just one regret I had that I did not get involved, but you cannot deal with everything especially when you have such heavy workload of your own. I simply put it down to their naivety and the fact the offence was not on us, still not good enough in my book a crime is a crime no matter where committed.

There is a lot in favour of knowing your patch as I had the fortune to stay in the same C.I.D. Office for many years. One extremely good conman over the years was a continual and very clever offender often moving well out of the area where he was unknown to commit his offences. Like all criminals they can perhaps sometimes get away with many crimes, but nearly all at one time or another become too confident and let their guard slip. When eventually caught their past comes to haunt them, no different to this man who always ended up with a two or three year stretch of imprisonment.

As he became more experienced he was harder to catch and not so easily convinced to be cooperative. We had a case where this man had been purporting to run a business and placed an order for £4000 worth of storage units, for delivery at a certain address which was false at a local trading estate. Naturally the goods, all at wholesale prices, were delivered and signed for. The offender met the delivery man outside the alleged address, which were actually empty premises. He helped unload the goods near the front doors stating they soon would be collected as he had customers coming later.

I made enquiries with several owners of businesses on the trading estate and although half the estate contained empty premises, I came up with a positive lead. One Director of this small company had been approached by a man asking if he could share part of his factory premises for storage. He appeared friendly and plausible and the man struck up a friendship. Despite giving him a name which later proved to be false, I was able to obtain a full description. In addition he had access to a transit type van. Putting all together I thought of the con-man we previously had dealings with.

Realising this man was wise to search warrants and had been arrested so many times at his home address, where sometimes incriminating evidence had been found, a different approach was needed. Instinct told me that he must be using his vehicle as the main core base of the sham. I continued enquiries and built a pattern of his movements and made a plan of action.

Together with another officer, early one morning, we set up observations in an area close to the location. Within a reasonably short time the offender turned up and drove onto the trading estate. He went near to the premises where I had made enquiries, which were found to be closed. We then both approached his van, which had stopped and I immediately recognised him as being the person initially suspected. He was arrested on suspicion of deception and I requested assistance. A subsequent search of the vehicle found documentation relating to other firms who had been cheated out of supplying goods, plus copies of invoices of products delivered which he himself had signed for.

It was established not only was the man breaching the director's trust in him using his warehouse, I later established he had also used his fax machine without his knowledge to confirm dishonest contracts. No goods were found in the factory, but I established they had all been sold on to innocent purchasers. Altogether well over £10,000 worth of goods had gone through this person hands which he had not paid for and had sold on. He was charged with several offences and again went back to prison for 3 years.

If not down to local knowledge and knowing how criminals think, just following my instincts this matter would have been harder to detect. Something the powers that be did not think of when creating tenure of post, as discussed more fully later. Many times I have voiced the phrase to catch a criminal you have to think like a criminal. The more experience I gained over the years it became much more apparent that a good criminal always had to think like a policemen, so in order he could plan accordingly and cover his tracks destroying and obliterating completely as much as possible forensic and fingerprint evidence and in later years trying to prevent leaving DNA which was indeed much harder and difficult to always achieve.

I remember driving out on enquiries in the CID car and stopped to talk with two resident beat officers walking together. The beats these two officers covered adjoined each other and both had been working the areas for well over two years. It was late 1995, and I mentioned to them if they knew the identity of two well established local known criminals who lived close to each other on their respective areas and to my surprise did not know what on earth I was talking about. I was utterly flabbergasted. These two criminals had form for armed robbery with violence and were heavily involved in organised crime and drug dealing plus many other criminal activities. They were the most active on the division and with them living on their territory and they had not even made themselves aware of this. What were their priorities surely you would expect police officers on the beat to be aware of such criminal characters. I suppose for this reason you can understand why a change was needed in future policing. What on earth was their supervision teaching them, show the flag, walk round, be noticed, hold hands and keep your eyes closed. Fantastic if you are in the Cotswolds or Lake District take in the views as well. Here they were in areas where crime was high and their involvement in detection of crime was zero. In my view every officer should learn the identity of all good criminals on whatever area they patrol be it walking the beat or driving round in marked vehicles.

Many senior police officers would comment there is more to policing than just crime, such as school and traffic duties, and ensuring good cooperation with the public at all times. One way of building a good rapport in my book is clearing local crime and any dedicated uniform thief taker would certainly support this method of policing every time, pity the other useless participants in the police force could not do the same.

CHAPTER 18

STUPID CRIMINALS

As referred to in a previous chapter I always carried two forms of documentation. They were an absolute necessity as explained in the following story having a blank witness statement in your possession, it was just perfect to commit evidence to words, where they later could not deny what was relevant and spoken at that exact moment. The other form as previously stated was a consent form to search premises. Having this item with you, this story is a perfect example of where being in possession of such a document at all times was of extreme importance.

I do not mean to be blasphemous but I am sure God must have put some people on this earth just to have a good laugh. We received information a drug dealer had quite a substantial amount of money at his home address. In fairness the information source was untested and was a little of a shot in the dark. I knew the man concerned and to my knowledge he had never previously dealt in drugs, only petty kinds of crime. I went together with WDC MYLES to his address where on arrival he answered the front door where he was advised we suspected that there were drugs and items associated with such activity on the premises. He was alone at the house and we stated that we wished to search the premises and he asked if there was a warrant. I told him that I was not in possession of such a document, but could easily get one, while other officers remained at the scene. I suggested it would save everyone's time if he consented, he could sign my consent to search premises form. He agreed and I stated we would be as quick as possible in carrying out a clean and tidy search. This shows the importance of being in possession of these forms at all times as I have referred to. This was especially true in this case as the information was fairly recent and we had no time to waste.

We went with him into the lounge and he just went ballistic, pulling out draws in the sideboard, throwing cushions from off all the settees. He threw out all the contents of cupboards all over the floor, in less than two minutes a tidy room became an utter tip, which was in a complete shambles. This was then repeated in the dining room, hallway and all three bedrooms including the kitchen where the contents of all the cupboards including food stuff were strewn all over the floor. Everything resulted in a gigantic untidy horrendous mess. It could have been a scene from a Christmas Pantomime or from a slapstick comedy show on television.

It did not prevent use from leaving no stone unturned, as we checked every nook and cranny in the search for the items alleged to have been present. Despite his cooperation, no money or drugs or such equipment for use in supplying drugs was found in any of the premises or the adjoining buildings or garden. I politely thanked him for his help, again fuming inside with intolerable laughter as was my colleague. What an idiot, I hope he enjoyed housework because he most certainly had his work cut out, all totally unnecessary.

Despite searching the house which was based on this colleague's information, having found nothing, we were subjected to a little unfair criticism in that we hadn't searched this area or that. We were just two officers, not the SWAT team, or the equivalent of a dedicated search team of some twelve or so officers and a sergeant, so we did the best we could under the circumstances. Okay a valid point where do you draw the line, do we get every floorboard up, find a false petition in a room concealed by hidden screws. Search behind the gas fire, inside the chimney, dig all the garden up in case money is hidden in a special place. This all had to be weighed against the credibility of the informant with whom I had no background knowledge and could have been even vindictiveness by him.

The officer didn't want to get involved as he knew the owner of the property, tough big deal. On more than one occasion I have locked up many people with whom I know and have had previously friendly dealings with, it's all part of the job. The same applies to informants who become too big for their boots and think they are above the law when they try to run you and dictate how you do your job. Not with me they didn't. These people just have to be put in their place. This officer wanted us to do his dirty work then becomes the nine o'clock critic, when he had not got the bottle to get involved himself. All talk and no action, to me enough, get lost, end of story.

There was another example of building a rapport with criminals, being fair but being ahead of the game. I was with Dc WATSON with whom I had worked with often over the years in uniform and CID who was also a reputable and experienced thief taker, until a few years later he fell on his sword in utter disgrace, but that's another story in this book. There had been a crude house burglary on a council estate when the offender had literally kicked off the rear door completely, in his attempt to gain entry. Not particularly the first class work of a professional criminal. He filled a shopping trolley which he found dumped in the street and used this to take electric equipment and a video recorder which in those days were £500 alone. Video players back then were a new commodity and always fetched money as they were good sellers, popular with fencers, persons who had connections in the criminal underworld, who could easily depose of stolen property.

We established exactly what had been taken from the house and our enquiries into this matter were completely routine easy and straightforward. Due to the incredible noise made which was during mid-morning, the burglar had been seen. He was named by two local neighbours, who did not wish to come forward due to any retaliation from the offender's family, as all were six pence short of a shilling, in other words thick, a typically stupid offender but one with a violent disposition.

Knowing the identity of this man we both made enquiries to find him and saw him a couple of days later. We visited him at his girlfriend's house where he invited us both inside. He provided both DC WATSON and I with a warm drink and offered us biscuits. Whilst there he was playing a video tape, but it was in a different machine, make and model to the one that had been stolen in the burglary. We had already established there was a VHS tape in the video player when stolen and enquired as to what material had been recorded. To our surprise the tape he was playing for us showed exactly identical programmes as described and obviously was stolen property from this burglary. We thanked him for his hospitality, but before leaving told him of our findings and that he was being arrested for burglary. A search was made of the house and other property that had been stolen was subsequently found, including the shopping trolley. The VHS tape was found to contain writing on the front label made by the son from the house burgled. As for the video machine, that had been sold on and was well out of the area. He was taken into custody where we had the pleasure of returning the compliment in providing him with tea and biscuits whilst he continued to tell us about other house burglaries he had done. He was charged and needless to say he later went to prison.

I had to smile some few years later I was shopping in a local supermarket in a nearby town when I saw this same man with his girlfriend in one of the queues for the till. He was some distance away and shouted out across towards me uttering the words, "I have been straight now since you locked me up for doing them houses" I said "Good to hear it keep it that way." I recall even now the expressions on some of customer's faces, when they realised that a convicted house burglar was shopping in the store. I believe his intentions of going straight were genuine, but he was the kind of person who was an opportunist and the temptation was always there of re-offending which he just could not stop. I don't think he ever stayed out of trouble. He came from a large family and his younger brother who was also a customer of ours kept up the family tradition of being a regular jailbird. You had to feel sorry for some of the family as I don't think they really stood a chance from the moment they were born.

As soon as they were old enough they all had to play a hand in putting food on the table and contributed anyway they knew how. With limited education the system had given up on them and so they walked the path initially with petty crime, which materialised into some serious offences for which quite rightly they deserved to go to prison. However a few years later two of the elder brothers went straight and actually got labouring jobs, so hats off to them, it just shows life is always full of surprises and that sometimes the impossible can actually happen. One shudders to think, that just over a few centuries back, some of these kind of poorly educated people, would perhaps have been hung for some of their crimes. Thank god we are no longer that barbaric. Many people still argue for horrendous capital offences such as child murder, serial murderers and terrorism that it should be re-introduced. I am sure if put to the vote of the real genuine public it would be restored overnight.

I recall being with Monty one day, when the younger brother of this family was at our station in custody for some criminal activities. He was being documented where his family background would be updated along with his antecedent history. In addition as normal practice, his fingerprints and photograph would be taken. He was in normal conversation and we both saw that he had a serious deformity to his one arm. Monty asked him how long his limb had been in that state and he explained it had happened some 6 months back. He stated he was in the street and under his parked car lying on the road, messing about with his exhaust pipe. For no apparent reason he put his arm out to stretch for a moment and the ice cream van playing loud music then travelled past and run over it. He stated it was his own fault he never went to hospital the bone had fractured and he never had it looked at. Consequently the arm had become deformed and he just accepted that was how it was to be and he had to live with it. He just laughed it off. You just could not make it up we were both in hysterics. You certainly cannot say this family were boring they were a barrel full of laughs, there was never a dull moment with any of them.

Staying with the same family at one time or another over the years we had locked up nearly every member for criminal offences. We knew how to deal with them and we were trusted to be fair and honest, they used to brag to their mates that they had been arrested by Dc WATSON and myself as we were highly respected in the neighbourhood just as if it was a feather in their cap being locked up by us the elite. You had to laugh but amongst some of their petty crimes, some sadly were serious and not at all funny for the victims who had been at the receiving end and for those offences they never got away with any of them. The main household figure in his late seventies suddenly died and sadly his kids who had followed in his career path, along with friends and neighbours all mucked in with the funeral arrangements. As a genuine feeling of compassion while we were in the area at the time of his funeral, Dc WATSON and I called round to offer our condolences with the family. Upon arrival our presence was appreciated by majority of guests and friends alike. I had to smile when in the vicinity of the church, in between hymns one of his old comrades shouted out to the horror of all present, "Well you bastards, you hounded him all his life and finally you've now hounded him to the grave. There is nothing more to say." Dc WATSON replied, "Amen to that." and I said, "Well so be it." That was it time for a sharp exit, as we politely walked away bowing our heads in dignity. Enough said, but it is fair to say they were all not bad people.

Mixing with the community was also important and my colleague Dc WATSON not only worked the area but was born locally which he used to his advantage. I recall being with him late on Saturday afternoon when we called to see someone at this local address where he knew the family. At this address the borders between both back gardens were secured by old internal doors being nailed together, now that's something you do not see at Homebase or B &Q. This was a household where you wiped your feet on the way out and when the front door opened I could understand why. The youngest daughter answered who was in the process of dying her black hair to peroxide blonde which was soaking wet and dripping everywhere. She was getting glammed up ready to hit the town and later the night clubs in hopes of bringing some unsuspecting fella home to mummy. While she was talking a large 5 hand horse walked from the lounge, apparently having entered from the garden. This very large horse made its way into the hallway past this charming young lady out the front door into the street across the road to the house opposite where neighbours took it into their garden.

We were then invited into the lounge and the lady of the house asked it we would like a drink of tea. Without being impolite I immediately showed my manners thanking her for the offer, stating that I had not long ago had a drink. I did however confirm my colleague would love a drink adding he took two sugars. We sat down on an old settee and members of the family settled down nearby sitting on a bale of hay which was positioned on the lounge floor. Upon being offered a drink in a chipped and dirty mug, when no-one noticed he poured the contents into a tub containing a large house plant. Having stayed there for several minutes we completed enquiries and made excuses to leave. You might say who lives in a house like this, but it was their way of life to them and was completely different to most people. Whatever our views we must always remember that we are all God's children.

One of the most stupid thefts I ever had occasion to investigate was committed by a well-known habitual thief. He was in the town centre and had visited a butchers shop and was standing in the queue to get served. An elderly lady was in front of him and placed her reading glasses onto the counter as she rumbled through her shopping bag for her purse in order to make the necessary payment. It was whilst she was pre- occupied in finding the money that the thief struck and stole the ladies reading glasses which he placed into his coat pocket. She left the shop and the man was served and also left.

The elderly lady soon realised her mistake and returned to the shop. The offender was well known in the town and one of the customers who had been waiting to be served was still in the shop and reported her suspicions, in that she thought the man had taken her glasses but could not really believe it.

The matter was reported to the police and I was out on the town when I received on the radio the alleged complaint with a description of the named suspect. A couple of streets away and I saw him. I went up to him explained what he was accused of and searched him recovering the reading glasses from his coat pocket.

He was duly arrested and taken to the police station. He admitted stealing the property and was charged with theft explaining he did it just as a force of habit and could not really explain of what use they would have been to him. It certainly would have been an expensive issue for the victim and just proves that some people will steal absolutely anything just for the sake of it. What an utter nuisance these kind of people are, causing distress and misery to these kind of vulnerable people.

CHAPTER 19

THE INTERESTING BEHAVIOUR OF SENIOR DETECTIVE OFFICERS

I remember a DI Barry JONES another officer who had rose through CID ranks who was smart sophisticated and clever who knew exactly how to draw the best from each individual officer. He was my sergeant when I first went into CID who was no fool, providing you were a good policeman and thief taker there was never a problem, if not you just did not survive. He would always get stuck in and help where necessary, he was one who had seen and done it and went high up the ranks later in service.

We were having numerous burglaries where a group of known men were believed to be responsible. A sighting was made and three of us attended the area. We managed to stop the suspect vehicle, which contained five black men who were each over 6ft and of proportionate build and completely un-cooperative.

DI JONES was with Dc WATSON and myself and between us we asked them all questions and got no response, the situation was getting nasty and we could see violence was going to ensue. All in all between them they had over 20 years of prison conviction sentences for all kinds of serious crime. If they had done nothing wrong then they should have been cooperative and avoided all this inconvenience for us, yet alone themselves. We asked for assistance and a dog handler and patrol car came. When the moment was right we decided to strike, telling them they were all under arrest on suspicion of burglary. We each selected one person to arrest, fighting started and eventually all were taken into custody and the vehicle searched. Despite no evidence being found to connect them with any burglary they all faced public order charges. Again refreshing to see such a senior officer get his hands dirty and stand his ground. If only some of the other senior officers had the same fearless attitude.

I remember we had a divisional exercise arranged by D.I.JONES where it involved the arrest of all active villains residing in our areas who were suspected of committing serious crime involving burglaries and robberies. One morning we went out after a major briefing and arrested all those suspected. A total of some 15 persons were arrested however the strength of some of the evidence in some areas was thin but it was necessary to act. Out all of those arrested four admitted responsibility for a robbery and serious burglaries and were subsequently charged and pleaded guilty. So the exercise was not in vain, with the amount of intelligence gathered also extremely useful and it tested the trust between all those arrested as to who had grassed them all up. I suspected really it was just this Detective Inspector playing his usual games with them all just to let them know who was boss and let them know if they are active they would get pulled. Whether it was down to his good luck or just sheer bluffing on his part resulted in several jobs being cleared. This kind of police work did bring results but as the years went on it was harder to get to the truth without sufficient evidence.

As time went on good detective sergeants were very few and hard to come by, compared to my younger days when you could see immediately that the sergeant who had been previously a detective in most cases filled the role perfectly. All this was because officers stayed in the positions or ranks longer and gained valuable experience and the job certainly was the better for it. Today promotion is all about money and does the job no good at all without such experience learned. To go from uniform constable to sergeant and then into a permanent CID role in my view was an uphill road which some never made. Equally so for officers of higher rank, as like in a factory, a shop floor Manager learned the skills of every department before taking overall charge. Same in my view applies in all walks of life today, especially the police force where learning whilst in the role is sometimes flawed and only second best.

Some old detective Inspectors hardly used their vehicles and I am sure most of them made bogus mileage claims, whilst rejecting working constable's everyday expenses in efforts to save money. I know this from first hand. One Inspector got moved over his expenses back into uniform and later got promoted to Superintendent. He even came back to our division seeing metal dealers around Christmas time in an attempt to scrounge a bottle of seasonal drink. Talk about jobs for the boys, he shouldn't have even been in the job in my book.

The other Inspector was signing my diary where valid expense claims had been submitted. I was talking to him and saw some of my claims were in his bin. He alleged by mistake and immediately reinstated them, but how could you ever trust a supervisory officer like him again. The actions of senior officers behaving in this manner were a disgrace to all the hardworking policemen of all ranks. Thankfully the police force had addressed these issues where possible and the practice was eliminated.

I worked for a police Superintendent who had served in the Complaints Department and had come to our station as Detective Superintendent. His main pedigree was dealing full time in Complaints against the police which was acceptable after all the public need protecting as well as police officers who had nothing to hide. Corruption must always be routed out with those responsible being punished, just like the person who makes false and frivolous complaints against the police totally wasting investigators time. They should also be punished.

The worst thing with this Detective Superintendent in my view was that not ever having done the job of real police work in being an operational police detective, as he was very rigid in his approach and perhaps a little narrow minded believing all officers were corrupt. Decisions made at the time are always done in the correct spirit but he was too critical in case he was seen to be at fault, so you could not expect any real backing in some of the complex issues of the job dealing with scum of society. At least you knew where you stood. In fairness I sure he had many other qualities but was on a completely different wavelength when talking crime and catching criminals as far as myself and other detectives were concerned.

If you went to this senior officer for advice it was a joke. You would relate the issues and concerns and he would ask you to come back later. What he would do is look at some case files he had collected from other staff, and refers to text books. Where with a man of proper experience it should already be in his head and any advice it should just roll off the tongue with confidence.

On the other hand it was so easy to deliberately approach the same man with a complicated set of circumstances, which you already knew the answer to. Just to throw all the questions at him and to see his response where he would cringe and stutter, was all worthwhile where you could see all the stress had been transferred to him. Great he got the salary for his role he might as well start earning it. These kinds of people were pathetic, but sadly there were too many of them. I would not want to follow him into the witness box, or have him back me up in a fight. I would rather have a good policewoman anytime.

Then I remember whilst I was night detective, I received good information where a man who had been on the run from prison for over 12 months. He was living in council flats at another area on the division and despite his circulation and unique description, with hideous tattoos on his neck he remained living at this old address virtually unnoticed. I spoke to the duty Inspector a former detective who in my view was like a fish out of water in this role as he was well above his station. He just didn't have it together and must have slipped through the net on the basis that it was who you knew instead of what you knew. I recollect he only had a short time in CID as Detective Constable whilst I was working the beat, but to me never set the world on fire and his role was merely a step on the promotion ladder.

As a matter of etiquette with this being a different area than my own, I asked for his assistance. This with a request to have some officers available at a given time during the early hours of the morning, where we arranged to turn over the suspected address. Despite this, at the appropriate moment he stated he had no one available. Strange it was the middle of the week and it was a reasonably quiet sub-division anyway. Still this was a typical negative attitude with him, so I took two Officers from my own station and went to the address without that shifts assistance. Suspiciously we were kept waiting after knocking the front door, before being allowed inside by a young lady living there. A thorough search was made and in the kitchen at a secluded space behind a warm air central heating installation, I saw two feet dangling. I told the man to get out as it was incredible he had managed to hide in such a small uncomfortable space. I recognised him immediately and he admitted escaping from prison.

He was duly arrested and the duty Inspector I had spoken to earlier insisted the prisoner be bought to his station. Sarcastically I informed him that the man was going to our station as I could not run the risk of any further attempt escape and thanked him for his none existent cooperation. In any case he was only trying to cover his tracks as after all he had egg all over his face.

I made sure the Chief Superintendent who was no fan of this officer, was made aware of the negative action taken. I had a printout of all the jobs his shift were sent to during that night which proved when he stated his shift was busy, it was a fragment of his imagination as even council road sweepers would have had more to do working nights. Needless to say he remained in that rank for the rest of his service, so sad for the younger efficient officers under his command.

With increasing experience not only did you learn to read the character of a criminal, but also that of all other people including good and bad points of colleagues. We had this sergeant on attachment that had never been in CID who was on rest day with a younger detective and had come in early especially to arrest a person in Wales. He was due to appear in the Magistrates Court at a popular holiday resort there and they were both awaiting a phone call which failed to materialise.

Coincidently another job came in also 150 miles away and so our Detective Chief Inspector then allowed them go on this job, rather than lose out altogether. So off they went and instinct told me if the job in Wales later came to fruition we would be lumbered with working late into the night. Needless to say this sergeant had failed to do his homework as it was not a morning court appearance their suspect was due to attend, but afternoon. At 4.00pm later that day, the call came through the man had been arrested and so my physic ability came into play which meant me and my colleague were asked to go instead, surprise, surprise.

In anticipation I spoke to our senior officer explaining that if we did the escort and the prisoner was cooperative I would conduct an interview and get all his admissions tape recorded in case he later changed his mind. The main point I was making that I just knew this in-experienced sergeant on attachment to CID would falsely believe I would have pinched his prisoner and I wanted this senior officer to be fully aware of this in case he started blowing a fuse, as this would certainly be a fine example of his immature nature. This naturally was accepted and the Chief Inspector appreciated our honesty and noted all comments made.

After a 200 hundred mile journey we eventually arrived at the seaside resort and visited the local police station. Opposite was a typical country public house and we decided to have a short drink combined with a sandwich. The room was packed with locals and the two behind the bar were in the same demeanour as the cliental. It was just unbelievable nearly all of them were completely drunk including the staff, it was amazing they had the energy to serve us and this was before 7.00pm in the evening. We had a quick drink and took our food with us, amazing all this opposite the local police station. Still nothing to do with us.

The man had travelled from a northern city under conditions of his bail. He was spoken to and admitted theft and disposal of a high class motor vehicle, so an interview under caution was conducted prior to leaving. On the return journey he was found to be cooperative and stated he was able to give good information involving criminals in the area where he lived. He was treated well and back at our station was bedded down for the night. He was not charged so it was possible for the sergeant to pick up easily from where we had left and I would pass on all the information that he was willing to give about other people. This was what I called teamwork.

After going off duty and returning back for the morning shift at 8.00am, I walked into the CID office and heard the sergeant running me down to the Detective Inspector, stating I had encroached on his territory in pinching his prisoner. Strange I just knew it was going to happen, I could read the character of this man something you only learn from experience over the years. My initial instincts were completely correct. How nauseating, I immediately retaliated and gave him an argument he could not defend, comparing him to a naive young recruit who in the first place could not get his facts right, who lacked courage and morale of being a team player. In other words in my book, he just had to be told, so if the cap fits wear it.

The sergeant instead of conceding how wrong he had been, then showed his true character and behaved like a spoilt school child, interviewing the prisoner and not gleaning any potential from him as a future informant. He stated he was apposing bail and keeping him in custody. I pointed out the man had travelled all the way the day previous, from a northern city to Wales to attend court. I immediately asked him to explain on what grounds and he just walked off. Needless to say the man got bail straight away as the reasons for keeping him in custody were as pathetic as this man's actions, which were utterly useless. That is what happens when there is no practical experience, but boy, doesn't the job suffer because of it. The Chief Inspector marked his cards and to my knowledge he never got a CID posting again, unless in later service he learned from the experience and changed his stubborn ways in dealing with people.

Then we had the Detective Sergeant who got promoted and came back to us as Inspector. He was rubbish as a sergeant as he worked with us then for a short time and made a complete mess of a fraud and was severely criticised at court, which circulated around the office like wildfire. His credibility was even worse as an Inspector. I remember him telling me he had to travel over a 100 miles to join a Masons Lodge where he could be accepted, in order to complete his ladder up the ranks. They say that being a

Mason does not make any difference, so why did he have to do it. Surely if he was good enough he could have got promoted on his own merits. It's a pity he couldn't have been stationed a hundred miles away, as instead of us having to put up with his negativity and lack of esteem.

He was one of the officers who would reallocate enquiries when approached by staff who were incapable or lazy. The worst nightmare was going on leave for 14 days, and returning to duty. In your absence he would book out a serious crime where there were numerous witnesses to be seen, all waiting on your desk for you to come back to, whilst at the same time the trail had gone cold. In fact, this serious robbery took place the first day of my leave, and was lying on my desk with nothing being done until my return. I used to document all the issues and send the crime report back. He did not even have the guts to challenge me of the report which severely criticised his actions.

I included not only whilst I was on leave the trail had gone cold, that it was an extremely serious crime and the victim deserved better. Witness statements taken as soon after the offence were extremely important and the enquiry should have been allocated to officers working straight away other than being book out to myself who was not due to return to duty for another 14 days. Showing his negativity, and un-professionalism he even booked the enquiry back out to me leaving all the bizarre comments for all to see. This just being one example categorising his inefficiency and incompetence. What a pedigree for a Detective Inspector on a busy crime ridden sub-division, sadly to say as time went on these type of overpaid Mason approved senior officers were even more common place, thank God for the individual senior officers who were the complete opposite.

If you went out on an early morning raid he took control and knocked at the front door was until it opened. When the door opened with all the aggravation it was if he had all the talent of a circus acrobat, he somehow did a backward flip and ended up at the rear of the queue waiting to enter.

When you had a journey involving travel of any distance he always insisted you went by train, causing you to work around train time tables, where a round journey by using the CID car including the taking of statements could have been completed in half the time. That was it no one else wanted him and so we were stuck with him until he reached sixty, or by some magical fantasy took early retirement. Another vastly over promoted individual.

In his role he would have favourites which I expected, but was clearly palmed off by a higher level when he had a dead wood detective friend forcibly transferred from another department. This detective constable only had experience which was limited to just fraud, an area in which he was obviously very capable and had worked for several years. For him to be side moved instead of receiving tenure of post, he was thrust to work in our busy CID office with all the changes in the modern policing world that he was incapable of learning quickly, which was unfair to other colleagues.

What I did not accept was behind your back without your knowledge he slotted you in to work a possible heavy working Christmas week on nights, when it was this his friend's turn all because of his lack of experience in all criminal matters. He had not even got the decency to ask you, which if he had of done would not have bothered me and would have worked to help out. This pathetic and underhand approach showed the calibre of the man. Why do him any favours, he certainly would not do you any. He was not fit to lick the boots of some of the truly professional officers, of all ranks I had worked with.

From the Serious Fraud office where this officer had previously worked, we had a detective sergeant working there, who had never been in CID as a constable and had no real experience in crime investigation. In an earlier chapter I told the story of when I was involved in a non-stop road accident where I was breath tested in accordance with the rules. This sergeant was at that time in uniform.

Strangely I never liked this officer, I was on CID attachment at his station and he was always jealous that he had never ventured into that department and enquired about doing a 3 month aide as a sergeant. I later discovered he did a short attachment and later he went on to serve in the Serious Fraud squad in the main city. Surprising really, as this man had never had any experience in these matters yet alone in working in a general CID office, which was the first step working in crime investigation. Then it all clicked this complete unit was full of officers belonging to the Masons, being members of Masonic Lodges from different areas. In fact later in my career I applied for a position in that very department where on your application form you were asked questions that the interview would be based on some Roman or Greek mythology which you had to learn off by heart. Strange, nothing

202

to do with your crime investigation experience abilities no matter how good or efficient you were. Naturally I was not fully prepared lost interest and could sense the corruption I was facing and the lack of trust and integrity. I attended the interview answered to the best of my ability, knowing I was facing a sham interview not being a Mason, I just did not fit in with their cosy outfit. I had a very critical report back on division stated I was unsuccessful. Thank God, how can you work with these utterly deceitful people.

Amazingly this sergeant had survived a serious internal investigation along with another uniform police woman on the same shift. Both had been investigated for being on duty together on a night shift in a marked police vehicle and were caught having sexual intercourse with each other by a member of the public. Thinking they had parked their vehicle discreetly not that that is possible in a marked police vehicle, they had both been disturbed and were caught red handed in a serious compromising situation putting the police force under severe criticism. Both officers received a warning and that was it, end of story. They even stayed together on the same shift and received absolutely no punishment whatsoever. Other officers would have been demoted, dismissed for serious gross misconduct in public office, thus confirming my suspicions he too was a Mason. Who says they are not protected people by being part of this secret society amongst our midst which I am sure still goes on today in many walks of life.

As with other experienced detectives younger sergeants at every opportunity tried to impose and take over some of our more intricate work involved with serious offences giving pathetic excuses of 'I need the collar', and, 'it will help my promotion' All good police work in my book is by getting off your backside and doing the ground work yourself, after all as sergeants, they had the pick of any the jobs that came in. There was no need to steal other officer's work with such pathetic excuses, so it just showed the morals of the men we were working with. All because the prospect of promotion far outweighed the idea of being just a basic policeman and dedication had nothing to do with it, in some cases only greed for higher wages. Then towards the end of my career someone suggested at a higher level, all posts in various departments become subject to Tenure of Post, as discussed briefly in previous and upcoming chapters. This was soon to become a serious downfall in my view in the history of positive policing and is discussed in vast detail later.

So you had to watch your back not only against nasty villains, but scheming jealous colleagues of all ranks who were just out for themselves. Thank God we had several reliable friends and workmates who balanced the equation.

CHAPTER 20

POOR POLICE WORK

As in all areas of police work there are instances of good excellent work which are always in need of praise and should never be ignored, like there are examples of poor police work. These bad issues I believe sadly should have been reported and even if raised as internal issues, to ensure they were never repeated again but were not. After all we should all learn from bad mistakes and be man enough to admit them from the lowest rank to the highest rank.

A few times I have always stressed there is no accounting for doing the basic fundamental enquires. As police officers we have tremendous powers and are privy to information and authority other organisations would not be allowed. This is why warrants have to be used sensibly and when obtained all address details have to be justifiably correct.

There is nothing more embarrassing when warrants are obtained and checks against the current occupants are taken for granted and not crossed referenced with current utilities suppliers or phones records and other sources currently in use against the present occupier. So when police in the early hours use forced entry and find they have the wrong address with pensioners living there instead of villains the action in my book is nothing short of pure neglect of duty and indefensible. The times that these incidents happened in my service were fortunately rare, but always involved officers who were lazy and should have known better. Not only did they just let themselves down, but the rest of us policemen who did our job properly and conscientiously.

One of the worst scenarios was when I was in the Intelligence Department of CID and a crime report came in from an officer on a shift who had attended the scene of several burglaries. Some twenty new houses had all be broken into in the course of the night and all main electrical fittings had been taken, cookers, built in washers and fridge freezers had all been stolen. The cost of the crude removal amounted to very serious damage in itself. Noted on the rear of the report was the address where all the items had been taken and stored in the large rear garden. No arrests had been made and no property recovered. These are some of the standards supervisory officers were allowing to take place. How disgusting. I went straight to the Inspector in charge of the shift and asked the obvious. Why no Scenes of Crime, or found stolen property not fingerprinted. The house was shared by a well-known burglar and his girlfriend yet no enquiries or arrests made.

He stated he would send officers down again and take positive action. This he did and the girlfriend was arrested denying all knowledge as to who was involved, but accepted she had allowed stolen property to remain in her garden. Enquiries were later forwarded to CID and I was sure despite my intervention the main offender was never apprehended by any officer. The girlfriend carried the can for receiving all the electrical equipment a total of some thirty or so items, cookers, fridges and gas fires. This was after all serious crime and the woman alone certainly did not steal the items herself. Yet her boyfriend a career criminal who regularly received heavy sentences for crime, had got completely away with it, as despite being named was never arrested and must have been dying with laughter.

The Detective Sergeant who was assigned to the case was fully aware of who was involved but was too interested in his own promotion. An experienced colleague of mine in an adjoining sub division Dc TRENCH told the story where he had apprehended a serious bank robber in the town, based on his own initiative and enquiries and had this sergeant working with him at the time who begged to sign for the arrest saying he needed it to boost his career. He later made Superintendent. Can you believe it, how times had changed, this to me was not policing and things seriously were in need of change. Perhaps I was becoming a little bitter and twisted, but I had seen so many bad examples of promotion where poor work was no obstacle. Yet if I had ever been subject of any serious complaint for even less issues, than as portrayed in their pathetic work practices, I would have had the sack. It does not bode well with all the good investigating officers who would have dealt with the issues correctly and got results no matter how busy they were when others get completely away with it.

After all we were always trained that people can always see good police work and also bad. Hopefully things have improved but I dare bet it is left to all the dedicated hard working officers who carry the job on and others who cover behind their good work. As with some of the promotion issues and bad practices the police force hopefully over the years since I had left would have recognised these problems and addressed them.

CHAPTER 21

INTELLIGENCE – SHOULD BE EVERY POLICE OFFICERS GOAL

From the time I first joined the police, from walking the beat, driving on panda patrol, to a rural beat and back to an urban built up town centre, intelligence always played a major role. When shared, as I have illustrated in many pages of this book, intelligence work works well in the detection of crime and many other areas of policing.

There is absolutely no replacement for having the right staff perform the right tasks. A lazy policemen on any beat is a no go situation and should never be tolerated anywhere. He should be made to improve or be sacked. No different to an inexperienced Officer out of his depth working a busy crime ridden beat will not ever bring in results. Some police officers love the excitement of shift work and attending 999 calls, fights, disputes and checking motorists, but I am sure throughout my story whilst in uniform you created your own interest in all the different avenues of police work.

I think some of the officers when I was last in service well over ten years ago, had not got a clue in how to work a beat, and just preferred normal patrol duties. In many cases today it is down to senior management where majority of staff is deployed. Walking the beat it was all down to getting the trust of the local people, being left to your own initiative providing over a realistic period of time, positive results were achieved. It was forever an ongoing and continual process for sowing seeds to generate further information from the public in order detections remain an permanent objective. Learning criminal connections between their friends and families, identity of nicknames, who is involved in which gang and which vehicles were being used. Establishing who is wanted on warrant, driving whilst disqualified, using and driving various vehicles was just basic intelligence. As were the identity of those involved with drugs and alcohol and who are your indecency merchants and where do they frequent. Persons, who commit damage, write graffiti and are suspects for arson. All these are intriguing issues for a dedicated police officer in knowing the area that you patrol. How some officers cannot work under these circumstances just baffles me. I wonder why some even joined. To walk a beat was far more interesting, than going from one silly job to another, some with blinkers on, driving all day and not know what was going on around you. The exception to those not interested were the other kind of uniform shift officers who were an asset to their role, also being as keen as mustard in spotting criminals making good arrests, where walking the beat did not come under their goal for job satisfaction.

I believe some officers had gone through majority of their service doing nothing other than work shifts, driving panda cars and walking different areas. For some they would do an extremely good job, but normally anything involving immediate investigation was impossible due to continual calls coming in from the public. I used to find that extremely frustrating, whereas those same officers found my role boring. If only they knew how rewarding being a beat officer actually was, resulting in excellent job satisfaction. Similarly in CID acting on your own volition and instincts in all areas of crime all contributed to intelligence gathering.

So now they have Intelligence Officers in most forces working on all divisions combined make up of uniform officers, civilians and detectives. This is a good step in one way, but officers worth their salt would not give away sources of information built up over long periods of time involving trust and integrity between the officer and the grass. Some require delicate handling, others allowed not to dictate the terms. But where you have some information no matter how small, that is not going anywhere, all should be forwarded for analysis, to help in building a bigger picture. So if say on most working days, every officer forwards important information regarding criminal activity, it is not long before targets can be suggested and drawn up for surveillance. Perhaps today things have improved in some ways, or possibly not.

As operational detectives we all had to perform a six month attachment to Intelligence and for some it would not be their favourite police role. Whatever you are assigned to, better to do your best based on your knowledge and experience, be self-motivating and set an example. We like most areas of the country were experiencing high volumes of sneak in burglaries. Mainly involving old people living alone some infirm, who unwisely would be entrusting to callers especially those who were plausible, making all kinds of realistic excuses to get inside and keep the occupants talking. Whist this was taking place an accomplice would sneak upstairs and other areas of the home, rifling through cupboards and draws, until finding hiding places these elderly people kept their life savings.

Really these sneak in types of burglary were heinous crimes which sadly robbed older and vulnerable members of our society, who lost all of their life savings all by just answering the door to a stranger. I am positive their actions were a major contribution to eventually causing the death of some such victims, as they never recovered the shock or financial heartbreak involved. In many cases I believe some of the offenders should have been possibly considered for charges of Manslaughter.

It was suggested that research be made into this area, so in my view anything that could bring about the detection of these crimes and the offenders to justice, was motivation enough for me to participate. I would give it my all, my best shot. Initially there was loads of different material available to me and with hard work over a hundred crimes all over the division going back over a twelve month period. I just used my practical experience, built up descriptions where given and words spoken, excuses gaining entry and how many offenders involved. Full details of each vehicle circulated nationally, as being involved in suspicious activities. Requests made for details of all occupants stopped to be returned for my information.

This positive method of action in my view was working and gradually I had report after report all coming back as being very useful, where I was able to build a picture of a gang of itinerants who were mainly involved. I had continual updates of similar crimes that were reported and some were linked either by vehicle, modus operandi or descriptions. During this period I went with my colleague out to various gypsy encampments. He was a West Indian mixed race detective, extremely likeable and a good friend and policeman, whom I have since learned had been promoted. So good to hear that news well done to him, they had definitely got it correct on this occasion in the promotion stakes.

The main issue was we were both dedicated to catching these individuals who were responsible for so much serious crime all against the vulnerable and elderly. As we entered the sites, some of the occupants knew who we were and I gave a bogus vehicle description never likely to have been there in the first place and of course knowing this, they allowed us to look around the site. What they did not realise was that I had all the registration numbers recorded into my concealed tape recorder and the speed we went round the site nothing untoward was suspected. This was repeated at other various sites. On the return journey my colleague had an extremely good voice, which was not wasted as he belted out good gospel songs one after another. He did not realise I had tape recorded him and still doesn't until this very day. I thought I might just see the funny side one day and kept the cassette tape safe.

Through putting together all our intelligence we now had the team involved and all the vehicles used. It was established they were covering more than three police areas and were very well organised. In addition they were visiting an accomplice who was serving a prison sentence for the very same crimes. A full report was circulated, for all forces and the Detective Superintendent was made aware. I had the pattern so well organised that every day I could update my files, with any new activity or new vehicle being used within just 20 minutes.

Although I had been doing this for a fairly short time, I knew in my heart that one day something positive would materialise. We had a new sergeant join the team and he really had no CID experience and although he was fully aware of the action I had taken, it to him was all unnecessary. He stated it was not leading anywhere and told me he was to see the Detective Superintendent, our friend from police complaints also without any former CID experience. Together they agreed it should all be stopped. So not to rock their fantasy world I just wiped it all off the boards and kept all the circulations sent internally and to adjoining forces. I also put in for transfer back to operational divisional duties away from the inexperienced clowns, who were playing at the role of trying to become experienced policemen.

Prior to this, I continued to have fun in my role before leaving which was always the fine balance between hard work and letting off steam. With all the dead wood around, you really needed to use your sense of humour, as without it working continually with some of the idiots would just drive you insane. We had four female civilian staff working in the office that were all very experienced, but hated Detective Inspector CLINTON. It was mainly the one girl, so I went up to her one morning and sat down at her desk. I just came out with it. I said," So why don't you like him, He never says anything about you." She replied, "It's just his manner, his attitude everything he says and does." I kept her talking for some ten minutes and the conversation was indeed not very complimentary towards this senior officer. So I then got out my tape recorder and re-winded the cassette tape of the conversation. She yelled out, "You've been taping me." I smiled and said, "Of course I have." She said, "What are you going to do with that tape." I said, "I am going to see Detective Inspector CLINTON and play it to him." She shouted, "Oh no you bloody aren't" I smiled to her, she didn't know I was joking, or realise I had no intention of doing anything.

So I started to walk away as if to leave the room and suddenly I was attacked by all four women who had tripped me up and were pulling punching kicking and biting my hand to get the tape. It was just funny as I thought whatever they would say if someone walked into the office. The commotion lasted about five minutes and I surrendered giving them the tape and was hysterical with laughter. All settled down, but this one married lady she just wouldn't forgive me. In the end I realised her birthday was close and organised a small collection, to her surprise she had a beautiful bunch of flowers delivered, the first time ever at work this had happened for her. That was it I was back in her good books. DI CLINTON never knew, and was none the wiser.

Then a couple of weeks passed and the West Indian detective was off on sick leave. That was it time for action. I dialled DI CLINTON on an internal line and when he answered I played this officers recording of him singing for at least ten minutes or more, a selection of his gospel songs.

No comment was made he just listened in silence as one of his officers was off sick and had called him on the phone to sing to him. Fantastic for morale, I never revealed it was me, and I would have loved to have discovered what DI CLINTON thought about it all. Memories like this never disappear.

I recall on attachment we had a young man from police Headquarters who was into crime analysis and for his age he was keen and hard working. Only thing was he did not have a very good bedside manner. Like with all staff, including supervision we all would take it in turn to make hot drinks when and where necessary. I recall asking this young man whom had the nickname 'Ethel' if he would like a drink of tea or coffee. He stated tea, white two sugars not too hot as he liked to drink it luke warm. Unlike anyone else there was no please or thank you and whether he was joking or not, told me to hurry up. That was it payback time, I made all the drinks but paid special care to his drink of tea. As I prepared his drink I cut open the tea bag and left just the tea leaves and added the sugar water and milk. I gave him his drink and he told me to put it down on the table. His manners again showed consistency with no remark involving any kind of thank you. I carried on my work and forgot completely the concoction I had served up, when all of a sudden he was talking with some senior officers and took a slurp of his drink where he suddenly spat all out as if he was haemorrhaging tea from the mouth at 100 mph. I burst into laughter and said 'Are you alright?' He said, 'No thanks to you.' I just stated 'Manners cost nothing young man.' and walked off.

It was several months later I was back as operational detective again and I heard that uniform had just arrested two men out of a car containing five, who had been committing sneak in burglaries. All of a sudden money was thrown into the air where eventually £20.000 in cash had been retrieved from neighbouring houses and gardens.

I later discovered the two in question were the main targets of my exercise and circulations and the accomplices who made good their escape, also should have been apprehended. After all their details were on display in uniform parade rooms and all CID offices so no one had any excuse. Even better if they had been tailed by the RCS regional crime squad. In this connection the wanted poster showed a full detailed package of the men, vehicles used, areas where crime committed and their modus operandi. This document called a Crime Information Bulletin, was sent to all areas of the divisions concerned, regional crime squads and of course police headquarters. In charge of the Intelligence was a Detective Inspector who had the same service as I, who was a pompous, smarmy individual apart from always being dressed in Saville row suites showed as much interest in his role as running a pig farming centre. He even had the audacity to change the wording of the report to make him look important and prove he had higher rank. I just thought him to be supercilious and idiotic and if he had spent as much time pushing for the regional crime squad to have picked up the targets, than he did just scrutinising my report this would have been more beneficial and worthwhile.

To prove the point when enquiries had been completed it transpired these two arrested had over £300.000.00 between them in various bank accounts. As for the other three who should have been rounded up as well, who knows what they had in their bank accounts from the types of crime committed. Averaging the proceeds out altogether I imagine £150.000.00 each, altogether totalling £750.000.00, in other words three quarters of a million pounds. All the proceeds of poor old age pensioners who foolishly saved for their retirement, keeping the cash at the home addresses rather than trusting the bank.

So all in all the Detective Superintendent, Detective Inspector and Detective Sergeant all responsible for Intelligence, who had not got a decent criminal brain between them, decided to scrap my line of enquiry. The two of the named suspects caught were named nine months earlier, and these overpaid morons did nothing in their role as supervisors. In my view they should all have been condemned for such negative actions, at the very least disciplined and demoted or kicked out of a criminal investigation role. In fact in my view, they allowed so much crime to be committed without taking necessary positive action and failed to support all the hard work done by those who worked with me on the fact finding analysis. These officers alone in my view could have prevented some of these crimes taking place by authorising and promoting extremely good intelligence work which to their utter shame was completely ignored. Yet if I had behaved in any way against similar circumstances I would have been disciplined for Neglect of Duty, which is exactly what they all should have been charged with under the discipline code. Not one of these officers had the guts to contact me and offer their apologies for neglecting all the hard work that my colleagues and I had done. It just shows the pompous integrity of them all, who should have hung their heads in shame. All this evidence of neglect, this could easily have been supported by the civilian staff employed in the Intelligence office who were aware of the hard work done and the negativity of these supervisory officers.

The pair of villains finally got convicted at Crown Court after pleading not guilty and both sentenced to lengthy terms of imprisonment. Of course what happened to the proceeds of their crime I do not know, but one would have hoped it was possibly returned to the victims of the crimes they were charged with.

Also for the two detectives who interviewed the two in custody, based on the circumstances of arrest and my intelligence bulletin, were able to charge them with offences and put them before the court. They both all did excellent police work.

This result had nothing whatsoever to do with the efforts of this trio of senior staff, who walking round the station full of their own importance and purporting to be policemen. These senior officers are no different to those in senior management in majority of our hospitals. The same characters who walk around all day carrying clip boards and hardly doing anything at all and paid very handsomely for it too. I also witnessed this first hand during my 10 years working in operating theatres in a large selection of major hospitals after leaving the police. Again the hard working medical staff in all areas, nurses and doctors and paramedics, just like the hard working operational police officers of all ranks, carrying the rest of these in charge of these vast areas forming part of our emergency services.

Some six months later the same useless detective sergeant was present in a meeting at the police station stating tenure of post was to be implemented, in that all CID were going back into uniform. I had left the Intelligence with the same idiot sergeant still in charge and guess where he was sitting, right behind me. I could not hesitate to point out to him, of how good detective work on his part, had allowed the gang to have continued committing crime virtually undetected, banking thousands of pounds and that summed up his detective work in a nutshell. This when they had all the ingredients formulated into a report showing all the hard work we had done, for which he was one of the instigators responsible for scrapping.

He told me if I continued he would discipline me. I invited him to do so. In fact I begged him to. Nothing would give me greater pleasure or comfort of standing before the Chief Constable apologising for my behaviour towards a senior officer of the next rank. At the same time I was exposing the actions of all the so called policemen who were unworthy to be involved in any investigation yet alone Intelligence. All this because they could not stand working with staff, lower in rank than themselves who were more experienced, just because they had a degree or had passed their exams. I came to realise sadly the police force at that time did not want dedicated thief takers, so sad for those who really joined for a career in detecting crime. I hope from all these experiences the police force has improved. However I am sure it is still the same, the brave hard working experienced officers of all ranks carrying the rest of them.

When I was in CID I would always liaise with the uniform beat officers and exchange information. What we should never forget is the police would never be able to do a thorough job without the enormous help of the general public.

Here we are, and back in 2013, and for the previous year there was one local police area close to where I live, which published annual reports now under the Disclosure of Information Act. It reported 29 House Burglaries, with None Detected, 30 vehicle crimes, with None Detected and 111 other offences of crime with only 29 Detected. Agreed it was an area of low crime, but what an earth are the local policemen doing. What intelligence is forthcoming to clear this sort of crime or what enquiries are being made cannot go unnoticed. All I know if I was in charge based on my experiences I would be extremely unhappy with such a poor detection results. Today some officers will argue that crime is only a small part of police work, but not in my book it wasn't and still is not today. Yet even in present day it is reported in the newspapers some areas of the country police forces still have extremely low, or no detections of house burglary. Whatever the excuses it is still not acceptable.

To be honest in reality in the one police force where I was stationed, upon the results being published the Chief Constable himself would have been knocking on the station door at 09.00 o'clock the next morning demanding answers and wanting to know why no crimes especially house burglary were not detected. What was going to be done about it. With strict measures put into place to ensure positive enquiries were completed and no stone left unturned in the detection of these crimes. How times have changed.

A few years later this same police force had a private resident, living on their patch who was a business entrepreneur whose business premises were in another adjoining police force area and situated some 4 miles from the force boundary. He had an office and factory complex with very expensive computer equipment installed valued over thousands of pounds. To compliment this enterprise the proprietor had excellent state of the art CCTV installed all linked to his home computer and mobile phone. During the early hours of one morning the alarm connected to the CCTV device activated on his mobile phone and immediately he checked his premises viewing the live footage where in clear colour video could see masked intruders who were all wearing face and hand covering concealing their identity, whilst they were in the process of disconnecting and removing computers and monitors from the premises. He was in actual fact recording the commission of a serious burglary live on his computer.

The offenders had no idea they were being filmed as the cameras were all hidden, so immediately this very concerned businessman telephoned the emergency services reporting the burglary in progress. This was received by that force control room who contacted the police station covering the attacked premises. Whilst he was still talking to the emergency contact, the person related the disturbing issue that the force covering his business premises had no one to send. How disgusting, someone could have got any police station surrounding nearby to visit, but it was not to be. The civilian control member in the offending force was rigid and made no attempt to get personnel of any kind to the scene.

All the time for a period of some 30 minutes, the business man was watching CCTV and the whole of his office complex was gradually stripped of absolutely everything. Was there some policy stating burglary of business premises was de-graded, as not important enough a crime for the police force dealing to attend, especially when all offenders could have been apprehended. Whatever the reason, later that same day the businessman had the television, radio and newspaper reports present and the whole matter was circulated throughout the media. A spokesman for the force in question stated the business man had been failed and they would review their procedures. I appreciate cuts have been made in police budgets, but you cannot tell me somewhere some officers could not have been dragged out of interviews or some job they were doing as this was a priority pending a positive result. What a state of affairs, I do not believe the offenders were ever caught and cannot state whether the businessman was at all compensated. Criticism of the police covering this incident was certainly not complimentary and in my day of policing heads would have rolled, how times change, not for the better and sadly there are far too many examples supporting extremely bad police work.

Police Forces are going away from having officers on the beat, its costly, not enough man power and whatever other excuses come to mind. It would be interesting to go back in time for the same area and see what the detections in crime there were some twenty years back. I would hope to presume the results would be a little more positive.

Although in the earlier days of my service the main source of drugs involved the illegal use of cannabis and marijuana which resulted at that time with the arrest of a select few who were using such drugs for personnel use. Other persons heavily committed in the unlawful importation into the United Kingdom and responsible for drug dealing and or possession with intention to supply obviously were committing more serious offences and were always dealt with by H.M.Customs and the Force Drug Squad.

One might argue that if the use of cannabis and marijuana had been dealt with more severely the current drug epidemic might not have been so bad. Today they treat smoking more strictly than they did dealing with drugs, no criticism of that it has made life better for so many. So why not do it with drugs even today. The softly, softly approach towards people from all walks of life, including colleges and universities, some of today's celebrities and politicians using and dealing in these drugs did not help in my view in curbing the problem. I suppose one day it will all be legalised still I can then go and buy a couple of grams of heroin instead of a packet of hamlet cigars which probably will have been banned. How crazy has our country become, sadly in so many avenues which would fill more than one book in detailing it all.

As back in the older days the petty crime was always treated serious, in a hope the serious crime did not materialise thus the punishment always then fitted the crime. So what happened, what went wrong, this is a debate in my view the do-gooders and the law abiding people will never resolve. I am sure if we did this country as they do in some stricter countries like Malaysia, the United Kingdom would be a much better place to live. This softness in the law has caused addicts not to be content with lower class drugs. In my view many went onto to harder and much more dangerous substances including heroin, cocaine and LSD and all the other concoctions formulated over the years. This has caused many users to become habitual offenders in crime to feed their addition.

Since retiring the problem has gotten far worse together with widespread prostitution and the use of firearms used by many drug gangs. Today we live in a dangerous society and well before we went into Europe I would often discuss free movement of people is fine providing we have good border controls, so the correct type of person enters for the right reasons. Now we have violent gangs of all kinds of criminals involving some people from different countries some entering our country for the sole purpose of increasing their illegal trade of drugs, firearms, prostitution and crime. All this being the number one cause of murder in the UK today and many being innocent victims. As if we have not got enough serious criminals already in our lovely country. Hindsight is a marvellous thing but I am sure most law abiding people, could clearly see where the authorities, human rights and politicians were all going so wrong, wished over the years the authorities had come down much harder with all criminals committing serious crime and using drugs of all kinds, which would have helped prevent the state of society today. These people in power in my view have nothing to be proud of.

If places like Malaysia is virtually crime free due to high profile policing and sentencing, then that is a price most people would agree is a price worth paying. It seems as if smokers are punished more these days and subjected to more laws than drug users, not that I condone smoking in public places. Whatever the authorities decide it is obvious we are not yet winning the battle with drug abuse in this country. On top of all these serious crimes, which paint a pretty depressing story, the police and security services have the additional risks in dealing with all the different levels of terrorism. Despite sometimes severe criticism, no one can under estimate the extremely excellent hard work that some police forces regularly put into effect in the fight to detect act of terrorism, which is something of which we can all be proud of as a country. We still have the best police force in the world but could be even better if some were allowed to police properly.

CHAPTER 22

MAGISTRATES AND CROWN COURTS

O ne of the best changes in the law in this country was the clause of double jeopardy where a person could not face proceedings for the same charge twice. This was not good news for the accused but good for justice especially where the case was serious and there was a strong case to answer. Like if they get off on appeal and further evidence comes to light to prove lying or wrong doing, that is only fair justice in my book. Same as perjury, or wrongly accusing someone, of falsifying evidence, all should carry strong consequences resulting in serious punishment. In a lot of cases when you enter a Court be it Magistrates or Crown Court there is an area of etiquette and rules of behaviour. Not wishing to demeanour any of the courts behaviour, but I decided upon cross examination to test the system, to see what if any, outcome would be made over my answer to a given question. It was at a time when defendants when in custody clearly wanted to get out and could not wait to involve themselves in writing out a written statement under caution.

The benefit of this would be that it was an opportunity to show in evidence exactly what the accused had done and to put into place any mitigation. It was especially useful when things were mentioned that were totally unknown and could later also be corroborated, thus the importance of the person being honest.

On the other hand, it was always a defence issue under cross examination that the accused had been coerced, threatened, promised favours or had made the statement against his will.

It is amazing how different defences are all bought about, and then following a change in the law the well-known defence never materialises again. One such defence was to Murder where they tried to prove the accused was insane, especially when the death sentence was the only end result. Then if established any final punishment would be in the insane asylum. Since the abolition of the death penalty, where the sentence is now commuted to life imprisonment, majority of the population of offenders, suddenly are not in sane anymore. What a fantastic feat of medical intervention. The defence suddenly changed from insanity to diminished responsibility.

I remember being in the witness box being challenged on one such issue that the defendant had been coerced into making such a statement, which was totally untrue. I answered the defence Barrister, stating I was absolutely flabbergasted at such a suggestion. I truly was and I even saw the Judge take off his reading glasses and look directly at me.

Then in summing up later at the latter stages of the trial, stating, 'Ladies and Gentlemen of the Jury you will recall Detective Constable LUNN was absolutely flabbergasted at the suggestion of any coercement in the taking of the defendant's statement'. I thought they don't miss a trick do they how they paint a picture from what has been said. It is a very clever profession in being part of a legal team. In any case he was convicted quite rightly by the jury and sentenced. Rarely today is a statement of this nature made, as video and tape recorded interviews have taken over the validity of such a document.

On the other hand I had a case where it was in complete opposite contrast. We had a regular female shoplifter under arrest, who was an alcoholic who had fallen from grace with her husband. She was living with another man, who in fairness had a difficult job on his hands, trying to get her on the right path of honesty. She had been in custody several times for stealing and was always trouble being disruptive and making threats for no reason to those dealing with her. She was finally given a suspended sentence on her last conviction. In less than a month she was back again causing trouble having been arrested from several stores. I decided to help the shift in interviewing her as it was clear she was not learning her lesson. She was then later charged and bailed to court.

At the Magistrates Court she pleaded not guilty and was represented by a Barrister, she had been allocated, all on legal aide at the taxpayers' expense. Under cross examination whilst giving evidence I was answering all issues connected with the case. All of a sudden he asked me if I had had any form of intimate contact with the accused at any time during the period I had known her. Being extremely cross and annoyed by this suggestion I made it abundantly clear I certainly had not encountered any such behaviour. I even retaliated stating, "Why have you, because I haven't." I suppose the Barrister was only doing his job but I resented such an implication without any grounds or corroboration, or worse still any redress whatsoever. She was found guilty and the suspended sentence was suspended again.

What a mockery of justice. As I walked out of the court building with my colleague, I passed by the defendant with her boyfriend and she apologised for her accusation admitting it was all false in an attempt to deflect against the strong evidence against her. I accepted her apology only because the boyfriend was a decent person. Clearly he was welcome to keep his girlfriend all to himself.

One of the funniest experiences involving Court proceedings involved a local man who owned a dubious company where he undertook possession of a stolen wagon load of motor vehicle parts. Someone who he would never suspect grassed him up and colleagues from our office were sent down to his premises. Altogether all staff was locked up, including a cleaner who eventually was used as a witness. All others were charged with the valuable theft and elected trial by jury. He tried to force the witness from making a statement, which failed to materialise. On the day of his trial whilst sitting in the dock before a prominent and most efficient Judge, held his tie up like a noose. It was this behaviour that was the grounds for the first warning of many which was clear from the Judge who was to suffer no nonsense.

As the trial continued the man went into the witness box and was cross examined and gave an enlightening performance. He was asked a question and repeatedly replied, "It's no good my friend I can't understand a word yow am on about." Despite the question being reiterated by the defence, the Judge intervened and said, "Mr. JONES, your Barrister has asked you a question now on two separate occasions in a fair and proper manner. I will in the interests of justice repeat the question so you understand clearly, "The question quite simply is ----------. Now what have you got to say."

Mr. JONES, which is a false name to avoid revealing identity, said, "I can see why yow am a Judge, I can understand yow, but I core understand him." Clearly this man was extracting the urine and the court was in complete uproar of his behaviour. He was told in no uncertain circumstances not to waste the time of the court and eventually the case was finally summed up by the Judge.

The jury went out and eventually returned with a unanimous Guilty verdict. Stand up Mr. JONES," You will go to prison for a period of 5 years." This defendant had sealed his own fate, as Judges are very powerful people and can use their discretion accordingly. Clearly he would at the most, may have only received 2 years, but due to his behaviour and total disregard for the respect of the court, justice was seen to be done. He may have been an incorrigible rogue but paid the price for his comical antics. I remember on previous occasions he would enter certain licensed premises and would treat all the children and sometimes their parents all to a free lunch and pudding. Clearly he had good points to his character but had his priorities in life totally mixed up.

CHAPTER 23

BAD POLICE BEHAVIOUR

Some officers were below standard who obviously should never have got through their probation, or indeed when after this initial period, joined the culture where they believed they were entitled to a meal ticket for life without doing the job that they were paid for.

It is easy to appreciate why targets were introduced which in my view should have happened ten years earlier. No hard working police officer would ever have a problem with this anyway, as it was designed to identify wasters. I remember an old experienced uniform Superintendent telling me the busier the station the easier it was for some officers to hide under the backbone of the hard working, as they were sometimes hard to detect. I can justify this, as later in my service at the police station where I worked in the early nineties, half the morning shift had left all their equipment in the parade room and had gone downstairs to the canteen for breakfast. Out of curiosity I decided to look through their pockets books to see how many individual arrests had been made of their own instigation or volition and I could not find one officer who had made such an arrest in the last three month period. Clearly we had a fire brigade police force who were at that time just attending incidents one after the other and some officers were not making any effort or looking for any arrests. As

I have said previously some of my best arrests in uniform, were when being sent from one incident to another, where you would see your burglars or thieves, but you had to know their identity or look for them in the first place.

When you raised the issue there was always excuses but no arrests in three months, clearly in my view there was something going terribly wrong. How was the younger officer going to gain experience, or become motivated in the true tradition of the policing, in learning how to investigate thoroughly and learn the instincts that come naturally to experienced officers. I clearly felt very sad for these officers willing to learn, with no one to show them.

I came from a generation where self-motivation was always a prime ingredient of being a reliable worker. Whilst throughout the country when times are hard, the police, fire, health and government workers always did a job on very poor pay and conditions, despite being criticised for being in regular employment. Since pay increases have been put into place, some people have joined for the complete wrong reasons, with some in order just to climb the ranks solely for higher wages. All with less given dedication than our predecessors as if working 9 to 5 was a given right and some officers having the audacity to say they could not work over, even when in the middle of an important ongoing investigation.

Some Officers would rather write the name of a suspect on the back of a crime report than actually make an arrest. Even when they clearly had the opportunity, they would use all the excuses possible they could invent, to avoid doing the job. In my view it was easier to complete an enquiry, rather than try to find a way out of dealing, which was always certainly more rewarding.

I remember one day I was with another colleague and we had arrested a young lady who was half way through her pregnancy, but the allegations were serious and needed to be investigated as soon as possible. We had four custody blocks within our division and I was advised whilst on route our station the custody block was completely full of prisoners. Another station had no police woman and the other two police stations were also full. Upon enquiring which station where we could take this young lady, we were advised to travel to another division where another two stations were found to be fully committed and had no spaces. We were involved on a merry go round where there was no common sense and we had to put up with this display of stupid political correctness, which I am sure was divisionally organised by Custody Sergeants. Yes they can be busy but certainly no more than other hard working officers. At least they were in the warm and had a different kind of pressure, less severe than being out on patrol.

The final straw made me tell the Custody Sergeant to expect me back at our police station and over the radio he was most indignant pulling rank, stating I was to go elsewhere but in fairness I was having none of this nonsense.

Upon arrival in the custody block he reiterated his demands and I told him I had travelled around the division like a headless chicken listening to all the pathetic demands of Custody Officers. He clearly could see she was heavily pregnant. I stated the woman had been in our vehicle for over an hour, had not been allowed any drink and that if he refused to deal and I had to take this lady elsewhere, I would not accept responsibility for any decline in health and any distress caused to the lady as I would blame him entirely. In addition I stated if he wished to discipline me, go ahead. So when faced with an issue of common sense he calmed down and bottled out. Yes they were busy, but not that busy they could not cope. We all have a job to do, but all the actions of the Custody Officers that morning, to me were just plain ridiculous, as they were acting very militant as if they would go on strike. Their behaviour was appalling and I would have given them all a written warning if I was in charge, as to their atrocious behaviour. Senior therefore did not mean Superior not in my book as respect for rank is one thing, but respect for the person is a completely different issue. This only comes with the background knowledge of the right person having experience, common sense and good judgment which is regularly put into practice.

Then another of my colleagues, who lived close by to us during our career, had completed his service and retired. Just as he had bought his new home his wife suddenly left him for a senior officer, who at one time was also a close neighbour. They both had been involved in a long term affair lasting well over 20 years, behind the backs of both partners. For a man of such rank, his actions were despicable and he continued in his civilian life still walking around with an air of pompous conceit, often miserable and very self-centred. If he had been in the military his behaviour would have resulted in him facing a Court Martial. It was a pity this scandal did not surface whilst he was still in service, as I am sure there was possibly an offence committed within the police Discipline Code.

In fact both ex-partners found out only through Dear John letters as neither person could not even tell them face to face, how cruel that was. I remember my wife and I both spent time consoling both injured parties who were upset and deeply hurt. The man recalling that he not got the slightest suspicion of what was going on between this pair, suddenly stated that his parents were at the home over this Christmas period some 18 years ago. It came straight back to him as his wife stated she was going to the neighbour's house one evening to see if she could help with the young child. Apparently his wife was in hospital having the day previous given birth to their second child. She went mid evening only to return late in the early hours of the next day. Her husband was working nights but the in-laws were suspicious in that she had spent so long in the same house with this married man. Naturally it all then fell into place, she had even been sleeping with this man at that time so long ago, and ever since.

Even though we had good relations with all parties, this couple had fallen in love and although these things happen but it was the way it was all bought out into the open, to be so cruel in the way they deceived their own spouses and way they told the heart-breaking news to their partners. No one is perfect in life but he lived all that time sleeping with another colleague's wife, his morals were just non-existent and he appeared not to show any remorse. At least the husband had survived a nasty suicidal bid, but at one time he was close to death having taken such a large overdose putting his life in jeopardy, and he nearly did not recover. He later met someone else and again found happiness in his life. As for the other wife I am sure she eventually rebuilt her future and moved on for the better.

The police force was a wonderful career and as interesting as you made it, but we have to applaud all our dedicated spouses who had to put up with late hours, missed events, times we had spent socialising and missed parenthood, especially working the most awkward hours possible. No wonder so many officers of all ranks just wanted regular shifts or 9-5 jobs.

All we appear to get these days is female police Superintendents and female Assistant Chief Constables hitting the headlines over a bust up at a social function. Both women were comparing the size of their breasts in full view of many people. They were seriously arguing whilst intoxicated, over the size of their assets and that one of them a mother of children stating she was adequately blessed and looked better than her colleague. Can you believe it, both in such responsible roles which deserved respect from all in society blatantly indecently exposing themselves in such a demeaning way. In my view being in such a privileged position they should have both been demoted at the very least and not allowed to keep such prominent jobs. Officers of lower rank would possibly have been sacked.

Then a Chief Constable of another force suggested that new female Muslim recruits should be allowed to wear the Burka, so as not to cause offence to the Muslim faith. These highly ranked officers who should lead by example, they are not even fit enough to fill the boots of many of our predecessors. Sorry but from the negative path they are purporting I can state from their behaviour in my book they could not even detect a smell yet alone a crime. How anyone with an ounce of common sense could support such a recommendation, but it was all treated as a serious proposal that easily could have been implemented. Imagine that, female police officers walking round with only a letter box available to the public that they can communicate from. What planet are these people on and what on earth is happening to our country, in making such absolutely ludicrous suggestions.

We have a police force in the UK that is constantly under the umbrella of the media and as such being on your guard keeping protocol and behaving responsibly in all areas of the public has never been more important. This is definitely the view of the very professional and hardworking police officers of all ranks who put their lives in danger and are well tuned in the activities of criminals, despite a fall in police numbers. These officers carry majority of the other officers who clearly fall short in the same standards and some are indeed a total embarrassment to the police force and the whole of society.

In the media recently a woman Chief Inspector having sex on duty allegedly several times in different locations with a civilian member of staff whilst on duty, who is under investigation. If proved or not the damage is done people get so very annoyed at these type of sordid incidents. Again in my view when on duty you are in the public eye, nothing wrong in letting off steam after a long shift, but there is a time and place which is not in the public eye. Officers taking selfies with mobile phones at crime or accident scenes is never a good idea and humiliating for all. No different to officers disco dancing in the street whilst on duty in full uniform many show their friendly side but crossing the line in my view with the public perception of the police force who are becoming a laughing stock with the public.

Then another force in the UK is considering allowing all its officers to have 2 days stress leave per year, when many do not even know what real stress or hard work is. We desperately need police back on our streets as a tool to detecting crime, yet another force puts a PCSO and uniform constable on the beat only as a stupid gimmick to pick up litter and bag it up with newspaper cover to suggest they are mixing with the real public. People would have more respect if they made enquiries into burglaries and felt a few collars, but no the powers that be decided perhaps this was good for public morale. How utterly ridiculous just shows the mentality of some of those in charge, more brawn than brains with what I believe hardly any police experience despite being paid very handsomely for the role.

CHAPTER 24

BARRISTERS AND SOLICITORS

As I became more experienced like other well established officers, you became the officer in charge with the case you were dealing with and fully responsible for presenting a file of evidence for the court. There was nothing more encouraging when you received a compliment from the Prosecution Barrister or Solicitor as to the high quality of the paperwork. This had important meaning that the answers to any possible query or question were all catered for, in that you had been completely thorough in all your research and enquiries, which had been appropriately documented. This is particularly true with any small report to the thickest file of evidence, which could land on either the Chief Constables desk or indeed with the Home Secretary or with the most Senior Judge in the United Kingdom. It was therefore important to present the best file possible to demonstrate your professionalism and capability.

Sadly towards the end of my career and possibly still today there are too many officers involved with no one taking overall responsibility. There is nothing better than dealing with something from start to finish. I can imagine there being some officers today having accrued some service, who have never experienced this kind of police work and have just played a small part of many as if you are completing a jigsaw puzzle.

I have already covered several experiences involving court procedures and it is easy to identify the good points of officials involved to those being underhanded, untrustworthy and unprofessional, this involving Defence and Prosecution Lawyers, Crown Prosecution staff and Police Officers. Over the years the police have had to get their act together, quite rightly especially with cases involving corrupt practices and unprofessionalism with many forces, with one force having the Serious Crime Squad disbanded. This did so much harm to public confidence and tainted everyone on that department with the same brush. In reality, majority were completely the opposite, sound professional officers with high standards, who had a career to be envious and very proud of. If someone walks free from a court or police station due to lack of evidence or other reason, especially if a prolific criminal so what. It can be very frustrating and you have possibly done your very best but that is not the end of the matter. They become over confident and believe they are above the law so they will slip up big style at some point especially if unknown they are targeted on surveillance operations when all their other crimes old and new can be re-looked at again.

Over the years it is also clear that some Defence lawyers have not played by the rules either, falsely claiming legal aid against fictious names of non-existent clients in addition representing offenders they possibly know are guilty. If this is true if accepting their client is guilty they go ahead to defend allowing him to tell open lies in court. Although I am sure this has not happened very often, instead of defending they really should advise the client to plead guilty or not represent them at all.

Some defence solicitors during my experiences would attend the police station and be present on interviews naturally representing their client's interest. Then when deliberate lies were taking place against the advice given by them, the Solicitor would pack his cases and stand up stating he could no longer represent his client. How honourable, no different to defence Barristers when in mid-stream of a trial his client is telling lies also in the same manner, against the advice given, and he too has packed his cases, apologised to the Judge for the same reason and left the defendant to represent himself alone. Sadly these instances seem to get less and less. These kinds of Barristers and Solicitors are the very best in British society and give real credence to a genuine not guilty person who they are representing to prove their innocence.

The police by this time had travelled along a bumpy road going from notes made after the interview, to note taking contemporaneously during interview, to tape and video recording. Not that the presentation of the evidence was called into question, but taken or recorded during the interview was more credible. In addition to disclosing any evidence to the defence before questioning, the police had become extremely more professional, in quite a relative short period of time, thanks to improvements in modern technology.

The work of some defence lawyers with generous donations from the legal aid fund has created many a millionaire legal representative. Some I am sad to say with no scruples touting for business involving foreign complaints against our troops, all under the alleged umbrella of the Human Rights Act. It was later established many were for frivolous claims against the public interest, all justified however under the current law so in actual fact they are doing no wrong. However it transpired in the main this one solicitor was found to be concocting false allegations completely, causing horrendous sufferings to families and relatives, when in fact the troops in question had done absolutely no wrong. This is all an issue of morality on both sides in the interests of fairness and justice and many good barristers and solicitors too would hate this bad apple of the legal profession. Let's hope one day he faces justice himself for his rotten and evil behaviour with a punishment he utterly deserves.

Quite rightly they claim they are only doing their job which is perfectly true, but it appears some of the practices that would not even have been considered years ago, are today the normal. Others abusing the legal aid system where one such practice involved a Solicitor who defended the murderer of an alleged victim of a Road Rage Murder in the Midlands area. At least twenty of their staff from this same firm was involved in creating fictitious records supporting legal aid and upon finding of guilt were all given custodial sentences, all just through unnecessary greed. Priming a client how to answer certain questions which the defendant should not be privy to is not within the guidelines, but in my day went on, on more than one occasion. It was obvious during the Solicitors private consultation, words had been put into the defendants mouth in which in his limited capacity never in the world of pigs pudding, would the illiterate individual have been capable of thinking out the same answer for himself. As stated fortunately this practice was only confined to the underhanded kind of defence team, as most honest Solicitors would not lower themselves to this poor standard of representation.

Educating a defendant how to dress, training them how to act and give evidence in court is something which really there is nothing wrong with, but should in my view be down to the discretion of the Court, as to whether this is disclosed or not. The Chief Magistrate or Jury would then get a fair view of the real character of the accused, again that is only my choice and would not be tolerated by some arguing it was perhaps unfair.

I recall we had a regular Solicitors Clerk representing a local firm who often visited our police station to defend clients. She always interrupted conversations regularly, challenging evidence at every opportunity, sometimes asking for different private consultations with her clients. Whether it was intentionally or not to break up any flow in the investigation, or just too slow matters down. Not that she was doing anything wrong, it was just tactics. In some cases if I was the accused I would probably requested a person just like her to represent me, after all she was making her presence known. In all honesty though, I would never allow myself to be in such a predicament as I consider myself to be law abiding.

As we drew towards the concluding part of the interview, I informed her client I had an Inspectors authority to search the home address of her client in his absence. He lived some 20 miles away and we stated it was to be done as soon as possible, even though it was mid evening. She spoke with her client and as a result insisted she was also present during the search. That was new to me, I had never been placed in that predicament before and being a fair minded person I thought, why not. My pocket book was up to date and so I recorded all that took place in showing true professionalism.

She joined me and another officer and we drove to the location, arriving just before 10.00pm. It was a two storey house with a cellar and large loft and in her presence I told my colleague, we will leave no stone unturned. Upon being allowed entry I served formal notice on the occupant. A thorough meticulous search was made of the two upper floors, attic, ground floor, cellar and garden. All was not exactly found to be the cleanest house in society and some rooms were equal to the grime buster's series on television.

During the search I seized various items all suspected to being stolen and to which questions under caution were put to the occupant. All details being recorded and duly signed in my notebook. We left at about 3.00am and finally got back to our station some hour and half later. This Solicitor stated," I will never, ever, ever go on a search again" I said, "Oh is that so." Talk about breaking a horse in, I think she got the message.

In addition we had many changes in the law under PACE, [Police and Criminal Evidence Act] where a person had to be released after 24 hours, unless a senior officer found grounds for extension. Obviously some cases did not warrant that, but cases that did it were obvious release was inevitable as we reached the given time limit. Some solicitors without scruples, despite being contacted repeatedly throughout the time a person was in custody, did not arrive at a custody block until the last one or two hours of this given time limit. Then they would deliberately prolong their consultation knowing a person would have to be released without any interview taking place. In the main without charge, which was very awkward when several joint offenders were in custody together, requesting the same firm of Solicitors.

This was only down to a small bunch of individuals and eventually as senior officers became more aware of their antics, guidelines were drawn up on policy to prevent any re-occurrences of these unlawful irritating practices.

During my time in the police, some solicitors would regularly advise their clients to make no comment, whereas others depending on the case would let their client explain what took place in their own words. Towards the end of my service more and more solicitors were advising their clients not to say anything, after all it is their legal right and it is up to the prosecution to prove their case. It was therefore extremely important that you completed all your ground work wherever possible prior to any interview. Sometimes you could only interview with the evidence available, but there was nothing wrong in bailing a person to return back to the police station at a later date when you have found more incriminating evidence. Then providing you have sufficient evidence you could obtain authority to charge, or failing that release.

It was refreshing to see that most solicitors whilst showing the main duty was to the court and for justice, representing their client on a professional basis was of prime importance arguing lawfully that everything had to be fair and just, but in the same tone not tolerate lies or any misconduct from them. This was completely opposite to the other kind of solicitor who would take a different approach.

I remember one solicitor buying one of his client's cigarettes and getting him food, whilst condoning his unruly behaviour, with continual bad language in the cells and during interview. He would continually allow and condone his client to spit or have tantrums, being disrespectful to anyone in authority and this included himself which was unacceptable. The custody sergeant or we as interviewing officers would then have to intervene in an attempt to quell such behaviour. This was extremely infuriating when the solicitor was talking to his client as if he was a person of great importance. I suppose in a way he was after all a good customer and earning his firm a fortune at the rate payer's expense from legal aid. Not that there is anything unlawful in that, but it goes against the grain when they do not control their client properly, when other good solicitors are so more professional and take control of bad behaviour. Then you have unruly juveniles in front of social workers, and legal advisors always foul mouthing, swearing at people in authority all condoned or accepted by the same regime. None of this really should have any place in the normal part of British society, but I suppose we live in a society where influence from other badly behaved adults, parents and everyday films which portray violence and bad language so easily picked up by the younger generation.

When dealing with solicitors especially over the years we had fairly good relations with some who were nothing more than likeable, friendly and polite, extremely professional very much perfect ladies and gentlemen. Not that on occasions we did not disagree which is healthy in any relationship. Naturally they would get to know your abilities and how you worked. This included how efficient and reliable you were and thankfully these kind of people more than compensated for the other extreme members of their profession who were always approached with extra caution.

CHAPTER 25

SERIOUS CRIMINAL OFFENCES WITH MORE THAN A TWIST IN THE TALE

One report of serious crime involved two fellow colleagues who both worked in our office, a DC John SOMA and DC Mike GREEN. These detective constables who were both young, dapper, extremely keen with a good sense of humour who like most of us at the time worked hard and played hard, but never leaving any stone unturned when it came to doing the job with regard to any investigation. It was such refreshing addition to our office as they were both popular with everyone and morale was at an all-time high after working for so many years with dead wood.

Both were working in the office together when a call came in of an armed robbery in progress in the High Street of the town. An offender had entered the premises of a TV Rental retail outlet brandishing a firearm and threatening two members of staff and demanding money. It was not known if the gun was loaded and real or if an imitation, but when confronted with such a weapon in a threatening manner the ordeal is no less frightening. Fortunately no shots had been discharged.

Despite the uniformed police officers and detectives arriving fairly quickly at the scene the offender had left having stolen some several hundred pounds in notes from the cash register. Both members of staff a man and woman assistant aged in their early twenties appeared to be shaken up over their ordeal, but refused to attend hospital maintaining they were uninjured and would be alright. They were able to give a description of the white man responsible who was not known to them but they believed would be able to identify if seen again. A full search of the area was made, with the assistance of the force helicopter, but despite frantic efforts to find him and no knowledge of any vehicle or possible accomplice' the man had eluded capture.

As with any serious criminal case Scenes of Crime staff attended, together with photographic officers, but after a full examination nothing of any evidential value was found relating to the man responsible. In those days close circuit television cameras just did not exist and it was just down to basic hardnosed police work to establish the truth. A visit was planned as soon as possible for both witnesses to attend police Headquarters where it was normal practice in such cases to view police photographs of suspects fitting similar descriptions and those with convictions for these types of crime.

Another good tool in the fight against crime greatly assisting police investigations was the weekly police series on television. This show was broadcast live throughout the region involving a number of neighbouring police force areas. It covered many incidents of crime committed within all the forces concerned and was in fact a mini version of the national Crime Watch television program. It went out on air shortly before the end of the daily evening news and had a very positive effect in raising the status of the crime to a higher profile in many cases jogging people memories in flushing out information from the public. Similar police television presentations were repeated in various formats throughout other regions of the U.K. sadly after a long period of time these kinds of local television programmes came to an end never to be replaced. This left a huge vacant gap in popular public interest shows where the public really could tune into a more thorough insight into local serious crime and assist the police. So strange when today television is trying to break into the success of regional radio with more local television stations, but I suppose like everything it all comes down to costs.

Within a couple of days of the incident DC SOMA and DC GREEN after making all the arrangements, transported both witnesses to force Headquarters to the Special Witness viewing facilities within the Photographic department. Coincidently this was the same day the live broadcast was scheduled to take place at the regional television studios highlighting the full circumstances of the armed robbery. A reconstruction of the crime had already been filmed using unknown celebrities in the form of uniform and detective officers from our station posing as wannabe actors. Despite this the end result was indeed very convincing and a very professional performance.

After viewing several hundred photographs independently both witnesses were unable to pick out any male person responsible and were exhausted from their ordeal. On leaving police Headquarters both officers thought some light liquid refreshment with a bite to eat, at a local lounge of a nearby public house would have a relaxing effect with both witnesses allowing them to be able to recuperate. Whilst relaxing the young male witness left his female assistant to eat her food, and went across to the gaming machine and this soon became the twist in the tale as the behaviour of both of them soon began to take on a surprising turn of events.

The man was feeding the machine with money and spending like no tomorrow well in excess of a person of his position. He was allowed to continue and was seen changing notes at the bar to get more coins, all going into his unknown gambling addiction. As for the other witness this girl was becoming more nervous with the pressures knowing the crime later that day was going to receive high profile attention within the media and it was soon obvious she was bottling this all up inside her. It became obvious to both officers that her behaviour appeared well out of character and that clearly she had something to hide. Talking with her there appeared to be some inconsistencies in what actually took place. They both sensitively queried what was wrong and what was causing her to be so upset. She soon crumbled to pieces from all the pressure and blurted out crying that it was all a setup, that there was no robbery the male assistant had taken money out of the till and to cover his tracks had invented the whole fantasy. She admitted having some of the money but it was clear the man was driving force in committing the offence. Both were told it was time to leave the premises, not before being also informed they were both under arrest for theft of money belong to their employer. They were returned back to the police station where later upon interview they admitted full responsibility and jointly charged with the offence of theft and bailed to appear at court.

Discussions then took place with DI David GLOUCESTER who insisted it was too late to cancel the television broadcast as just within under an hour and a half it was due to go out as scheduled, so both officers still had to attend as if nothing had happened. Normally this would never happen but what the public didn't know they could not grieve, in any case having pulled a few strings to get on the show so quickly it would have been against protocol to have done otherwise. I recall having to smile when they both later told me the appeal went out as normal, but with the crime all being made up, yet alone detected there was little doubt that there would be any calls coming in from the public. For nearly four hours afterwards the phone lines had to be manned, turning out to be the most boring part of the investigation with no response whatsoever. Nevertheless it was still an ideal opportunity for each officer in turn to have the luxury of speaking to their respective wives in lengthy telephone conversations, a rare event indeed for a hard working operational police Detectives. Both offenders finally appeared before court where they were sentenced the man received prison, the female accomplice was dealt with more leniently.

DI GLOUCESTER was an ambitious, likeable and respected senior officer. I only ever had one grievance with raised words with him throughout his whole period of supervision at our station. He was being informed some untruths by a uniform sergeant who was on attachment to our office and unaware I had already had informed our detective Chief inspector of the consequences of this officers stupidity. Naturally not knowing the whole picture he was listening to some incriminating action for which I completely exposed as naive police work and his complete in-experience for an officer of the rank of sergeant working in CID. This sad incident is covered in a previous chapter, where DI GLOUCESTER completely exonerated me for any wrong doing or un-professionalism.

However a few years later, shortly after I retired I was informed news of the tragic death of this senior Officer, who I believed had also risen to the rank of detective Chief Inspector. I was unsure if he was still a serving officer or if he had also retired, but I knew he was a married man with a son who was possibly then a teenager. Apparently he had been having an extra marital affair with a woman and was torn between them both, with other unknown consequences, the pressure affected him and in a fit of depression sadly took his own life. I was told he was away on holiday with his wife and possibly his son, when he left them in the car to return to the holiday home to retrieve some property. All of a sudden the sound of a shotgun being discharged was heard coming from the premises and then there was silence. His wife returned to finding his lifeless body with the gun he used for shooting on the land, lying on the floor nearby. What a terrible experience for all those left behind, nothing is worse than committing suicide, but it only takes a second especially when you are unable to confront your demons and speak to someone for help. Whatever he had done wrong, he was otherwise a good person and very much missed.

We had various other criminal enquiries between us all within the office but sadly for us remaining, both these officers later got promoted to Sergeant and moved on to other stations. Nothing could replace the good times we had working together.

In police work you always come across those who believe they are above the law, none more so than the persons who have neglected their business through drinking. Instead of being in charge they were always absent when needed. At every opportunity this Boss would sneak out of his store, to drink in the bar of his local public house, then when the wheel comes off and things go wrong he expects you to move heaven and earth and use every means possible to sort out the problem. This includes him suggesting bending the rules, twisting the truth to sort his problem out. This kind of person never listens and only ever learns from his own mistakes when it is all too late.

At these premises one such incident cracked off which was discovered by mistake. A woman in her early thirties was employed in a type of warehouse shop open to members of the public where majority of goods were close to wholesale prices. The business had good potential and a strong turnover due to a family involvement, however the proprietor having a drink problem had become complacent in the trust and running of the business. When the girl could not turn in one day due to unforeseen circumstances, she was not able to cover her tracks from the day previous. The partner in the business took over and found a discrepancy in that £200 in cash was missing from the previous day's takings and covered up showing refund for that amount on the till roll. He quietly examined previous till roll readings and unearthed an explosive situation where this action had been continually repeated all the days the girl had actually worked, going back over a fifteen month period. He spent the remainder of the day analysing the figures but every time he reached the same result, over £40,000 had been taken over this fairly short time and could not be accounted for. As usual in these situations no proper audit or stock taking had been performed since the girl had started.

That's where I came in, as the matter was reported direct to me later at the police station. Both partners realised that their business future was looking bleak, you cannot suffer that amount of loss and survive and that was without knowledge of any other fiddles that may have taken place. It transpired the three days each week she had worked £200 in cash had been taken out of the till. The amount taken was just shown as a deduction or refund, so this record balanced with the theft, when cashing up at the end of the day. Not rocket science, but in a position of trust and going unchecked it did not take long to escalate out of control.

I discussed with them a plan of action, go and arrest her straight away or put in monitoring equipment. The best action in my view was to allow her to work when she returned for her next shift and complete a spot check on the till as she finishes for the day. In her current behavioural pattern it was likely another discrepancy could be found in line with all previous actions and then we could recover such money in her possession. Either way it was going to have to involve her coming clean to prove majority of the crime. Deciding the latter approach was the best way, I arranged to be available from midday, on the day she next worked.

The man who had found the discrepancies was appreciative of the advice and agreed the way forward. As for his partner, he was becoming outspoken and making improper suggestions to get at the truth. He was told any investigation would be by the rules as the culprit after all was no wiser to the crime having been discovered and to leave everything in the hands of the police and not obstruct justice. After all this was a crime that could have been easily preventable, if proper procedures were fully implemented, as allowing so much cash to remain in the tills was a temptation in itself. The man said he would talk to his partner and we would go ahead with the planned action but I had a gut feeling the main Boss could not be trusted as he was well known locally for being obnoxious and pig headed and just would not listen.

When I arrived at work the following day, I received a telephone call to visit the business premises. Apparently the one partner had remained at the warehouse most of the night, and had been drinking heavily. When the girl arrived he asked her to drive him to a supplier and was a passenger in her vehicle. The calmer man had asked me to attend and told me the facts, he was concerned as his partner never normally left the business premises and he had been gone for most of the morning. It was fast approaching midday, so I took full details of the girl and the vehicle she was driving, I was about to circulate them to patrols, when the vehicle with both occupants returned.

As I approached the vehicle, both the man and girl got out and came towards me. He had obviously told her I was a police detective and had made it known she was suspected for taking all the money. Speaking to the girl she added he had told her to drive but she had been detained against her will and threatened by him. As a result I called for assistance and both were arrested, the girl for theft and this man for kidnapping. At the police station it was established the man had told her to drive to an isolated spot high in the hills in the middle of the countryside, where he there made her suffer the ordeal that the family had lost everything through her thieving. At this location he had threatened the girl with a knife as she had a superficial injury to her neck caused by the sharp blade. In addition he also made continued gestures that he was going to end it all, and take her with him. She apologised and admitted she was sorry, but was frightened by his behaviour and despite her ordeal she was relieved it was all over and that she was safe and well. She was bailed pending enquiries and taken to hospital by a policewoman.

Having full control of the case I was approached by a young detective sergeant who was only out for himself and not even in the same league of any of his predecessors, who were well above his station genuine and totally approachable. He begged to get involved stating he needed the collar, only I knew his move on me was far more sinister as his intentions were only to take charge and purport all the job was down to him. You get to read people like this just like a book and he had the aura of untrustworthy written all over him. In later experiences my foundation for such suspicions came completely true. I falsely told him I had assistance and went to another of the more confident and trusting detective constables and worked with him instead. As for this man, he was interviewed and charged and remanded into custody.

Despite good sound advice given to him the day before, this man clearly could not leave matters alone and for the police to deal. He thought he could take the law into his own hands so became the author of his own destiny and lost his good character to a criminal conviction and later received a suspended prison sentence.

I can understand his predicament with the business but he had to shoulder part of the blame for relying on drink instead of failing to thoroughly check staffs actions and balance the books. The same could be said for the girl her behaviour was inexcusable also, ruining a family livelihood which not only employed her but several other people, who had all since lost their jobs as well, all because of her dishonesty. Although she made admissions under duress when abducted, she later accepted all the actions came to the surface due to her behaviour. She later reiterated her involvement for the theft in the presence of her Solicitor, as she wanted the matter to be dealt with so she could move on. Although such a large amount of money was involved it was inevitable such a stupid act involving such a series of thefts would eventually come to the surface. Her bank accounts were frozen and although not all the money was recovered civil proceedings had commenced against her. She received a sentence of imprisonment.

We had another Detective Inspector in charge at that time, who was close to the end of his service and put out to graze at our busy sub division. The trouble was he had about another eighteen months to go and still lived in the fifties, talk about dead wood coming back to haunt you. I strongly suspected the boyfriend of this woman was in on her theft involving £40,000 in monies and despite attempting several times to complete enquiries I was formally told to halt enquiries as the matter had been investigated sufficiently. I did attempt to resurrect the enquiries despite the advice but I was called into the Office and warned I would be disciplined for failing to obey a formal order. So after all he pulled rank again, not to compliment the course of justice though as in my view this was a serious criminal matter that deserved full investigation. He was the same DI who I found had thrown my expenses in the bin when he himself would claim for absolutely everything and this issue is discussed later. This Detective Inspector possibly had achieved many good results over the years and at one time was a good and efficient officer but he was well past his sell by date and could have retired at 25 years' service.

As for the Detective Sergeant who wanted to assist and get involved, my foundations for not trusting him later proved well founded and fully substantiated. Getting over my refusal to let him get involved in my case this officer, later became a team player with a Dc Geoffrey COLE who features in dealings with a murder enquiry in which he became the arresting officer. Yet less than a year later he was moved from CID into a uniform role, not the pedigree of such a fine allegedly professional and dedicated officer. Clearly the behaviour of these so called trusted officers was coming to light resulting in their well-deserved tragedies to materialise in their day of reckoning.

These officers worked with a woman detective officer who had earlier allowed me to investigate the series of thefts of newly made settees. This enquiry later escalated into a series of systematic thefts of property from the manufacturer, which all came about through just one dodgy private sale of a stolen settee which I referred to earlier. This female detective constable was a very industrious officer and had wished that I would work with her, following the promotion of WDC Myles to uniform sergeant. I had to think long and hard, I had been in CID for several years and although I felt privileged in being asked to work with her, she was single, enjoyed socialising, and it quite simply was not the lifestyle I really wanted as I was reaching towards the end of my service.

My wife had tolerated long hours and far too many periods where overtime was not a choice but a necessity to stay on duty to complete exhaustive and urgent enquiries into so many protracted and difficult crimes. In addition to these long hours we had various functions where with retirements, promotions and transfers were occurring all too often, many collections of the years where I had made donations which were just a re-occurring one way street as far as I was concerned. I therefore decided to work with another male officer which in the end was the right decision made.

With WDC Myles we both investigated the arrest of a female who was in custody together with her husband, for offences involving theft and burglary. The female prisoner had given me the odd snippet of information over the years, but was a dangerous individual and needed to be handled firmly and professionally. Some might say she was an attractive young lady, but her reputation always preceded her, which was a warning signal in itself. With a string of ex-boyfriends all of dubious character and a reputation for not being the cleanest female on the planet. This was coupled with the fact that she and her young spouse had recently committed numerous offences of crime together. Her husband too was also of the same mould equally as nasty and had untrustworthy streak written all over him.

Prior to their arrest, I had in no certain terms seriously warned the female officer teamed up with Dc COLE that she had information but advised them both of her pedigree to tread carefully as she was crafty and conniving person who could not always be trusted. This was just like some of her information, sometime accurate and rewarding other times dubious which had to be looked at from arm's length and judged on its merits. If dubious information tread very carefully or perhaps better not proceeded with for obvious reasons, but she and her husband did have their fingers in several different interesting pies. As for the detective sergeant, he also received the same strict warning about this husband and wife team. This officer with Dc COLE and the female officer all worked as a team. Whether they took my advice or not, was not my concern.

With WDc Myles we commenced interviewing the female prisoner over her involvement. She admitted her part in the crimes, but then on a taped recorded interview suddenly gave explicit information concerning the detective sergeant. She blatantly accused him of having sexual relations with her several times at her home address. As a result we stopped the interview and bought the matter to the attention of a Senior Detective officer. The facts were noted and we returned to the Interview Room and informed the prisoner of the action taken. She was later charged and bailed, along with her husband. No other allegations were made, the detective sergeant denied fully any involvement.

Whether this was true or not or if Dc COLE was involved was never established. However the damage was done and this conniving married couple established where the detective sergeant lived and confronted him in the presence of his wife. They re-iterated certain facts of what had taken place at her home, resulting in his wife moving out and taking her children with her. They later divorced. Whether or not the truth came out or not, but the damage was done. No-one is perfect in life but what was abundantly clear was the fact my advice was totally ignored which was given genuinely and in good faith. Sadly this detective sergeant suffered the break-up of his marriage, which may have already been on the rocks and the allegations made were the last straw. He later was promoted to Inspector so he finally got his wish, what a price to pay.

I arrived at work the one day on the afternoon shift and a crime report appeared on my desk to investigate, classed as Aggravated Burglary. This is a very serious crime where entry has been forced into a building in this case a dwelling house, with either a weapon of offence or where force has been used upon anyone using any article as a weapon of offence. Upon conviction this offence carries life imprisonment.

It was easy to detect that this crime had been around the office well before I came on duty, as some officers knew more about it than I did and they were very sceptical about it, or did they just not wish to get involved. Either way it fell on my shoulders to investigate. They were dubious about the circumstances and the complainant who was a solicitor's clerk lived on our area where the alleged offence happened. She worked in one of the law practices in another town on the division, where they dealt with many rogues who were appearing at various courts on criminal matters.

All I could hear was 'I don't believe that', or 'I would not touch that with a barge pole'. That was mainly the reaction I got, no wonder it ended up on my desk. I told those with negativity, 'Well are we judge and jury now. What do I just file it and do nothing. It will be investigated properly and I shall keep an open mind as to where the truth lies. To do nothing is neglect of duty and I bet some of you would just love me to be disciplined. Even more sinister what if it happens again and next time serious injury occurs or even death. So what choice do I have?' It suddenly went quiet I think I had won the argument.

Basically as far as I can recall a man knocked on the main door to the property. It was late evening and upon the young lady opening the door he immediately forced his way inside and attacking her straight away. He made threats using some item in the home I believe that he used as a weapon against the victim. She lived alone and was in her early twenties and speaking to the uniformed officers that attended was hysterical. Not physically injured as such but really badly shaken up and frightened. As far as I can recall she was accused of being responsible for some wrong doing and was grabbed violently where she was threatened with injury unless she helped them in what they wanted. Whatever the circumstances it was clear something was going in which she was possibly involved in, or was it a case the offender had got the wrong person. There was some suggestion possibly he was accompanied by another man although she did not see him.

Together with another officer we saw the victim as soon as we could and went through all the details step by step. She stated she had not done anything wrong and that she was attacked for no reason, but was utterly scared and frightened that he and his accomplice would come back. I asked if she had any idea who he was and obtained a detailed description. She stated she had seen him once before and believed she would be able to identify him again. I took a written statement from her and arranged for her to be taken by a woman detective to force Headquarters to look at photographs. She spent most of the morning there and was able to pick out a suspect, who was known to us.

The suspect turned out to be well known to our office, a nasty devious individual with numerous serious convictions for violent crime. He was very well known to Dc GLOVER. I wonder why he was not given the crime to investigate, the plot thickened, and you had to work with this office when half were still dead wood. His main friend was equally as dangerous with criminal convictions to match, all mainly for violent crime too.

Whenever this man was arrested it was always a major police operation with several uniform officers, a dog handler along with CID all visiting his home address all together. I asked my detective sergeant for assistance, who conveniently stated he was otherwise engaged. He had nothing on in my view of any importance and easily could have assisted but chose not to. I wondered why?

With Dc Mike GREEN and a young policewoman on attachment we drove to the suspect's house. Upon arrival his wife answered the door, followed by the suspect. I remained polite and introduced myself showing a warrant card. I asked if I could speak to him as a matter of importance and could we come inside. He looked around and was bewildered no other police were present. I explained it was necessary to interview him about a matter we were investigating and would he accompany me to the police station. He asked what it was about and I stated I would explain fully the facts back at the station. He invited me inside and stated, 'you've got some guts coming here normally I have half the police force here. I could give you a bloody good hiding even now if I wanted'. I stated that's up to you but that would certainly not help you and of course they all know where I am.' I addressed him by his first name and stated,' I do not work like that. I liked to keep things simple and only arrest at home when absolutely necessary'. If he chose to attack me so be it, either way it would only make matters worse and not necessary. I stated we had called without notice if he wanted to have a drink or a wash to refresh himself so long as it did not take too long as I wanted to get this over as soon as could. He obliged had a drink and came with us voluntarily to the police station.

I took him to one side and stated that being in the police station I had a duty to place him into custody for the purpose of conducting a formal interview under caution. He could have a solicitor of his own choosing and I would be completely fair with all my dealings with him. I formally arrested him for the offence and placed him into custody and his solicitor was called out also to attend. In the meantime, I was back in the CID office awaiting his arrival when I was advised there was a violent disturbance in the police station. Apparently his father had arrived and had vaulted over the station desk trying to free him and drag him out of the custody office. Other officers restrained him and he was put back into the public waiting area. I was asked to come down as he was demanding I speak to him. I immediately came down to the front office and approached where I spoke with him alone in private. I explained his son was assisting with our enquiries that he had been formally placed into custody relating to a serious allegation which I was unable to discuss. I informed I had arranged for his solicitor to attend and reassured him I would deal with him fairly but could not give any more information than that. I stated he was welcome to stay and that the solicitor would probably fill him in with all the facts later. He wanted assurance he would not be beaten up and I stated I have never met you or your son before and that was not my way of working and never would be. He seemed okay and thanked me.

I briefed the solicitor on the allegation his client was facing and after his short meeting with his client in the cells we conducted an interview. All the evidence was put to him and he denied any involvement in that he had an alibi for the time the offence was committed and would give the details later. He stated he knew the victim, as she worked for the solicitor who was representing him in the same law practice. With the allegation being serious, even though he did not make any admissions a decision was made at a senior level for him to be charged and that he should appear in custody. His previous convictions were also serious and it was suggested he could interfere with the course of justice if released. The solicitor was fine with this and despite objections he was remanded in custody to be committed to Crown Court for trial.

During the course of continued enquiries, a girl friend of the victim attended the police station and requested to see a woman detective. In confidence she stated that her friend had confided in her she had been raped by a man who was possibly an accomplice of the man who was still in custody along with all kinds of threats. She was petrified and even though she could give a partial description, she did not want to pursue it as she was scared of the consequences and the fact the person in custody had so many dangerous friends. The victim was later seen and initially denied all this happening. She then implied even if it did I will not take it any further. Despite senior officers getting involved she would not pursue it under any circumstances.

The alleged offender then provided an alibi that he was in bed with a girlfriend unknown to his wife at the time of the alleged offence. This was confirmed by his wife who stated her husband had confessed to the affair during a visit with him on remand. Something he would normally never ever do. He was eventually released on conditional bail pending the trial and no further incidents were reported.

A few weeks later we attended one of the higher tier crown courts and the trial began. The young lady gave evidence and underwent a lengthy cross examination. After hearing all the evidence, the Judge made a ruling that the jury find the defendant not guilty. He stated the witness presented her evidence to a high standard and that the police could not be criticised in any way whatsoever as they brought the case quite justifiably before the court and the identification process had been performed correctly conforming to all the rules. He based his ruling on the fact there was an element of doubt on her interpretation of the suspect, who clearly had been seen previously by her at the solicitors office when he was attending on a previous matter. There was an element of doubt she may have convinced herself this was the same person which may have been purely coincidental and as a result would be very unsafe to convict. He was free to leave the court and awarded costs.

No further incidents were reported and she later left the employment of this firm of solicitors, working for another firm well out of the area. The Judge had been informed also of the full facts. Whether or not this alleged victim was holding anything back, I did not know. Not to identify the alleged rapist was another area of contention, but bearing in mind the pedigree of these criminals that was to some degree also understandable.

The only thing that was suggested by Dc GLOVER was that she knew both men and had received from them valuable stolen property and had failed to pay them. Was this the reason for the forced entry to her home where threats were made? I believe they may have searched the premises too but this was denied. Was she raped or did she go along with it as she may have known them far more closely than she was saying. Keeping an open mind it did make sense, was this alleged victim hiding some devious activity which she was involved in. Whether this was true or not, again we did not know. It was possibly feasible or it could have been a seed planted by them in the mind of this detective to create doubt after he was far closer to these criminals than his working colleagues I was sad to say. Also coincidently to get someone to admit they were having an affair is another ploy often used by clever criminals which often can be irrefutable without other strong evidence coming to light to contradict the issue put forward. Either way I did not really have any option but to let the law take its course. It was a matter for the court to decide. I had done my job properly, without criticism and accepted the result as no slur on my integrity.

Eventually Dc GLOVER retired and one day this man who was acquitted came to station to see me. He had an associate who had been on the run for some time and was wanted in connection with a serious offence of grievous bodily harm. He had stabbed a man and was hiding from the police and he wanted me to deal with him and that he would get him to surrender to me. He stated he would come clean and was aware he was facing a heavy prison sentence. He just stated that he trusted me to be fair and bore no grievance to the previous arrest that he had been involved in. I agreed and true to his word he turned up at the police station and his friend surrendered himself to custody, He admitted the offence and was charged where the court gave him conditional bail. He pleaded guilty and as he anticipated went to prison for several years.

As for this man whom she had picked out, he had served three years for a serious warehouse burglary in another force area. Apparently he and some others had a large van and were stealing a huge amount of televisions and computers from these premises and were disturbed by police. He was approached by a police woman and he came across as being the perfect villain being caught red handed in his dirty dealings. He said, 'Fair cop, I will come quietly I will not cause any trouble'. Then whilst this officer was off guard he belted her repeatedly in the face with his fists, causing horrific injuries and rendering her unconscious. Other officers attended but they had abandoned their van and with others left the scene in another vehicle. Apparently there was evidence left at the scene, either fingerprints or something else to identify him. They later arrested him on our area where they charged him with burglary and grievous bodily harm. He pleaded guilty and was sentenced. In actual fact in my view he deserved double the sentence given to him for this deplorable attack on a young female officer. As for his colleague I would not have been surprised one instant if he had not been with him on that job. He too had numerous criminal convictions for very serious crimes of violence, and had served lengthy terms of imprisonment.

I remember dealing with an extremely nasty road accident when I was in uniform some years back just before I took control of my own residential beat. I was driving the police car and was sent to deal with this road accident. A Ford Capri had been stolen moments earlier and driven at high speed on one of the dual carriageways away from the town centre. As the stolen vehicle drove fast along a steep dip in the road, it accelerated at high speed up a hill where it was required to stop at the junction to another main road. At that time a family motor car was approaching the junction from the opposite direction. It was being driven at normal speed by a man, whose wife was seated in the front. Two young children both just under ten years were seated in the back.

As this family car was about to pass by, the stolen Ford Capri was approaching that fast the driver had lost control and it left the road for a short while and nose-dived directly into the vehicle containing the family of four. How on earth they all escaped was nothing short of a miracle, seat belts were not invented then, but it would be debateable if in this instance they would have been of any use. All were severely hurt and suffering shock and covered in blood.

The driver who was believed alone just abandoned the scene and made good his escape. There were no witnesses, to the actual accident. Emergency crews attended, ambulance and fire engine. The victims had to be cut out of the vehicle, and the other vehicle had to be disentangled from the same wreckage. This was one of the worst road accidents I had ever seen in the whole of my police career and sadly I have seen a few, but in reality it was a crime scene and warranted CID involvement but things did not work that way back then. To me it was not only a serious road accident but a very serious crime. As with a fatal road accident the victims are deceased and nothing can be done they have lost their lives. As for this family they were all in excruciating pain and screaming in agony and yet the ambulance crew could not get any access into the vehicle until the fire service had completed its task of dismantling the wreckage. Removing the stolen vehicle and using cutting equipment to get the poor family out. Although their injuries were not life threatening, amongst them they had multiple fractures and broken bones and internal injuries.

I was joined by several other police officers, including the sergeant, Inspector and dog handler. The area was searched across neighbouring fields, with patrol cars scouring the area for anyone who could have been responsible, who also may well have been injured. Despite hospital checks then and later no suspect was found attending casualty.

This road accident occurred well before the arrival of police helicopters being used by the police force, how useful that would have been back then. The stolen vehicle was checked by Scenes of crime for fingerprints but that too resulted negative. What a shame DNA was not invented back then with luck that possibly would have flushed out the offender.

I requested urgent enquiries be made at the scene where the vehicle was stolen. It had been taken from a town centre public house car park and I ask enquiries be made there just in case some information was forthcoming. The pub was packed and mainly the cliental were all from the criminal community. Sadly nothing of any use was forthcoming. The victims were all taken to the local hospital and were kept in until they each recovered. Altogether they spent between them several weeks in hospital recovering from their injuries and convalescence was much longer when they returned home. We had press releases, requesting information as to the identity of the offending driver, all meeting with a negative result.

Despite continued enquiries on every spare moment I had nothing was forthcoming. A few weeks later I established the man who was a friend of the person charged with aggravated burglary, was drinking in the town centre public house the night the car was stolen. There was some suggestion he was the thief and driver responsible. He lived in the direction the stolen car was being driven, just about a mile from where the road accident had taken place. He had convictions for joy riding and at the time was a disqualified driver and always nicked Ford Capri vehicles. I regularly liaised with CID in particular Dc TRENCH who was so thorough a detective and cooperative, feeding him continually about this awful tragedy involving the poor injured family. Despite continued enquiries he did have a well-established informant come forward with information that this was the man responsible. Dc Trench had not given his name to anyone and this source confirmed his identity as being the same person. As much as we both wanted to lock him up and convict him for this serious road accident, we had not got the slightest scrap of evidence against him. Later more than one source confirmed the same information, but it was all hearsay. This cunning devious criminal would not admit to anything unless confronted with overwhelming facts that gave him no choice, so sadly that was the end of the matter. I bitterly regretted we were not able to detect this awful crime, but I am certain in my view we found the right culprit.

All I can say is all these people who commit evil sinister crimes and get away with them, I just hope they receive just rewards another way. At the time they are at death's door about to meet their maker I sincerely wish they have repeated flashbacks of all their terrible crimes and evil they have committed. Continually wandering was there any punishment if there was indeed an afterlife. If so I would not want to be in any of their shoes facing the unknown.

This pair of well-known criminals continued to be active and were arrested several times by the regional crime squad as they resorted to committing serious crime on other divisions, and other force areas. In fact they even went across to France and carried on their trade there, but to my knowledge were never arrested abroad. This was the same pair of criminals I related to in a previous chapter, when two officers were walking together on adjoining beats where these active criminals lived. Although having patrolled their areas for a couple of years they had failed to find out who they were or even get to identify them and monitor any activities or associates. How appalling was that. Even worse in today's modern policing I would bet over half the officers working the area did not know them either.

After several years after retiring, I was with my son out one Sunday for a lunchtime drink and inside the bar of a local respectable public house. As I was getting a drink they both came up to me and spoke. I was friendly and polite and stated I had retired and that for several years I was working in the main Operating Theatres in areas of the main city. They asked if I missed my job and I explained I had seen it done it and was achieving so much job satisfaction caring for those less fortunate than ourselves. We parted on good company, not that I would ever trust them or turn my back on them. Today I still bet many police officers have never heard of these two criminals who I would imagine have not retired from their very lucrative profession.

The only time I had any real grievance with D.I. CLINTON was where a young lad was charged with Robbery. He made partial admissions but his real involvement did not add up. The more I thought about it, the more I realised it was necessary to solve the issue once and for all by having an Identification Parade. This was despite the person charged being named by a witness to the actual crime. Apparently she recognised him from her school days as both lived in the same area. I told D.I.CLINTON instinct told me something clearly did not ring true and in the interests of justice it was essential we should satisfy ourselves, as the offender had no previous convictions. If it weakened the case so be it, at least we could inform the Crown Prosecution Service and get any prosecution halted and the case discharged. It later turned out that this would have been the right course of action, but it wasn't to be.

He stated based on the evidence we were right to charge the offender as he had a case to answer. To have an Identification Parade can strength the evidence if he is picked out, but weaken it if he is not and advised against it. I had no choice I had to accept his decision but I was not at all happy with it, as it twanged my conscience.

A few weeks later we were called to Crown Court as he had pleaded not guilty and again I thought well I can only let the court decide on the issue providing justice was done in either finding him guilty or innocent if he was not responsible. If this was the case why admit any involvement. Perhaps he was naive or did so under pressure. On reflection I thought to myself, did he warrant someone being with him to give him advice, or should I have insisted he had a solicitor which he refused. We never stop learning and hindsight is always a quality we always cannot draw on.

As the defendant arrived with his family, the main witness who named him also entered the court building. Straight away she came up to me and asked if that was the young man we had arrested and charged who was standing the other side of the entrance hallway. I stated he was and she suddenly blurted out, 'Oh my God I have made a terrible mistake. It is not him, he has the correct Christian name, but it is another lad who was in my class at school. He has the same first name I just got mixed up with the surnames.' She then told me the surname of the youth she was referring to as committing the robbery. I stated I understand thank you for telling me, a genuine mistake on your part.

I immediately advised the barrister of this development and later before the Judge the case was dismissed. I went to the accused and apologised, but stated I was only following the evidence that was provided. I also explained why admit to something when you were not involved and he stated he was sorry too. Either way he was okay and the family were thankful this witness had come forward.

At the end of the day we had a robbery that was now un-detected so I continued enquiries as the witness was adamant who the real culprit was. It was just that she got the surnames mixed up. Although I had to include this information in any future file of evidence I arranged the person now suspected to attend the police station. This suspect was arrested and was on bail for other offences of theft and robbery. I advised him to have a solicitor and later during interview he admitted fully the offence. He wanted to clear his slate and this offence was one other offence outstanding. He went to court and pleaded guilty receiving custody.

Since that time the law has changed. Any issue of identification must be clarified with an Identification Parade taking place whatever the circumstances.

CHAPTER 26

MURDER INCIDENT ROOMS WHERE TEAMWORK SHOULD BE AN ESSENTIAL PRIORITY

To try and get detectives working more closely they decided to have divisional C.I.D teams and although they had the pick of most major crimes, in fairness it did produce good results, but there was still secrecy and jealousy amongst staff. Hard to believe when we are all fighting the same enemy, the common criminal whose lifestyle is continually funded by crime.

I recall one such day when I walked into the main arena where some fifty detectives were seated and working. One obnoxious detective whom we later worked with, was a DC Steven RAY who was well liked but also extremely moody and could change character in an instant to being friendly and amusing, to the complete opposite. At times he could be good fun who loved to give the banter out, but could never take it himself. Only trouble his good days were infrequent as he was forever sarcastic and miserable as if the world was on his shoulders. I recall he shouted out to me aloud in front of everyone, in attempt to grab attention. "LUNN if you get any bigger round the chest you'll need to wear a bra."

The room just exploded into laughter all at my expense, but suddenly went quiet in anticipation of my response or reply. They need not have worried as I maintained the entertainment in the highest tradition of the police force and replied back to him. "Well Dc RAY from what I hear is, if you take any more women out you'll soon need a Dog Licence."

According to the Clap-o-meter my reply was a roaring success. This detective wished he had not opened his mouth as he went bright red with embarrassment and was completely lost for words. Unknown to me however, was the fact that just the day before this man's girlfriend of several years, had packed her bags and moved out of his home forever. How sad, but I had no regrets. What do they say people in glass houses shouldn't throw stones? I kept the smiles to myself.

It is sad all the good morale created out of these events is not portrayed in everyday investigation of police work. I had moved into an office where initially there were a percentage of officers who were dead wood, together with the antics of Dc GLOVER and Dc PEGG. Several years had passed but there was always someone still there waiting to stab you in the back or steal your hard work as their own, without any scruple of remorse.

We had the murder of a Local Government Officer who had met a man whilst closeting in some local toilets. The victim was gay and was touring round looking for someone to befriend. This he did and invited the man back to his home address to participate in gay sex. All did not go according to plan as when they started to become intimate, the offender just lost it and realised he could not cope with the situation. The only way he was able to confront his behaviour was to lash out, which he did with a blunt object, crushing the skull of the man he had met, until he was dead. He then panicked and left the scene. It was not until he had failed to turn up for work the following day that a visit to the address of the victim was made and the gruesome discovery found. A murder enquiry was started and this involved several of us mixing with people from the gay community in an effort to trace the offender.

Over the years I had built up good relations with several people including the friends and family of two men living together who were openly gay and well-liked and accepted by most of the people in the neighbourhood. Through this together with another detective I was working with, we made significant progress in putting together the identity of the offender and due to both men previously giving me reliable information in the past, I had no doubt that our enquiries would be fruitful in getting a result.

Our prediction came true, after we finished duty they both later attended the police station where in our absence they provided detailed information concerning the identity of the murderer. Dc Geoffrey COLE with another officer acting on this fresh source traced the man who was duly arrested by him.

In addition to forensic evidence and the murder weapon being found, the offender eventually admitted full responsibility. As the man was charged with Murder and later documented all he could do was laugh and joke as if he had not got a care in the world and failed completely to show the slightest hint of remorse. He eventually went to Court where he was found guilty of Murder and given life imprisonment.

On refection it was good work by those involved, but I later established not all was fair and above board. Both men who supplied the information had initially attended the police station asking for my colleague and I and all this was hidden. They had taken over our initiated enquiries and dealt accordingly, normally that was fine, I did not mind that as it was not my nature to be jealous.

What I didn't cater for was the actions of Dc COLE who had transferred from another department and as stated was taking over purporting that he with another had done all the spade work which was strictly untrue. We never had a mention of our initial visit to the two men who were the final source of the information, which was under-handed in my view. Still if you wish to work like that in a team you do not survive for long as you cannot live off the backs of other people's hard work forever.

What he had were similar hallmarks of Dc GLOVER and was certainly a person who was out for himself and all the glory he could muster. I think this was a pattern that materialised from other places where he had worked and he did this on more than one occasion against other people I had dealt with in taking over. I wouldn't have minded if he had been open about it, after all I did not have a single thing that I needed to prove to anyone. I could stand up against the best of them as I had done so for several years, but most of the staff I had worked with had become friends as well as colleagues.

Dc COLE was not aware I had established the truth to where he had obtained this information in solving the Murder given by someone asking for me at the police station. On reflection although

I was annoyed by his impoliteness, I did assist in a final interview with him, but prior to this, the accused had already admitted his part earlier. I could not see the point of my involvement at this stage unless it was to address a twang of guilty conscience. The main thing was the matter had been cleared which was important for the family and friends of the deceased.

As for the Murder Team, we all attended a function held at a local licensed premises in celebration of the crime being cleared, which was usual in those days. Dc Cole and others arranged for the two gay men to attend, after all they had been so helpful and to create a bit of fun both came dressed to the 'nines' as women wearing smart outfits, wigs and full make-up with bright red lipstick. The one man was what can only be described as 'very fetching' and amazingly attractive in his get up. As for the colleague who arrived with him, he fitted the bill in his shapely attire except for the fact he still had his moustache which can never look right when purporting to be a female.

Nevertheless I just had to smile when the most attractive of the two men, went to the bar and had his arm around the younger detective in the team who worked with Dc Cole and began whispering to him 'sweet nothings'. Perhaps he was bowled over with so much attention from such a good looking woman! He certainly was engaged in deep conversation giving the impression he had pulled and even engaged in kissing this person.

It was amazing he did not recognise him as being the same person who was initially at the police station when the information was given. Especially when standing directly next to them both was the other gay man with the moustache. Clearly this young detective had a lot to learn, or did he know something that we didn't. Either way it was a good laugh, pity we had no cameras. After some twenty minutes both so called women revealed their true identity by removing their wigs, where we all fell about laughing as the young detective became as red as a beetroot in the face with embarrassment, completely lost for words and obviously very gobsmacked. Later he denied anything was untoward but the incident stuck with him for several weeks despite his continued protestations that he was acting in all innocence. In other words he either clearly knew what he was doing, or was totally shown up by his behaviour that he was once speechless. I suspected the latter.

Back on the sub-division reverting to normal duties, WDC MYLES and I had team up with the new DS Tim BOOTH who was assigned to his new partner Dc COLE. As stated we previously were an efficient working duo and I think the move was unnecessary in any case it was not the best, as it did not work as both these two new colleagues were alien in our organised approach to investigation. I think it was to stem some jealous conflict among certain staff, but also something was not quite right between this other pair as to both WDC MYLES and myself they were a little like chalk and cheese together. Out of the two DS BOOTH was more approachable and trustable.

Later my woman detective friend got promoted which she richly deserved and it was not before long I took a break from operational detective duties and commenced an Intelligence Role which I relate to in a previous chapter. DC COLE was able to work with someone else, in any case I was well shut of him, in my book sadly he was as disorganised as DC GLOVER used to be and exactly the same happened to him. Not everyone likes paperwork but if not looked after properly especially in a detective role it can result in the ultimate downfall and this coupled with stealing other staff's enquiries and informants just for glory was indeed a recipe for disaster.

This behaviour continued and several months later when all the Office were out attending a social function with our wives and all travelling together by coach, the unbelievable happened. Again Dc COLE and another well-established detective officer from the same Division had learned of a Murder which had just been reported to the police. We were all off duty and it was nothing to do with us, but no, these two wise guys just had to get involved, where they directed the driver of our coach to stop outside the house, at the scene of the murder. A uniform Police Officer was at the door and detectives at the scene were awaiting Scenes of Crime and a Forensic Team.

I couldn't believe it when they both went inside to have a look round, all as an ego trip and career boost when in actual fact it was just plain simply unprofessional. What good could they do other than contaminate the actual scene, with a strong risk of obliterating evidence in the form of foot or fingerprints or disturbing any DNA evidence. Eventually they both left and we continued on to the function, but I was damn sure I was going to divulge all that had taken place at the first opportunity with senior officers, but someone had already beaten me to the post.

I was aware both officers were to be reprimanded for their actions. Whether this played any part or not I don't know, but despite all the recognition received in the other detected murder Dc COLE was later eventually moved sideways back into a uniform role. If only his values had been more sincere all he could do was take, take, take, when the role in CID always demanded give and take coupled with honest teamwork. At times he was the most capable kind of officer and often willingly helped other staff. He clearly was deep down a nasty individual, not listening to my advice given about the husband and wife team of burglars who were indeed dangerous informants. Going into the scene of a murder against all the protocol of a Murder Investigation was so childish and immature. In addition taking credit for non-existent in depth enquiries into the murder, my colleague and I had completed in identifying the murderer and taking the glory. My comparison with him and Dc GLOVER was spot on.

In any case it was his own fault in being removed in some cases he was hard working but he loved to pick his jobs, neglecting many matters on his desk which he failed to ignore. Some being very important issues and needed proper investigation and more controversially some commitment to the people who had reported matters of crime for proper criminal investigation. On this basis he was a disgrace.

After attending the function on the evening with our wives and girlfriends we knew exactly what faced us the following morning when a Murder Incident Room was commenced. This related to the murder of a middle aged lady victim who had gone out the night previous early evening to play Bingo, but had forgotten something and returned home. Upon arrival she entered by opening the front door, but someone was already there and had gained access, believed with a duplicate key. She was immediately attacked, again with a blunt instrument and received fatal blows to the head and body, where she was found on the floor in one of the rooms in the house.

This was the same scene visited as described by the two Detectives who were off duty and out for the night with us all socially. Why do things like this happen, better to be caught red handed for burglary than face any murder charge. This is where they cross the line as it was not necessary to take anyone's life in these circumstances, but sadly happens all too often in still many cases in present day.

With the Incident Room in the process of being set up I was now in an Intelligence role where I had joined DS BOOTH. Although we had not worked long with each other we had several interesting cases between us and being a mature person it was refreshing working with someone again on the same wave length.

So the hunt was on for the offender and all avenues of enquiry were meticulously being explored. The role was completely different to the investigating side of police work, and although it was another learning curve I was pleased it was only for a short period of time before later returning as an operational detective. Like all Incident Rooms, officers are seconded from neighbouring Divisions and it was inevitable DS BOOTH was to meet with some of his former colleagues. So he did and they were having a friendly chat. He was the sort of person when he speaks positions himself close to you where you cannot escape. He talked endlessly about everything totally unimportant until you run out of excuses to escape his presence which was becoming more and more infuriating, especially when I was always an industrious sort of person. Apart from this one irritating factor, which I suppose we all have, he did however have a good sense of humour and was well liked and was good at his job. I have to admit apart from joking about his conversations he did have some good stories to tell. He just had a terrible habit of striking up lengthy conversations at inappropriate times.

I remember he had been talking for up to nearly three quarters of an hour and was stopping other people from working, including himself which was a bit annoying. I remember picking up a chair and pushing it across the room towards him and saying,' Well if you don't wish to work you may as well sit down and talk. I'll remind you, this is a Murder Enquiry.' That did it. He had not got an answer, unless he was begging for further criticism and finally he started to do some work. He just needed to get his priorities right as time for socialising was after work or when the murder was cleared. There was an atmosphere for a short time, but miraculously I don't think you could ever offend him and things soon got back to normal, even if I had been a little blunt.

Eventually a former lodger who had stayed at the house a couple of years previous had been traced. His fingerprints were found in incriminating circumstances and he was subsequently arrested and later admitting to being responsible but denying murder. He was charged and pleaded not guilty to Murder where the jury rightly found him guilty. He received the mandatory life sentence.

CHAPTER 27

TENURE OF POST AND ITS CONSEQUENCES

When I first completed my police probation in 1972, the doorway was open to new horizons. I could take my promotion exams, or decide to eventually transfer to the Traffic Department, Dog Branch, or Scenes of Crime Department. In addition there was the Criminal Investigation Department or CID branch which ultimately offered further avenues with attachments to Regional Crime Squad and Drug Squad, or I could continue in my current role. After all I had barely any real major experience and you cannot grow an old head on younger shoulders overnight. In any case I was new in a job I loved and learning and gaining experience became an utmost priority.

Moving to my own beat was a privilege back then being so young in service where I enjoyed a mixture of unusual offences. Upon transferring in a Metropolitan police area was completely different although comradeship was exactly the same if not better. Working such a busy multicultural area also provided me with new skills providing enormous knowledge in investigating all kinds of crime and different offences. The most important talent that I developed was being able to thoroughly investigate activities of criminals, assess and evaluate evidence combined with intelligence where I had a successful reputation of being a good thief taker. I always felt comfortable treating all individuals in a fair and honest way including both victims and offenders alike.

Transferring or being promoted into CID as it was classed at that time, as a detective was my ultimate goal where every day was a completely different challenge which sometimes pushed you to the limit with heavy workloads and long hours. This role was not something that many police officers would wish to swap with, but then it was their choice as they too were in the kind of role they enjoyed within the police service. Most officers in CID all came with different qualities and agendas. Having become fully established and efficient detectives, some were on the promotion ladder for sergeant and above. Other members were encouraged to develop their skills into drugs, serious crime or fraud. A small selection of CID staff were just happy fulfilling their role as detective using all their talents on an everyday basis in detecting crime until they retired.

Many I have known were as keen on their last day of service as they were their first. They were first class officers of all ranks like many of our uniform colleagues, who had completed their careers and were able to hold their heads high in the true wording of reaching a profound sense of achievement.

In all police forces within the UK all senior officers, being above the rank of sergeant could remain in the police service until the age of 60 years before retirement was compulsory. As for sergeants and constables uniform and plain clothes had to retire at 55 years. In fairness anyone serving 25 or 30 years of a busy hard working career, had seen it done it and should have got the ticket, but everyone had different ideas. As with life there is always something to look forward to within the future, especially using all your skills and drive to travel in whichever direction is attractive to each individual.

We had a Chief Constable in charge of our force, who introduced Tenure of Post, possibly with some higher intervention from above. This policy was not adopted by all police forces, mainly the large Metropolitan areas followed suite as the London Police were one of the first. This meant that if you had chosen your career to be in a specialist department it no longer applied, as after a decided period of time you were required to return to normal uniform policing duties. This I think was one of the most demoralising of issues ever to face the police force and resulted in a mass exodus of personnel retiring. If someone had chosen a career path such as Scenes of Crime, Dog Section, Traffic, or CID as was widely encouraged early in my service, it would have resulted in devastating consequences for that individual. In selecting this career path it meant in most cases the right person interested and suitable for the job was correctly found. In majority of cases that person went on to become hard working, successful and fully experienced in such post and if not there was always the alternative of being returned to a uniform posting.

What was the point of transferring a valuable hard working and loyal traffic officer to uniform shift duties when he had experience in motorway policing, vehicle inspection and other unique qualities. Exactly the same applies in the case of moving a detective to doing uniform duties involving traffic duty at a busy crossroads or attending domestic issues between parents.

All these officers being supervised by a police Inspector with far less service and experience, who has never completed a major criminal investigation and only knows how to give orders. What a complete waste of talent and experience.

If any police officer had decided to go down the career path of being specialised, then he could be moved back any way on the whim then of a senior officer just because your face did not fit with no redress whatsoever unlike demotion. No one would ever mind if the officer was lazy and failing to work efficiently, but not against the opposite kind. The old saying but very true words of just like an old machine, if it works leave it alone. Could you imagine tenure of post in the Nursing profession, Fire Service or any other major industry there would have been complete uproar amongst all the work force. I cannot help thinking that it was because some senior officers felt seriously threatened although this would most certainly be denied. Many had in my view climbed the promotion ladder too quickly and lacked many qualities of other experienced staff. This is a view reflected by many former senior and lower rank officers alike who have now since retired.

In most police forces you could not escape the fact that a good experienced detective was on a par to at least a uniform officer of the rank of Inspector. Not that anyone of that rank would agree, but they would be quick enough to try and pick your brains. Just because they were senior Officers did not mean they were superior, which some clearly fantasised they were. However such tenure of post never applied to senior officers being reduced in rank, moved or demoted unless due to discipline. It was if upon their 12 month period of probation to demote them, on the basis of their inefficiency was an affront to the promotion boards.

It became apparent some younger officers were being promoted to Sergeant and Inspector with less than six years' service, with Chief Inspectors and Superintendents also being promoted much younger. There were a few exceptions where some young officers learned quickly and adapted admirably, but this was the exception rather than the rule, with so many I feel who were lacking in the many natural qualities our predecessors carried. It is easy to see why this occurred looking back on several of the stories I have told where it is clear and absolutely obvious of officers being over promoted. As stated back in the amalgamation of police forces in 1974 nearly everyone who had passed their exams made it into the next rank, some to their credit but many regardless of experience or suitability. Tenure of post was principally in my view introduced where some senior officers who had rapid promotion were clearly very inexperienced in various areas of basic police work and did not like officers of lower rank having more knowledge or skills than them. In any case there was always plenty of movement between departments created through general wastage with retirement, promotion and transfers for it to be totally unnecessary.

I can and have given several examples involving many good staff, especially Dc TRENCH who was one of the loyal and hardworking officers, whom I as well as Monty and other officers had the pleasure of working with many times over our careers. His experience reflected in the detection of very serious sexual offences as outlined in Chapter 15 and Chapter 5. This detective Officer had spent twenty plus years in CID and would never fit in the deadwood category that fitted so many other policemen yet alone some senior Officers. Dc TRENCH had attained 30 years at the age of fifty and wanted to stay on another five years and was still as keen as mustard with an enviable energy and talent for crime investigation and could easily lose many of his senior contemporaries on this level playing field. This extension of service was acceptable and approved, but because of tenure of post it could only be served in uniform, where he would work under several less qualified officers of various ranks many of whom he could easily eat for breakfast. What a complete waste of such an experienced officer. Such a talent that was soon zapped up by defence lawyers who offered him a job immediately against ever employing the wasters that created the rules in the first place.

Many officers of similar calibre who also chose this same career path achieved identical pedigrees of success, in which they too should have been very proud. Unfortunately they left these Metropolitan Police Forces in droves, some establishing separate careers, others justifiably through ill health caused through stress due to so much upheaval and negative attitude in uncompensated wasted careers and hard work.

Less than five years later with serious crime on the increase, they had to bring back into service many ex-detectives and other experienced uniform Officers to support the thin police line in a civilian role, how sad was that. Clearly their policy of Tenure of Post was a disaster and those responsible in my view for this all had egg all over their faces. Some existing staff were lacking in the necessary experience required putting those with any real ability under pressure. At one time the average length of service for a detective constable working in CID was three years in some locations of these police forces. Nothing wrong with that as they will learn with experience but it becomes difficult when there is a restriction of staff available able to pass on their skills. Hopefully since that time things have improved.

The people responsible for such decision had caused so many good officers to resign or retire under health grounds. Needless to say the Chief Officer at our local force at the time, who implemented this and the closure of so many police social clubs, received his knighthood so well done to him. What he did to the existing high moral never recovered. The annoying issue was many of our smaller and efficient local police forces left their personal unchanged and maintained existing higher moral for everyone and had improved efficiency which in itself spoke volumes.

Now here we are in 2017 and guess what, the London Metropolitan Police Force has 600 vacancies for detectives. Undoubtedly this process will continue in other large Metropolitan police forces too. This speaks volumes that many officers from the uniform rank and file who did not want promotion did not want to bother with CID to be moved back into uniform some years later, just too demoralising. As a result of this they have now put out job vacancies for members of the public with the right qualifications to apply for the post of detective constable without ever served in uniform or gained any experience from that role. Will they be exempt from Tenure of Post, absolutely. How can they be put back into uniform when they have never done it in the first place?

What an absurd waste of money training all these officers who had achieved very high standards, against those promoted being members of the Masonic lodges. This was an absolute joke, being over promoted even more so as they climbed the ranks. All which can be verified by decent hard-nosed detectives and police officers who carried the rest of them who were in-experienced and in-capable of achieving results. That's where tenure of post should have been applied routing out all these wasters who had been over promoted and were an embarrassment to all.

Now today, believe it or not I was informed recently, whether it is correct or not, these Metropolitan police forces are wasting even more money. After a severe reduction of staff implemented by the Government, many have had no alternative but to hire ex-working detectives through an employment agency. This to make up the extreme shortfall created by Tenure of Post something they will always deny, but irritatingly true. No different to the Nursing profession and possibly Social services and Education, all using employment agencies to fill posts with high quality staff and with enormous exuberant fees. This including the police force, no wonder we are in one total mess today in policing. Too politically correct, and under the thumb in my view from Government control or intervention. Long gone are the days of high profile policing, where the criminal was always afraid of arrest for every crime committed. To fire brigade policing taking details, reporting crime and doing nothing, to enforced performance targets all created in my view because of poor supervision. Clearly they have recruited some who are incapable of being efficient police officers. Education is important, but having an honest background with a good head on a recruits shoulders combined with drive and tenacity to succeed is just as important. As well as being able to think on your feet make sensible decisions and most of all being cable of profiling the movements of all criminals and other offenders is a priority.

Obviously some recruits will have the right qualifications and may do well but all the degrees in the world cannot replace common sense and gut instincts that come with local knowledge and experience. Something the modern police force today seriously lacks. Other recruits will just be there just for the money, dictating what hours they work and having the same qualities of many who were classed as graduate entries who never get the grasp of basic police work and are carried in their profession by the more dedicated and experienced officers. Many of the qualities and examples I have included in the various stories that I have written.

This just shows what a ridiculous policy Tenure of Post was, although this would never be admitted. Causing mass exodus with many leaving the job causing so much upheaval and demoralisation in being put back into uniform. So many fully experienced officers with their talents wasted, from Dog Handlers, Traffic Officers, Scenes of Crime, Fraud Squad and Regional crime Squads, and of course many hardnosed, hardworking detectives and many officers of various specialised squads and departments. Many of these fully dedicated officers, knew their traffic motoring skills, dog handling control following scents of criminals. Along with visits to crime scenes securing and preserving evidence. Detectives who knew their patch, and liaised well with uniform colleagues. Regularly identifying all criminals actively committing crime, and those who were also career criminals.

All because some senior officers who were threatened by those in lower ranks having more experience and common sense in the career path they chose. Some of these staff would never have been capable of filling these roles anyway and when you look at the reduction of experienced officers all over the country, I feel the police force is under more pressure than ever before and is in one almighty mess. Thank God for those brave and dedicated officers who do mainly dangerous and unseen work that helps justify the existence of so many inexperienced officers.

To add insult to injury, in my view, now direct entry to the police force being open to new recruits to join as senior officers with absolutely no experience whatsoever. I suppose they can get away with this now as many already in these posts who have been over promoted have hardly any real experience anyway in my book and are allowed to learn by their mistakes, but at what cost to fellow colleagues and victims alike. What a shambles, we appear to be definitely heading in the totally wrong direction.

I am sure there are many suitable people in high management positions in the private sector, but most of these are already working in the no blame, no responsibility culture and being very handsomely paid for it too, along with annual bonuses and other perks never available to lower staff. I wonder how they will address the strict Discipline Code which applies to all officers when the rules have been breached or not put into practice, or have failed in their position of authority to supervise correctly any investigation or incident. Perhaps they will try legal aid and hide behind a Barrister or Solicitor and say absolutely nothing, then inevitably where possible sue the police force like so many others for exuberant amounts of money. Just like their colleagues in other civilian posts.

What a shame we could not promote people based on their real experience and natural qualities who have continually proved themselves in the post they are successful in and for a change definitely give real value for money.

I cannot help thinking, in my view, too many senior politicians in Government are running all the main everyday policing operations, something which should be left to individual Chief Constables responsible for their areas. Like Religion, Policing should never be mixed with politics, the law is the law for everyone to adhere to and no-one should ever undermine that authority.

CHAPTER 28

MEMORABLE FUNNY MOMENTS WORKING IN CID

Through majority of my service I have enjoyed the privilege of working with some of the most experienced senior police officers, who had excellent organisational skills in creating motivation and giving credit in rewarding hard police work and instilling discipline when necessary. Shrewd forthright reliable and trustworthy, born leaders who would not suffer fools lightly, who had no time for tittle tattle behind peoples backs. They were unique and would stand by you if you were in the right. Sadly these characters were few and far between, and an ever decreasing commodity as younger and less experienced staff joined the ranks.

One of the better soldiers was a Detective Inspector CLINTON whom I have referred to previously. He was always approachable, a good practical policeman himself, who understood the difficulties facing an operational detective in every day policing. It was always a breath of fresh air when he was in charge he always drew the best from everyone and for all the time I worked with him the morale was as high as the ceiling.

I remember going to his office one day in a deeply serious manner, albeit this part of my character was in disguise as my objective was to challenge him over unfairness between the ranks. It stemmed over a certain issue where I insisted we all have lockers in the office as we had nowhere private for our clothing and personal items. He listened sympathetically and I pointed out how comfortable he was in his office, as he had his own personal wooden wardrobe. So I then said, "What are you going to do about it then Sir?" He replied, "Absolutely nothing, now fuck off and stop wasting my time." I left the room unsurprised after all I was only winding him up, but I was determined not to let this matter go away.

The next morning before he came into work I put all my belongings into the one side of his wardrobe, in readiness to continue with my plan. He arrived and later that morning I went to go out to continue enquiries calling into his office. I said "Morning Gaffer, how are you this morning." He made his usual friendly reply, until I went up to the wardrobe in the corner of his room and he said, "What the fuck are you doing." I said, "It's alright don't worry Alex, from now on you are sharing my wardrobe with me. Make sure you keep things tidy." He said, "Like fucking hell you will." I said, "I know my rights, under Health and Safety all staff must be afforded lockers or wardrobes. You can share mine until you get one Sir, I will see you later."

I just walked out in hysterics thinking all my stuff would be thrown out. When I returned later all was still in place and he stated he would see what he could do. I wasn't really bothered anyway as it was just a good laugh. Anyway he had the last laugh because three years later and we were still without lockers.

Just like when I got my Long Service and Good Conduct Medal from the Chief Constable. With the medal I also had sets of ribbon denoting the significance which was to be sewn onto uniform, but being in plain clothes it didn't apply. So I got the ribbon and with bulldog clips I attached a ribbon to each of the lapels on the front of my coat.

I walked into Detective Inspector CLINTON's Office again and said, "I have now been awarded the Police Long Service and Good Conduct medal for having been a good serving policemen for over 20 years. I now wish to be treated with some God damn respect." He said, "That appreciated Dc LUNN now fuck off." So much for that, it was good to be awarded with a medal on behalf of the Queen, God if only she had known how I was treated.

He was open to bribery though as a few months later I was due to attend a Senior Detective Refresher Course residential for three weeks and really did not want to go. It was Easter and he said he would pay me to work the Bank Holiday on Good Friday. I said, "If you can let me work the Friday then you can give me the Monday as well. He mumbled to himself and sniggered and said," Go on then." Deal done, I paid for it though as I had the hardest weekend working, as the cells were full with all kinds of criminals who had committed a wide range of offences. Still at least the time went quick and the money compensated for the cost of socialising whilst in attendance on the course.

The funniest memory was when I was dressed up as Father Christmas and we all went to the Indian Restaurant. We were all off duty from the office as another Station was covering, but it was one the best and most memorable of parties. We had all walked to the location taking a borrowed shopping trolley of beers, lagers, selection of spirits and house wine. We used to know how to have a good time. In my sack were some of the most disgusting presents imaginable, all carefully selected by the DI and myself.

As I stood up handing them out, I gave the perfect presentation, a telephone Directory for one colleague, stating "You are such a boring bastard, now go on have a good look through and see if you can ring some poor old fucker up." WDC MILES had an associate detained in prison and we gave her a free Visiting Pass. I had handed out majority of the presents, some of the more disgusting ones I cannot even comment on.

For another colleague DS BOOTH his present was an ill-fitting shirt which we had purchased from a charity shop, which to his surprise came in more useful than he would ever realise. When I had finished, he stood up and said, "Hi Santa have a Christmas drink on me." I saw that he had one of my shoes as I was wearing wellingtons and he passed my shoe over which was completely full of beer. Big mistake I was on a make shift stage and higher than him, it was inevitable where it was going to end up, I had the perfect aim as I poured it directly over his head and shoulders.

Now you don't see Santa do that very often, the place was in hysterics, as it went all over DS BOOTH drenching him and completely soaking all of his shirt and tie. He had no choice but to wear his present in which he looked utterly ridiculous and bursting at the buttons. He took it all well, he had to he had no choice.

We all eventually left and I remember the next morning waking up. It was my day off and I had burned all the side of my lower arm. I had put my arm round the metal Balti dish and despite it being red hot at the time of my inebriation I had never realised contact had been made with the skin, or even felt it. The alcohol obviously was a good local anaesthetic. The funny part when I got home having been given a lift the lights were out and I went next door in case my wife was visiting. The young 4 years old boy answered the door and his mother was present and confirmed that my wife was not there. I returned home and shortly after my wife joined me she had been with one of the other neighbours.

Next day, my wife she spoke to the lady of the house I initially visited and she recalled the conversation that had taken place. She became aware I had called there looking for her just shortly before she arrived home. She just burst out in hysterics as she started to tell me just what the little 4 years old boy came out with. He said, 'Pissed as a Parrott he was'. Obviously referring to my demeanour and we both could not stop laughing. Imagine some couples they would have horrendous domestic quarrels and here my lovely wife was laughing at the very appropriate comment that was made. Marriage does not come better than that. Of course at the first opportunity a meal for two was arranged on her at my expense.

Today some police forces send Christmas Cards to suspected villains stating comments such as, "We know that you are active and we are watching you." This sort of nonsense in my book is a complete waste of time, better to build evidence and give them a nice surprise instead by feeling their collars even better if done on Christmas Day.

Then we had DI MOUNT my first boss when I went into CID who was there to sort out all the dead wood. With most of the staff in need of a cultural change, this was soon provided. Dc GLOVER and his cronies all used to drink at the same public house and there was the Licensee with all different road signs removed from all areas of the country and displayed throughout his premises. His punters used to steal them and he paid out in order to add to his dishonest collection.

DI MOUNT was a man after my own heart, he had to sort the wheat from the chafe. In the presence of all the staff, on his first invited presence in the public bar Dc GLOVER decided to impress his new chief of CID and introduced the licence of this establishment to his new boss. However he could never anticipate how this meeting would backfire so much in his face. This Detective Inspector immediately but politely told the licensee to get his coat on, as he was under arrest for handling or receiving stolen property. After all no one was above the law and the licensee was openly bragging about his customer's antics. Even better Dc GLOVER was instructed to deal and he had no choice but to interview his former drinking partner. What a way to show who was in charge. Dc GlOVER clearly had egg all over his face. It was all resolved with the publican attending court, where he was fined and naturally lost his licence and indeed his job running the public house. All property which proved to be extremely expensive, being restored to the various local authorities concerned.

Again we had another issue where a police officer was suspected of stealing cigars from the bar of the police club. He would be working nights and rumour had it, despite being a member of the committee, he was regularly taking products without paying. Unknown to staff, video monitoring was installed and the officer was caught red handed. He was then interviewed by two senior officers and had been directed to attend the station whilst being at home after finishing the night shift. When confronted about not paying, he referred to a pre-written note in his tunic stating he had taken the cigars and had intended to pay later. Officers went to his home to retrieve the note which obviously had been all cleverly well thought out by him. It's a pity such ingenious thinking could not have been put to practical police work, but then again he was more of a sports enthusiast than an operational police officer.

They had both sadly jumped the gun and had egg all over their faces. In reality they should have created a pattern over a short period of time and recorded all sequence of events. This then would have cooked his goose with no promised payments ever forthcoming coupled with no mention to anyone of taking cigars. His excuses would have fallen on deaf ears. It was surprising how naive the investigating staff were, as by following this course of action this corrupt officer he would have been guilty completely of theft. Whether or not he was responsible they could not confirm, as there certainly was not sufficient evidence to formulate any charges. He was moved anyway to another division and normally would have been taken off operational duties, but he hadn't patrolled the streets for many years.

This was another officer who had found a cushy little role for himself whilst majority of other good staff carried him. So he was moved to the Courts complex on this adjoining division where his role today is completed very successfully by civilian staff. Hindsight is always a lesson that we all learn by our mistakes the annoying thing was this officer used to participate in all aspects of sport and this certainly came before police work, that's if he ever did any. Just a complete waster, in my view I had not ever seen any decent police work done by him in over 15 years. He was paid the same as us all and in my view, was working under false pretences, yet there were plenty like him. Why put yourself in any kind of predicament which involves suspicion of being dishonest.

He had this position in the courts and I remember seeing him in the police room one day as I went in preparation for a trial. He always made a joke of C.I.D. and other hard working policemen and whenever he could, would try to run most police officers down. Payback time, in front of the whole room which was full with staff, I asked him if he knew where the cigar machine was. All went quiet with him becoming red faced and to add to his pedigree I said I was going into one of the Courts and if he wanted to follow me I stated I would show him where the witness box was situated. He hadn't got an answer for that either, no wonder I don't believe he had stood in one since the creation of decimalisation.

CHAPTER 29

A SELECTION OF
INTERESTING MURDERS

Murder today sadly is commonplace, accepted, tolerated, committed through hatred or greed but affects everyone. It involves the friends and family of the deceased who are also victims, including the family of the accused, everyone is traumatised and all suffer alike. No one wins. All that is inflicted is a lifetime of pain, which for some never ever goes away. Some people quite rightly belief an eye for an eye, meaning a life was taken so the offender should pay with their life. This decision can be difficult and people will debate forever on the rights or wrong of it. Certainly with cold blooded murder and serial murders the argument becomes stronger. Where the answer is, I don't honestly know but either way there appears no deterrent.

When I was a child I was bought up to be law abiding and back then people were executed for murder. Just the thought of this, when a child, of someone being executed just made your blood run cold with fear. In fairness the offence was always headlines in the press and news on the radio and television so there was no escape in not having the slightest knowledge. Right up until the moment of execution. Then we had the death penalty abolished and the sentence was mandatory, life imprisonment.

Today there are more murders than ever and the sentences are ever decreasing, as if it all goes into a multi-marketing package to get the best deal on the length of sentence. Sometimes justice is served, sometimes not.

I suppose we are all here for a reason and for some, a lesson has to be learned. Perhaps forgiveness should be more forthcoming, especially where a sentence has been served without protestation, but only when total remorse is revealed by the offender and all is believed without doubt. All I know is back when I was a child and people were hung, I vowed I would never, ever, lower myself to commit such an act and believe it or not, my principles haven't changed. I could just not ever do it, just like so many other people in this world. For some it's a fine line that is crossed where they lose control but no matter what the excuse, to take someone's life, unless in an act of self-preservation is totally wrong. That is where you have to live with your conscience and I am sure no matter what the punishment, whether you ask for forgiveness or not, you have to live with this every day of your life, until the time comes that you meet your maker.

Dealing with murder can be intriguing but basically it is a sudden death of a person killed with intent, involving wounding or grievous bodily harm. So the enquiry takes on the form of any other investigation such as grievous bodily harm with intent, but the victim is not here to give any statement, so that's where the competent skills of the qualified Pathologist, and Forensic Teams have such a major part to play. With DNA evidence becoming more and more accurate, this is now extremely vital, together with close circuit television cameras. Playing the role of Detective and Coroners officer is a combination I feel all officers should experience which together is excellent groundwork for C.I.D.

Over the years there have been miscarriages of justice in many cases of crime, but none more serious than being wrongly convicted for murder. I suppose for as many that have got off on appeal we have to believe that all were innocent, or is it a case they have got off on a technicality or not been truthful in the first place and that some are still guilty, or where some are just plainly innocent. On this basis the abolition of the death penalty is fully justified, however there is a strong argument for child and serial killers or where horrific torture preceded murder for the death penalty to be restored. After all advances in all forms of DNA have proved invaluable in the detection of all serious crimes, in many cases conclusively proving guilt without any shadow of doubt. In addition any other set of circumstances surrounding other serious or brutal murders, based on overwhelming evidence involved, could be considered by a panel of Judges for final outcome of sentences. Unfortunately we all understand that in society here and throughout Europe we have a collection of seriously weak Judges who would never participate in considering the death sentence.

For this to take place however the Human Rights Act would most certainly have to be repealed but then that's another issue we could discuss all day. All I know if it was put to the vote of the people majority of the public would definitely vote for abolishment or strict amendment of the Human Rights Act and the death penalty would be restored overnight. A lot of do-gooders in politics believe they do an excellent job and maybe some do with certain issues, but I feel we have crossed the line completely where today there is no respect, discipline or deterrent to crime, especially with prisoners who re-offend. All I know is, for as much as these kind of people need help guidance and support, it has to be balanced with a strict course of punishment for those who deliberately fail to accept the alternative.

Today there are tremendous pressures on the police who only have a given time to keep people in custody and quite rightly cannot charge without sufficient evidence. When I first joined the police force it was unheard of for a person strongly suspected to be responsible for murder, to be given police bail pending further enquiries to return at a later date to a nominated police station. Yet as time went by especially in my early years in CID, it became a natural consequence of events. Today it is a regular practice as officers are continually working against the clock which starts as soon as a person is in custody. The only problem is in my view, the defence can use the excuse to state that the offender was not a danger to the public, whilst out on bail, especially where there is no repeat performance. Nothing should diminish the grotesque horrors or main ingredients of the crime when final sentencing of a guilty person is made.

In most major television programs we always see the senior interviewing officer as being a Detective Chief Inspector or above. This was true many years ago but for the last ten years of my service and to present day, majority of all interviews are undertaken by Detective Sergeants and Constables. This makes real sense, as senior officers have a major role in running and taking charge of the enquiry, using their administration and organisational skills. Interviewing of prisoners and witnesses is a major part of a detective's working day, their basic bread and butter stuff, to which they are well tuned in to, providing an experienced professional performance, whereas senior officers in this regard, due to their job description, are a little out of touch with.

One such case of murder was where the body of a woman was found at the family home. It was initially a suspected suicide, as the deceased a married lady had used rope tied onto the door handle and thrown over the other side where a noose was round her neck and death by hanging was suspected. In addition her bible had been left open half way, as if she had prayed before taking her own life. But things did not ring true, she was of Catholic religion and suicide is a totally unacceptable practice. In addition to this she was of Italian origin. The husband was subsequently arrested on suspicion of murder and interviewed by senior officers. He denied all knowledge and after being in custody for a substantial period of time was given police bail.

Forensic evidence later came back of an incriminating nature and a few days after, the husband was re-arrested. Whilst on bail he had been allowed access to his three children, wrongly or rightly. With hindsight in my opinion he should not have been released at all and perhaps the forensic process could have been expedited. In any case he finally admitted he had made up the whole scenario in that he had strangled his wife and faked suicide by tying her onto the door.

Whilst on police bail he went back to live at the family home fortunately he loved his children, but in my view at this stage of the murder enquiry they were extremely vulnerable as the pressures of what he was hiding could have played on his mind and easily resulted with further tragedy, but that was only my view which was not accepted by senior officers at the station. A strange development was found with this case, as I had arrested his nephew a year earlier for burglary offences and when completing this lad's antecedence he stated his father, who was a brother of the murderer, had committed suicide a few years before, death being due to hanging. Perhaps there was something in the family genes that centred on this morbid way of terminating life. There was no doubt of this person's intentions in murdering his wife, the mother of his three children. He pleaded guilty and was sentenced to life imprisonment. Due to him being released on bail and spending time with his children, encouraged grounds for appeal. This said and the case was later reheard and reduced to manslaughter and after serving a relatively short period he was released from prison. He later again had custody of the children. Whether this was the right or wrong decision who am I to say. I often wonder if he was not given bail during the enquiry, if he would have stayed convicted of murder.

A year later we had another murder where the husband had beaten his wife of over 40 years with a handmade wooden baton. Nothing was apparently wrong in the marriage and the husband spent majority of his time in the tool shed in the garden. Unknown to his wife the man was premeditating murder as onto the lathe he was making the wooden baton, as he had decided this was to be the weapon he would use. He beat the poor woman about the head and face in that she was totally unrecognisable and subsequently died of her injuries.

He was arrested and believe it or not, gave a full account of all his actions, right up to the final deed. He was sentenced to life imprisonment, but again a perfect example where no one wins. Both sides of the family including surviving parents, children and grandchildren all had to rebuild their lives with the loss of a loved one and the imprisonment of another. I believe a few years later the husband was finally transferred to a Mental Health Unit, clearly not a case for instigation of the death penalty.

We had another murder which involved a young man in his twenties. Quite sad, but then was he the author of his own destiny. For a period of well over two years he was behind all kinds of serious crime in the neighbourhood where he lived, from theft to robbery and aggravated burglary. He basically terrorised the community and although he was arrested and charged with various offences, his involvement was always minimised, when in fact he was the initiator and brains behind the events that occurred.

His main target would be the homes of old people where he would threaten them with violence in return for payment of their life savings and this was blackmail of the most serious kind. His method was mainly picking on the vulnerable and was a form of guarantee the police would not possibly be involved, or being old and infirm people their recollection of events may result in being confused. It was not until after his murder that many of these matters were reported to the police which plainly showed how terrified he had made his poor victims, who had paid money some serious amounts to quell his evil threats.

One of these same crimes however he decided to approach a man younger than himself, in his early twenties who lived alone in a one bed room flat. Like with all his victims he would enter their homes initially just to talk, where the conversation would become more sinister resulting in him making threats to maim or cause serious harm, if his demands were not met. Clearly he appeared very cool and calculated in planning his every move and was well out of control. However when he returned a couple of days later to the same address, to collect monies which he been promised through threats and intimidation, he was to have the surprise of his life, his death. He had made a pre-determined time for revisit and was allowed into the man's house. He had demanded the sum of several hundred pounds, to be paid by the victim, which of course the young man just had not got access to.

As a result of this form of attempted robbery and blackmail, unknown to the offender the victim's father was in the adjoining room lying in wait to come to his son's defence when necessary. When he threatened the young man with a knife the father suddenly appeared and told him, 'you live by the sword so you can die by the sword.' He had a ten inch Vietnamese razor sharp fishing knife and rammed it deep under the offender's ribs, twisting and pushing hard as it went into his upper chest in an attempt to stop any attack on his son. The offender stumbled from the house just managing to climb into a waiting car driven by an unknown accomplice and was taken a short distance to a nearby hospital. As he struggled to get out of the vehicle his condition was rapidly deteriorating but managed to get inside on foot into Accident and Emergency Department, where he fell onto the floor in a bungled heap and drew his last breath. He was found to be DOA meaning Dead on Arrival. The man's father was arrested and admitted self-defence, however he was charged with Murder and later was found guilty and sentenced to life imprisonment. On appeal it was reduced to Manslaughter, followed later by a further appeal where Self Defence was allowed and he was finally released.

Although I can say every murder is sad, in this case, no law abiding person I ever met, would ever say it was not self-inflicted to some extent. All the local criminals came out in droves to attend his funeral and rumour had it one of the biggest villains in the area financed the whole proceedings. In any case as a pure epitaph glorifying his nasty criminal career his family who were also suffering, would have loved to have written on his tomb that he robbed the rich to give to the poor, but on that basis it was possibly an insult to a proper Robin Hood. The deceased was pure evil in his commission of his crimes and in a way received his very own death sentence. All I know is that crime in the area he last lived, diminished completely shortly after his death and this in itself spoke volumes.

The great challenge of being a police officer and certainly a detective was that you never knew what to expect next. I was always totally committed with high volumes of work, with lists of jobs to do, and persons to arrest, all which had to be prioritised. A perfect example of this, was one Saturday evening I was about to take my wife out, together with her parents, when I made the mistake of answering the telephone. Not that I mean that the job always came first, but the night had to be cancelled as I had to report immediately for duty.

I attended the police station, where I discovered we had the murder of a young man in his early teens, who had been the victim which involved a fight between two Asian gangs at a large social event where the Mayor of the town was also present. Several people on both sides were in possession of knives. Altogether at least twenty men were detained in hospital some with life threatening injuries, but fortunately all survived.

At the police station were several hundred people who had all been to this entertainment event where the incident had occurred. It became apparent that possibly 700 people were involved and initially no one appeared to be telling the truth. At the time of the murder it transpired we had 699 suspects, all of whom tried to tell us they were in the toilets with the deceased lying stone cold on the dance floor. It was decided a quick brief interview was held with all, obtaining details of their identity. Where anyone was found with injuries or blood on their clothing, they were immediately arrested for ancillary offences of assault. So in addition to the deceased, and twenty plus injured people in Hospital, there were a further fifty men arrested and placed into custody. In addition we certainly had our work cut out with several hundred witnesses still to be spoken to on a thorough basis, as no one was coming forward with a clear picture of exactly what had taken place.

I did not realise that this enquiry would last at least four months and this meant all my existing work had to remain untouched for me to pick up again, except for essential matters which were redirected to other staff. Is that pressure or is that pressure, but there was not a thing I could do about it. I just thrived on the adrenaline factor of dealing with everything that I could, and let everything take its course.

Eventually as each day went by we finally pieced together all the ingredients. Working on this enquiry I had enormous pleasure in working with an Indian Detective Sergeant, who apart from being extremely intelligent, with a nose for sniffing out liars and detecting crime, was well versed in writing, reading and speaking nearly all of the Asian languages we were ever likely to come across. This was an absolute necessity and was of the highest priority to aid the enquiry in a positive way. He was born in England and could not have presented a better example for all those who originated from his parent's country land. In addition to all these qualities he had a perfect understanding of the English language and had a sense of humour to match. Everywhere we went in pursuit of those responsible for the murder whenever anyone spoke out of turn whilst being questioned or spoke another language in our presence to someone else, he immediately picked up on the issue and addressed it. Slowly but slowly we were able to piece together the sad events of that evening and get to the truth of the matter but it was initially a little like pulling teeth to get at the truth. I wished he had worked with me full time. During the four months we were together we bonded a working relationship that was to last for several years later until he transferred elsewhere. I also became an expert on selecting good Indian food. Apart from several people being arrested and interviewed on suspicion of murder, we eventually narrowed down the list of main suspects to a total of three who were finally charged with the murder. In the end following a trial at Crown Court, due to knives being used by all, to such an extent, it was impossible to prove which stab wound, by which person, caused the actual death of the deceased.

On this basis we could not prove individual offences of murder or manslaughter and all three were found not guilty of these two main offences, but guilty to wounding with intent to cause Grievous Bodily Harm. This in itself also carried life imprisonment, however they were given lesser but long prison sentences which reflected fully on their involvement.

As with any drawn out murder enquiry depending on the amount of Staff involved we always had a social event naturally to celebrate a successful enquiry. In other ways this was to commemorate working with detectives from other stations, where good acquaintances had been appreciated, with excellent bonding for future relations. In any case a detective Superintendent was paid expenses for this kind of celebration which came from a special fund and was an excellent way of looking after the troops and maintaining morale. It was sad that as the years went on from various investigations into murder when we went from cracking open a bottle of whiskey or two in a quiet but friendly celebration, to celebrating in the politically correct way of having tea and opening a tin of biscuits. Wow, how exciting that was, they never show this kind of fantastic celebration in any current television police series or dramas it just would not win any Bafta's at the annual TV awards ceremony.

Dc THROWER, my pal joined us on several enquiries and it was good to see that he had not lost any of his detective skills and abilities, or indeed his sense of humour. One such Incident

Room I remember him working with another colleague similar to ourselves who was Detective Sergeant. He phoned up the Canteen Manageress in advance one day purporting to be a Detective Superintendent, who was visiting with another Senior Officer, my mate, and was enquiring as to what was available on the current menu. She related all the delicious recipes over the telephone and he replied that he did not want any of that rubbish. Steak was the order of the day together with requisite bottle of good house wine, as he was entertaining another Officer and they certainly did not mind paying. A time was agreed for the meal and later that day they arrived.

I remember walking through the canteen at the time, where they both sat down to a white table cloth, china crockery and silver service cutlery and were receiving waitress service. They were both in hysterics hardly able to contain their laughter and I of course couldn't help but smile, also from inside on their ultimate achievement. It was just so funny. No one ever knew. It was just like when they all walked out of the canteen on being give false instructions at my instigation, rushing to attend the parade square. All so I could jump the queue to order a bacon and egg sandwich as I wrote about in my earlier uniform service.

Another occasion sadly I was not privy to, was when the same pair attended a Christmas celebration at a local public house upon clearing another murder. Some of the police women decided it would be quite appropriate and seasonal to get all involved in the spirit of Christmas in singing carols. There was a piano in the corner of the room and they were desperate for someone able to play.

The Sergeant former bogus Superintendent immediately purported that Dc THROWER was an accomplished pianist and as they quickly organised carol sheets in anticipation of a good choral evening, they were all in for a total shock. Naturally my mate could not play a note yet alone read from any hymn sheet. If anyone has ever seen that wonderful moment in the Gerard Depardieu movie Green Card, my friend gave a truly unforgettable performance where he was just banging his hands down on the piano keys in a boisterous manner nearly drowning out all of the singing. Consequently he was showered with nuts, crisps, crusts or anything in easy reach of being thrown, that in itself just pure unforgettable entertainment. Who says no one should celebrate.

If we carry on in this country without any change in the justice system, I can foresee in the UK will have in proportion for the size of the land as many murders as in certain parts of America. Officers instead of being given burglaries, robberies, wounding and assaults to investigate, with they will be allocated their own murders to deal with like our counterparts in the USA.

Majority of so called do-gooders will argue about it's a fact of life, our ways and lifestyle have changed, it's the culture now, anything but being positive to resolving the outcome, which should be tackled now and not twenty years along the road. New York cleaned up its act some will argue whether three strikes and your out is morally acceptable, but they all knew the rules before they were broken. In most cases today citizens can walk around Manhattan with relative safety, more so than in some big cities in our country. I think the best example is Malaysia which is one of the most crime free countries in the world. Somehow the UK, USA, and majority of the western world went sadly very wrong. With knife and gun crime resulting in so many murders each and every day, there appears to be absolutely no deterrent, but hopefully it is never too late to implement change.

CHAPTER 30

LIFE'S NEW EXPERIENCES

U pon leaving the police force, I was just over 50 years old and new ventures lay ahead. Either I could relax, play golf or become just a couch potato, or I could motivate myself on learning a new career. I had no degrees or formal education qualifications but I had a wealth of practical experience and determination to succeed.

I can say for throughout all of my service, except for the last 12 months I fully enjoyed nearly every moment. I always thrived on hard work and always accepted a challenge directly up to the day I finished. From initially joining a privileged public role working with experienced officers of all ranks, sadly the level of supervision over the years was very mixed and in some cases extremely poor. I would have loved to have completed my full 30 years' service, had it not been for that reason coupled with low morale caused through tenure of post. Although there were still good supervisory officers the situation had deteriorated and was not getting better.

Over the years I often reflected the times when I was in the county forces and would go out on patrol from my beat station, even though I had done my 8 hours and not to claim overtime just doing the job I loved. Walking the beat and working the shifts were the some of the best days and could never be replaced. Despite the rocky path early in CID mainly caused by jealousy, nevertheless I persevered and became all the better for it.

I was respected by many genuine people and I gave full respect to senior officers deserving such credit and other colleagues officers of my rank both uniform and CID. I approached every day as a completely new challenge but the negativity set in not with my working abilities, but listening and having to side with issues that were nothing whatsoever to do with good policing practices. I have many friends still in the job and those who have left in similar circumstances who would support me completely regarding the principle issues in leaving.

One has to say providing high wages, does it attract the correct type of entry into the police force. I honestly do not know, but we all have to live comfortably in the balance of work we are doing. I know many staff would not take a drop in wages like I did from being a butcher when joining the police. In later years, it was all about getting to the next rank for many when some staff were not even good enough to hold the position they had been given in the first place. In the end it got to me and my health was suffering. I suppose I looked too closely at some of the poor standards of work taking place which I have honestly portrayed. This was a sad reflection against some of the excellent work done over countless years by so many professional highly experienced officers and things clearly were no longer the same. I decided to get out and cut my losses but it came at a financial cost. So in fairness I took a drop in wages to join and a drop in wages to leave. Still I could live with that. Some officers quite deservedly had fatter pensions than I received, but unlike some officers I know I earned every penny of mine.

I would rather do any job and work hard, learn new skills than stay in a profession where you had to kiss backsides to be in the running or be considered for favours. I felt so sorry for all the good staff that had to work in the environment that I was so pleased to leave. I just missed the comradeship of the many friends and acquaintances I had met over so many years.

Many officers of all ranks planned their future, some were already making moves well before leaving and providing it did not detract from their work, I suppose no one could blame them. What is not right is when they get jobs promised covered by a formal interview when perhaps it was just down to a nod and a wink in a major prominent position possibly due to their connections with the Masons in roles they simply did not deserve. The powers that be can say well that simply is not true. When you have a Detective Inspector commenting he had to go to a London City masonic lodge to become a member to assist in his promotion, one wonders exactly where the truth is, we may never know. When I think of all the leaving presents over the years that I have donated to when I myself never had a formal leaving do due to illness, I can still hold my head high in knowing what I personally achieved was a price worth paying.

Within having been retired a short time, I discovered D.I. CLINTON, who had been a most practical and well liked officer his wife worked as a senior Nurse in a sister role at our doctors practice. My doctor was very pro-police and was aware of my past and my then current working within the operating theatres. He also was a close friend of D.I. CLINTON. He explained that in the final part of his service this officer had been seconded to the West Indies island of St Lucia where he took the role of one of the Chief Commissioners of police, with all the expenses and privileges that go with such a position. I thought well what a reward for such a highly respected officer who clearly performed well during his service. What a change especially when this role indeed was one which was normally reserved for the more pompous officers and considered as 'Jobs for the boys'. He certainly did well.

Even more so one day, when I was seen at the surgery by his wife who confirmed the story and added that his friend throughout all his service, also a police Superintendent in our former force also received this identical posting. Both were serving together on this Caribbean island together for the same period of time. You could not make it up, I bet the powers that be never realised that, or did they. It just makes you think what goes on in such high circles, still good luck to them for achieving the impossible. What a different lifestyle to us under dogs.

I decided to firstly try the basics with computers and I enrolled on a course and received qualifications learning new skills. In between time I decided to apply for work in the hospitals, after all I had enjoyed the professionalism having close working relationships with Doctors and Pathologists and all kinds of nursing staff. I initially was interested in becoming a Theatre Porter or Nursing assistant, giving be the opportunity to care and look after patients able to give them dignity and help with all their problems of serious illness or with fears of facing surgery. Just that smile or friendly short conversation to put them at ease and feel better was so fulfilling in job satisfaction it made everything worthwhile. With no vacancies anywhere I just accepted anything they could throw at me. I started doing housekeeping, cleaning private wards and also working in the canteen. I served meals to patients and worked on the reception in the Out Patients Department and also performed stints on the main hospital switchboard. I took on the role of cleaning the Operating Theatres, until eventually I was offered the role of Theatre Porter. It just shows if you put yourself out, whatever age you are, with determination and luck with the right approach, whether you start again at the bottom rung you can always climb the ladder through hard work, patience and politeness.

In addition to this I was always looking for other similar situations of a more permanent nature and became interested in applying for a Civil Service Post in Child Maintenance, not that I told many of my former police colleagues. There's nothing like being a jack of all trades and master of none, but giving it your best shot. I joined several Nursing Agencies and before long I was working in all kinds of different hospitals. Over several years I have seen nearly every kind of surgery. From major heart, liver and kidney transplants, to heart bypass, heart valve replacements and Neuro [brain] surgery.

In addition this included all kinds of plastic surgery, involving breast augmentation, rhinoplasty, liposuction and gastric band surgery. Not forgetting eye, ear, nose and throat surgery, hysterectomies, gall bladder and major removal of cancerous tumours to smaller biopsies. I became a fully trained Theatre

Assistant and qualified in my duties involving Orthopaedic Surgery, where I have seen hip and knee replacements, arthroscopies of most joints, hand and foot surgery, Spinal surgery and amputations of limbs.

In between all this, for about five years, I alternated both jobs together. I had the benefit of working in Operating Theatres two days a week and the remaining week for the Civil service. When I worked for the Civil Service as an Administrative Assistant in dealing with Child Maintenance. This was an area of enormous patience in dealing with the frustrations of parents, some of whom were continually at loggerheads with each other. During such period the worst experience was using two completely different computer systems, together which both kept failing and still are today. Against the background of an old complex maintenance formula being put together by politicians of all parties. They themselves I believe in my view may have tried to have a complicated procedure, purely as some would be prospective customers or clients. Needless to say a new fairer system has since been introduced, which really should have been the formula in the first place. As in the Police Force, Civil Service and Hospitals I always enjoyed good relations with hard working colleagues, albeit with many other members of staff being complete shirkers and wasters. Again in both these professions I made many friends and also enemies prepared to stab you in the back at the first experience. However I had more that plenty of experience to live with these horrible characters who were totally unaware of my pedigree in life.

Far more important was the job satisfaction of locking up serious criminals and recovering items of sentimental value for all kinds of victims, to getting proper maintenance payments for children. In helping ill persons wherever possible, especially when facing major or minor surgery and helping them to overcome their fears as far as possible. In my role as a Coroners officer helping bereaved relatives through the most anguishing and traumatic times of their lives, trying to come to terms of losing a loved one at whatever age. All these kinds of experiences have been extremely rewarding and have hopefully served me well to being a better person.

However even when retired it is amazing how your all round skills, suddenly come to the forefront when experiencing everyday problems. As my wife is a smoker I always purchase them for her when required, although she does not smoke many per day, but stopping completely I believe after some fifty years would be a major shock to her system and create more problems than it would solve. Either way she enjoys a quiet relaxing smoke at various intervals during the day and why shouldn't she if that's what she wants.

So when at the local supermarket I picked up a pack of 100 cigarettes, when doing the remainder of the grocery shopping. Not smoking myself when I got home my wife informed me I had completely the wrong brand they were to small and too strong a cigarette and not being opened she asked me to exchange them when I could.

The very next day I went back to the same store with the un-opened pack of cigarettes. I explained to the assistant behind the counter and she asked if I had a receipt, as she could not change them without one. I stated normally I did, but I paid cash, so I thought one was not necessary, but even so no customers served in front of me the day before were offered a receipt and none asked for one. This was the same for the 5 years I had attended the store. The young lady re-iterated that she really could not exchange the pack without a receipt.

Thinking on my feet despite a queue of customers behind me, I stated what if I visited your store say yesterday and I was a person with a grudge against the store. She listened and I stated that if I went up to the meat counter and poured some chemical over all the meat display contaminating all the food what you would do. She remarked, 'What Has this got to do with cigarettes.' I politely stated that the Management would scour the CCTV situated in the relevant area to catch the offender who had caused the damage. She nodded in agreement. I stated well if you can do that, go back through your CCTV here to this time yesterday and scour the footage, and you will see me handing the cash over for the cigarettes, and not being offered or given a receipt. Then you can agree with me and change the cigarettes for what I normally buy for my wife. She burst out laughing and stated you win and handed me the correct cigarettes in exchange. As I have always said there is always more than one way of skinning a cat.

So now close to my mid-sixties, the kindest of compliment I was ever to receive involved a patient, a man who was in his early nineties. He was frail and unsteady on his feet, but as sharp and alert as a man half his age and had attended to have an epidural injection into his spine. He was situated in the Anaesthetic Room where I was going backwards and forwards from there and into the theatre assisting in different roles where I could. He recognised me and demanded to see me. My colleague who was a practical joker, told me this patient knew me and wanted to speak. I was having none of it as he was smirking so I ignored him completely. When it was all over he was taken to Recovery and reiterated his request in that he wanted to see me without exception and would not take no for an answer.

Naturally I was intrigued and left the Anaesthetic Room to go and see him. He stated, "I know you young man." I thought his name was a little familiar but just couldn't place from where. He then put me out of suspense, telling me some 40 years previous he had interviewed me on a Police Recruitment Board and was then a Deputy Chief Constable of the police force I had enrolled with. With him being 90 plus years of age with some obvious medical problems his mind was as sharp as anything and his memory just amazing. What a character I had not seen him since that that time. He stated he was aware I had transferred forces early in my police career and stated he remembered me clearly. What a marvellous human being. I can only say I must have made a very good impression, or was it bad one. I'll never know.

Indeed all I know is that I have been lucky to have taken part in some of life's most interesting experiences and challenges. I do not ever take for granted anything in life and clearly appreciate those less fortunate than myself. This to meeting some of the best and worst characters you could ever imagine. Why in life when you do not judge anyone, you are judged yourself by others, who have no open mind or do not know the full story of any of your achievements, or are jealous or conceited in thinking they are better and have done no wrong themselves. The old but very true saying is that people living in glass houses should not throw stones but so many do. Whatever anyone has done wrong in their life we are all here to learn and show our forgiveness.

So what is next, as I move into old age I think being a self-employed freelance writer will do for a start. Shall I keep writing true life stories or perhaps a little fiction a little more stress free I imagine, God willing?

Printed in Great Britain
by Amazon